A Company of One

A Company of One

*Insecurity, Independence, and the New World
of White-Collar Unemployment*

Carrie M. Lane

ILR Press
AN IMPRINT OF
CORNELL UNIVERSITY PRESS
ITHACA AND LONDON

First published 2011 by Cornell University Press
First printing, Cornell Paperbacks, 2011
Printed in the United States of America

Library of Congress Cataloging-in-Publication Data

Lane, Carrie M., 1974–
   A company of one : insecurity, independence, and the new world of
white-collar unemployment / Carrie M. Lane.
      p. cm.
   Includes bibliographical references and index.
   ISBN 978-0-8014-4964-2 (cloth : alk. paper)
   ISBN 978-0-8014-7727-0 (pbk. : alk. paper)
   1. Displaced workers—United States.   2. Unemployed—United
States.   3. White collar workers—United States.   I. Title.
   HD5724.L276   2011
   331.13'7973—dc22   2010040739

Cornell University Press strives to use environmentally responsible
suppliers and materials to the fullest extent possible in the publishing of
its books. Such materials include vegetable-based, low-VOC inks and
acid-free papers that are recycled, totally chlorine-free, or partly composed
of nonwood fibers. For further information, visit our website at www.
cornellpress.cornell.edu.

Cloth printing   10 9 8 7 6 5 4 3 2 1
Paperback printing   10 9 8 7 6 5 4 3 2 1

Contents

PREFACE

In the summer of 2009, the United States unemployment rate reached 9.4 percent, its highest level in more than two decades. New filings for unemployment continued to rise, while the number of long-term unemployed (jobless for twenty-seven weeks or more) hit 4.4 million. In total, more than 14.5 million Americans were out of work, with more than four job seekers for every open position.[1] Amid a deepening global economic crisis, ongoing national recession, and imploding housing, stock, and labor markets, the situation seemed unlikely to improve any time soon. A director of the Center for Economic and Policy Research commented, "It's really just about as bad as can be imagined.... There's just no way we're anywhere near a bottom. We'll be really lucky if we stop losing jobs by the end of the year."[2]

Like most Americans, I read reports of the deepening employment crisis with growing unease; I also read them with an overwhelming sense of déjà vu. As disturbing as this situation was, it was also eerily familiar; at that very moment I was completing a book—this book—on another moment, one not that long ago, during which U.S. workers were being laid off by the tens of thousands, flooding into a labor market already decimated by recession, national crisis, and the implosion of a different (although not that different) kind of bubble.

Since 2001, I had been researching the experiences of white-collar high-technology workers in Dallas, Texas, who were laid off during the volatile first years of the twenty-first century. I met with job seekers in coffee shops, restaurants, bars, churches, libraries, civic centers, conference rooms, and their homes, all with the goal of understanding how this new generation of workers felt and thought about their layoffs, the process of looking for work, and the experience of what became, for most, unexpectedly prolonged unemployment.

I did not initially set out to study unemployment. As a cultural anthropologist, I have always been interested in how people make sense of the world and their place in it. Since my undergraduate years, I have been drawn not to exploring the worldviews of exotic natives in far-off lands (to borrow a tired and problematic trope), but to trying to identify and understand the cultural beliefs and behaviors of those middle-class Americans whose way of life is often dismissed by academics as too banal, obvious, or distasteful to merit extensive study. And so my natives have always been, to a great extent, people like me: middle-class Americans with college educations, men and women, often white, whose beliefs and lifestyles are commonly referred to as the stuff of "mainstream" American life.

It was only after college that I began to focus on issues of work and the meaning it holds for those who perform it. My first job upon graduating was with a nonprofit research and consulting organization that works to advance women in business. I enjoyed the job and supported the organization's mission, but was frustrated by how little the statistical research we specialized in (such as counting the current number of women CEOs and tracking the percentages of women of color employed in executive positions) actually told me about what work meant in the lives of the men and women we surveyed, and how issues like gender, race, and class shaped the nature of contemporary white-collar employment. On returning to graduate school, I sought to answer those sorts of questions and ultimately specialized in the anthropology of work and the middle class, and U.S. cultural and business history.

When I began this project in 2001, the country was reeling at the sudden and generally unexpected failure of myriad dot-com start-up companies whose flat organizational structures and self-consciously casual corporate cultures had only recently been touted as the future of the U.S. workplace. My original plan was therefore to study those dot-com companies that survived the crash of 2000, where workday realities, I suspected, would represent a more complicated picture of what, exactly, the "New Economy" workplace was ultimately going to look like for U.S. workers.

I chose Dallas as my field site in part because previous studies of high-tech workplaces and workers had focused almost exclusively on California's Silicon Valley.[3] Dallas's large and varied high-tech industries and work-force—concentrated primarily in computing and telecommunications—scarcely rated a mention in scholarship on high-tech hubs; those who had looked southward tended to rush past Dallas on the way to its southern neighbor Austin, which had a smaller but decidedly sexier dot-com–based tech industry. By producing a historically situated ethnographic study of the Dallas tech workforce, I hoped to offer a comparative perspective to existing research on Silicon Valley while focusing attention on this dynamic but under-studied region.[4]

To that end, I began my fieldwork in September 2001 by attending the meetings of various high-tech organizations and professional associations in and around Dallas, looking for contacts in whose companies I might conduct fieldwork. Events ranged from early morning lectures by industry leaders, to mid-day seminars and panel discussions, to late-night happy hours for informal networking among self-proclaimed "geeks." Most events found me, Styrofoam coffee cup in hand, awkwardly attempting to insert myself into an ongoing conversation or to forge a new one with a fellow solo attendee. Like unpopular kids at a high school dance, most new attendees (ethnographers included) welcomed any sort of contact during those first awkward minutes of networking. In such a setting, once the introductions are out of the way, one tends to make what conversation one can with one's current partner. Although these forums were ostensibly for business people to make contacts, broker deals, and trade industry gossip, many of the people I met were actually unemployed, having been recently laid off from companies in the ailing telecommunications, computing, and Internet industries. At each event, I inevitably crossed paths with at least one person who wanted me to help them network into a company, while I was hoping for the same sort of assistance from them.

I therefore did a lot of talking, or listening, about layoffs—both why they were happening and how it felt when they happened to you. I soon found myself gravitating more toward unemployed attendees than employed ones, as I became convinced that the more fascinating and relevant story about high-tech work at the turn of the twenty-first century was taking place outside corporations rather than within them. My research focus shifted accordingly, and I began what would become three years of fieldwork (the details of which I outline in the introduction) on unemployment and job seeking in the Dallas high-tech industry.

As anthropologists have long acknowledged, the work of ethnography might begin in the field, but it hardly ends there; most of us begin to make real sense of our findings only as we attempt to shape them into publishable scholarly form.[5] As we go about doing so, our informants continue to live their lives, sometimes in ways that complicate and even invalidate the narratives we try to craft around them.[6] When I concluded my fieldwork in 2004, for instance, the U.S. economy was improving; many of my informants had found reemployment, and those who had not were generally optimistic about their prospects. And yet their stories do not end in 2004, and therefore neither could mine.

I wrote much of this book between 2003 and 2005, and then I set the project aside for a few years while I began a new teaching position. When I returned to the manuscript in 2008, the economic sands were shifting once again, prompting inevitable questions about how the new downturn might complicate or confirm my earlier conclusions. My central goal is to accurately document the experiences of a particular group of job seekers at a particular moment in time, yet the benefits hindsight can offer are too great to ignore. In this book I therefore seek a balance between reconstructing the world of high-tech job seeking as it was during my initial fieldwork (2001–2004) and critically examining that period—and my own and my informants' perceptions thereof—in light of more recent events. (Much of the statistical data I present, for instance, is specific to the early 2000s in order to provide an accurate picture of the economy and job market interviewees faced at the time they lost their jobs and set about finding new ones. When possible, however, I offer updated figures alongside them for informational and comparative purposes.)

To that end, in the fall of 2009 I conducted follow-up interviews with a small number of primary informants to see how their lives and careers had progressed over the five years since I last interviewed them. Those updates, which are presented in an extended epilogue, offer not only a fuller picture of how individual job seekers have fared since losing their jobs nearly a decade ago but also new lenses through which to view the data presented in the main chapters. They also offer revealing and unsettling evidence as to what lies ahead for the millions of Americans who, as I write this preface, are just beginning their own journeys through the world of job loss, job seeking, and prolonged unemployment.

Acknowledgments

My greatest debt is to the many job seekers whose candor and generosity made this project possible. Their experiences and opinions are the heart of this book; without them, there would be no story to tell. I am especially grateful to the small group of primary informants who served as sounding boards for my ideas and interpretations throughout this process—sometimes challenging my conclusions, other times supporting them with new stories and information. Although I cannot thank them by name, I trust that each of them knows how much I appreciate their invaluable contributions to this book.

I received financial support for this project from a variety of sources. My initial fieldwork was partially funded through grants from the National Science Foundation's Cultural Anthropology Program and the John Perry Miller Fund of Yale University. I was also fortunate to receive support for writing and revision through a Robert M. Leylan Writing Fellowship from Yale University; an Intramural Junior Faculty Research Award from California State University, Fullerton (CSUF); two awards from the

California State University Special Fund for Research, Scholarship, and Creative Activity; and an Untenured Faculty Development Grant from the CSUF Faculty Development Center.

I presented preliminary and evolving research findings in many forums, including meetings of the American Anthropological Association, American Studies Association, Society for the Anthropology of Work, European Social Science History Conference, and the University of Texas at Austin Graduate Program in American Studies; I also spoke by invitation to the UCLA Department of Anthropology's Culture, Power, and Social Change Group, the Dallas Area Social History Group, and Yale University's Market Culture Group. These talks helped me develop and hone my arguments in conversation with scholars from a variety of disciplines, and fellow panelists and audience members offered excellent critiques and suggestions for further study. I also appreciate the generosity of those scholars who contributed to this project by sharing with me their own works in progress, particularly Professor Meghna Virick of San Jose State University, and Daniel Marschall of George Washington University.

I have had the good fortune to be surrounded by talented and supportive colleagues and mentors at each stage of my academic career. When this project was in its most nascent form, Jean-Christophe Agnew, Nancy Cott, and Mitch Duneier offered much-appreciated words of encouragement and valuable ideas for expansion and revision. I also benefited from the feedback of scholars who responded to drafts or excerpts of this work, including Barbara Ehrenreich, Katherine Newman, and editor Donald Donham and two anonymous reviewers at *American Ethnologist.*

I am especially grateful to Kathryn Dudley, who for many years has inspired and challenged me in equal measure. It is impossible to quantify the innumerable ways Kate's involvement has shaped and improved this book. She has been a constant source of encouragement, pushing me always to look deeper and think harder. I am continually thankful for her guidance and for the example her own work provides of how engaging and important ethnography can be.

This work has benefited in more abstract ways from my ongoing involvement with the Society for the Anthropology of Work. As a member of SAW's executive board and reviews editor for the *Anthropology of Work Review,* I have been exposed to the latest and most compelling work in my subfield. Working with SAW also has its more personal rewards. It is an honor and a pleasure to be a part of such a vibrant intellectual community, and I am particularly grateful to and fond of Michael Chibnik, Csilla Kalocsai, Ann Kingsolver, and Jim Weil for making SAW such a fulfilling component of my professional life.

From the moment I met her, I knew Fran Benson would be my kind of editor, and indeed she is. Her enthusiasm for this project has meant the world to me, and this book is infinitely better as a result of her work and that of her colleagues at Cornell University Press, especially Katherine Liu, Cathi Reinfelder, and Susan Specter. Fran also did me the favor of enlisting John Van Maanen to read the initial manuscript. His thoughtful suggestions for revision improved the text immensely.

A professor once told me that when deciding which jobs to apply for, interdisciplinary scholars should ask themselves who they want to see at the department mailboxes every day. He intended the question to help me sort out whether I saw myself as primarily an anthropologist or a cultural historian (anthropologist, it turns out, regardless of what department I teach in), but I found a more useful answer upon joining the Department of American Studies at California State University, Fullerton. Were someone to ask me that question today, I would say that when I go to the department mailboxes, the people I most want to see are my colleagues Allan Axelrad, Erica Ball, Jesse Battan, Adam Golub, Wayne Hobson, John Ibson, Elaine Lewinnek, Karen Lystra, Terri Snyder, Mike Steiner, Pam Steinle, and Leila Zenderland, and our incredible administrative staff, Carole Angus and Karla Arellano. (I am particularly grateful to Erica Ball, Adam Golub, and Leila "Scissors" Zenderland for reading and commenting on portions of this book.) My colleagues provide me every day with inspiring models for engaged teaching, rigorous scholarship, and true professional service, and I feel fortunate to be part of this convivial, close-knit community.

I thank my parents, Ginger and Jim Lane, for instilling in me and my sisters a love of reading, for teaching us that education should be its own reward, and, although it annoyed me to no end at the time, for making us look up everything in the *World Book Encyclopedia*. I am thankful to them and to the rest of my wonderful family—Jim White; Tawny Lane and Arlie Nuetzel; Heather, Mike, and Megan Olson; and Anita Wellings and her family—for their love, wit, and encouragement over the years. I am grateful also to Steve Roman, for his wise and gentle guidance.

Guy Chet has been my most enduring booster throughout this process, reading multiple drafts of the entire book and battling valiantly (if not always successfully) for the inclusion or deletion of at least a thousand commas. Ours is a rare and special friendship, and for it I am forever grateful. To my other wonderful friends—especially Ahmed Afzal, David Christian, Emily and John Coppock, Lana Dalley, Shannon Kemper, and Charlotte Moore—I offer my enormous thanks. They are lovely, and true, and my world is infinitely better because of them.

To Matt Sterling, I offer my thanks, along with my heart, for his patience, love, and hilarity, and for everything yet to come. And, finally, thanks to Alice, for being my dog.

A Company of One

Introduction

Fortitude, Faith, and the Free Market

Although he worked nearly every night for a year waiting tables at a steakhouse in a suburb north of Dallas, Alex Brodsky[1] never thought of himself as a waiter. Instead, he says:

> I knew with absolute certainty that if somebody were to take a snapshot of this I could look at this and say, "This is not my life." Because I knew that while for a living I was waiting tables, I was not a waiter.

When I first met Alex in the fall of 2001, he had been out of work for six months following his layoff from an Internet consulting firm. The layoff was not a complete surprise, but Alex and his colleagues were frustrated with how the episode was handled. As the dot-com bubble crashed around them, the company's upper management had assured employees that their jobs were secure until the very day they laid off the entire office.

> I felt like a victim insofar as that the CEO of our company did lie to us. They did deal with us dishonestly [but] I didn't feel like life had dealt me a

hideous hand. I wasn't so interested in that. I was just figuring out, so what do I do now, what do I do next? What can I do? Let's figure that out and get on with it. I never had this sort of "why me?" [response]. The level of victimization that I felt was very aimed and directed at somebody who had done me in a less than pleasant, honorable way, but even then, I was asked to sign paperwork that said I wouldn't come back and sue the company—and it turns out I would have had grounds to—but even when I signed the thing I thought to myself, you know, hopefully I'll be working somewhere else. My effort and energy belongs to them, not this, so I signed because I thought, right or wrong or indifferent, I don't want to get involved in this. I want to move on and do something else and be doing something I enjoy instead of getting caught up in this vindictive, vengeful crap. I find it fairly easy to cut my losses, and I think I always have. There's a point where basically it's just not worth the effort, and the effort you're giving this is effort better spent doing something that is more beneficial to you.

Alex, who was about to turn forty when he was laid off, believed that next job, the one to which he felt his effort and energy truly belonged, would come along quickly. In his four years at that firm, Alex said, he had established a reputation—locally and internationally—as a leader in the emerging field of information architecture (IA), which entails overseeing the development and management of website navigation systems and design. Over the next months, Alex submitted hundreds of resumes through job search websites, attended job fairs across the Dallas–Fort Worth area, and participated in a variety of networking events for high-tech professionals. He contacted his extensive personal and professional networks, apprising them of his new situation and asking for leads and contacts. He had one interview, but the job was in California, two thousand miles from his parents and in-laws, in a state where his wife Hannah, a high school English teacher, was not licensed to teach. He withdrew from that search, but the company's interest reaffirmed his optimism that, despite the saturated job market in high tech, a new position was just around the corner.

And then came the terrorist attacks of September 11, Alex said, "and this sort of pall just settled across everything and everyone." Estimates of how long the average job search in high tech should take stretched from three months to six months to twelve months, and then people stopped making predictions at all. As the months passed, Alex found it difficult to maintain his initial optimism.

I was going to some of these job fairs, just walking in the front and turning around and leaving because there might only be ten or twelve positions open and there would be 150 to 350 people standing there and I was just not going to crawl into the herd....And as also happens when you're unemployed, you reach a point when you start to get tired of the sound of your own voice. You get tired of telling your story....Because there are days when you feel like you're in a big crowd shouting at another crowd. Everybody in your crowd is shouting across this chasm at this other crowd that's not listening. It's really difficult some days.

The frustrations of unsuccessful job hunting were compounded by unexpected back-to-back crises. On his way to a job fair in late September, Alex was in an accident that totaled his car and sent him to the emergency room with multiple broken ribs. The family was left with one car and sizable medical bills; until he sought out an alternate prescription, Alex's pain medication made him lethargic and depressed. At about the same time, the couple's two-year-old daughter Ella became unexpectedly ill and had to spend a few days in the hospital; she recovered quickly, but there were bills from that as well. Already struggling under existing credit card debt, the couple declared bankruptcy. Although relieved to be out of debt and "back at zero," the family still struggled to get by on Hannah's teaching salary alone.

Unemployment was running out...I knew that I had to make X amount of dollars in a month for us to be able to pay the bills. My primary goal was to put us in a position where we didn't have to move [from the house we were renting]. We had some things people would call luxuries, like cable TV, a cell phone, things like that. We haven't had to give up any of that [but] we've reached a point financially where...I just had to do something else to bring in some money. I decided to go back and start peddling steaks.

Very quickly, Alex said, he "found out why a lot of middle-aged guys aren't waiting tables." The job was physically exhausting and emotionally demanding. "You do a lot of smiling and waving at people who desperately need the shit choked out of them. That gets tiresome, particularly when you're in an environment when you've taken an 85 percent cut in pay....You laugh. If you didn't laugh, you'd cry."

Alex had actually worked at the same restaurant nearly a decade before. Following a layoff at age thirty, at his wife's urging Alex went back to school for his bachelor's degree, taking his first-ever job waiting tables to supplement Hannah's teaching salary. He quit upon graduating; on his last night, he bought a bottle of wine for his last table of the evening and told them, "Barring any serious reversal of fortune, you will be the last table I ever wait." Ten years after that night, sitting across from me at a café in a strip mall that runs alongside one of Dallas's many freeways, Alex said,

> And of course that word, that phrase, has just been haunting me. "Barring any serious reversal of fortune." Well, yeah. I would call this a serious reversal of fortune.... To go from holding forth at a boardroom on Madison Avenue to holding forth at table 42 at the Big Red Steakhouse in Plano, Texas—quite a big difference there.

Yet when he discussed that reversal of fortune, Alex did not rail at the company that laid him off; he did not critique the broader economic, social, and political forces that contributed to the dot-com bust or the post–9/11 recession; he did not lament the increasingly insecure nature of corporate employment. Instead, he optimistically invoked the power of the individual to withstand—rather than oppose—such periods of hardship. "Things will improve," he said, "if you make opportunities for yourself. But in the meantime, you do what you have to do." "If there's been a mantra," he says, during his time out of work, "that's been it. Do what you have to do."

***

This is a book about Alex and people like him, people who espouse a doggedly resilient faith in their ability to improve their own circumstances by doing what they have to do.

And yet it is also a very different book, one not just about a particular group of struggling tech workers, but about an ideology, a way of thinking about the world, how it works, and the rights and responsibilities of those who inhabit it. More specifically, it is about a neoliberal faith in individual agency, the logic and efficiency of the free market, and the naturalness of the status quo system of insecure employment. For although neoliberalism is now widely believed to have failed as an underpinning for public policy, I argue that it continues to play a powerful role in shaping the lives and worldviews of individual Americans. When they discuss their lives, layoffs, and careers, and when they articulate their expectations of their employers, families, and future, these job seekers express a decidedly neo-liberal set of values and beliefs, although that is not a term they themselves employ. They believe in the efficacy and justness of the free market; they favor individual responsibility over collective action, support economic globalization (even when their own jobs head offshore), and dismiss most forms of government intervention and collective activism as ineffective, if not injurious. As they see it, most problems, no matter how entrenched, can be solved through the combined efforts of individual agency and a functioning free market. Finally, they have a great deal of faith—in the value of their work, in the long-term buoyancy of the U.S. economy, and in the promise that the future holds for those who keep that faith despite the sometimes heavy costs they incur in doing so.

In some respects, this is an odd time for a new study of neoliberalism, the presumptions of which are said to have been thoroughly belied by the "Great Recession" that began in 2007 and rapidly destabilized national economies and financial markets around the world. Even Alan Greenspan, former Federal Reserve chairman and perhaps most influential imple-menter of neoliberal economic policy in the United States, has admitted to being "shocked" by the flaws revealed in free market ideology, "the whole intellectual edifice" of which, he believes, "collapsed in the summer of [2007]."[2] In addition, a host of works, most notably David Harvey's *A Brief History of Neoliberalism,* have already traced the roots, applications, and implications of neoliberal thought and modes of governing in the United States and elsewhere.[3]

Existing works, including Harvey's, tend to frame neoliberalism as the brainchild of a loose assortment of economic elites who use that ideology to recoup, retain, or enhance their own power and prosperity. Neoliber-als, in these accounts, are the corporate titans and political leaders who push neoliberal policies (or at least push policies in the *name* of neolib-eralism) that promote free trade, globalization, and individual respon-sibility while restricting or eradicating state provision of social services. Harvey also argues that "Neoliberalism has, in short, become hegemonic as a mode of discourse. It has pervasive effects on ways of thought to the point where it has become incorporated into the common-sense way many of us interpret, live in, and understand the world."[4] But who, exactly, is the "us" Harvey references here? The main characters in his own history are politicians—Margaret Thatcher, Ronald Reagan, Deng Xiaoping, Augusto Pinochet, Bill Clinton, and George W. Bush—a group hardly representative of those he describes as held in the sway of neoliberal hegemony. *One Market under God,* Thomas Frank's examination of the United States' romance with free-market ideology, offers a slightly expanded cast, but one composed primarily of free market gurus and poster boys like Bill Gates, Warren Buffett, Tom Friedman, and Tom Peters. Still unaccounted for are non-elite people who are said to actually employ neoliberal ideas to make sense of their less public, less glamorous, less lucrative daily lives.

Scholars have started to address this gap through ethnographic accounts of individuals and communities living under what has been termed neoliberal capitalism. Ethnography, with its emphasis on long-term participant-observation and open-ended interviews, is uniquely well suited to this task. It allows researchers to study the particular ways in which ideas and policies are experienced and understood within distinct cultural settings. Ethnography also makes visible the nuanced, culturally specific ways in which people resist, adjust, and embrace prevailing logics. The edited collection *New Landscapes of Inequality,* for instance, elucidates the ways in which neoliberalism builds on and exacerbates existing racial, gender, class, and sexual inequalities.[5] Most essays in the volume concentrate on exposing the extent to which society's most vulnerable members are further victimized by neoliberal policies, practices, and discourses. Two chapters, both set in Chicago, focus explicitly on the processes by which some people in the United States (in these cases black residents of a gentrifying neighborhood, and Latina/o high school students) have come to embrace ideologies that explain structural inequalities in the language of individual responsibility.[6] Although the volume represents a significant contribution to ethnographic examinations of the contemporary United States, it depicts a world populated mainly by affluent boosters and indigent victims, overlooking the experiences and ideologies of the many people situated somewhere in the middle.

A 2007 study by anthropologist Biao Xiang does examine how pro-market, individualist ideas and policies affect those less neatly positioned at either end of the economic spectrum, although not in the United States. Xiang follows Indian information technology (IT) workers to Australia and back as they navigate an increasingly global labor market.[7] These workers espouse a powerful faith in the power of personal merit and the naturalness of the hierarchy according to which their work is valued (or, more accurately, devalued). As Xiang deftly illustrates, however, the celebrated flexibility of the global New Economy is, to a far greater degree than IT workers themselves acknowledge, grounded in more mundane and unequal material realties.

With this book, I set out to continue the important work of documenting, in empirical detail, how individualist, pro-market ideologies shape actual people's lives and worldviews through an ethnographic study of white-collar U.S. high-tech workers who lost their jobs in the first years of the twenty-first century.

As I note in the preface, my fieldwork commenced in 2001 when I began meeting and interviewing unemployed tech workers. I met some interviewees at professional events and found others through online discussion groups and electronic mailing lists directed to Dallas tech workers.[8] Word of mouth played a central role, as interviewees put me in touch with unemployed friends and former colleagues. The leaders of various professional associations, networking groups, and job search seminars generously permitted me to attend meetings, introduce myself to the group, and invite job seekers to participate in my research project. One group's founder kindly used his regular column in a local tech magazine to solicit interviewees on my behalf.

My most important field sites, however, both for recruiting interviewees and conducting ongoing participant-observation, were groups and events directed at unemployed tech workers (as opposed to professional events intended for employed persons that job seekers might also attend). As I describe more fully in chapter 4, many organizations in Dallas, most of them not-for-profit, offer educational, professional, and social support to unemployed workers, and a good portion of them cater specifically to people looking for work in the admittedly blurry category of *high tech*. What constitutes "high tech" depends on whom you talk to. I use the term to encompass the industries of computing hardware and software, information technology, telecommunications, and Internet-related businesses. Most interviewees worked for high-tech companies, but a few did high-tech work at non–high-tech companies, such as managing databases for a bank or designing a retail store's website.

I conducted continuous fieldwork at these events for eighteen months in 2001 and 2002, returning regularly for visits and updates with interviewees throughout 2003 and 2004. During that time I observed the meetings and events of more than two dozen different groups geared to the unemployed, some on a weekly basis for more than six months. I attended job fairs, job search training courses, and networking events, which ranged from formal, organized affairs to raucous happy hours. With event leaders' permission, I usually announced to the group that I was an anthropologist interested in interviewing high-tech job seekers for a research project and invited interested parties to approach me during or after the event. I ultimately spoke with more than four hundred out-of-work tech professionals. I also interviewed leaders of local high-tech events and professional associations as well as career counselors, recruiters, employed executives, and the spouses of some job seekers. Their insights and experiences provided an important complement to job seekers' own accounts, sometimes echoing unemployed workers' perceptions and other times refuting them.

I also conducted open-ended interviews (shaped by individual exchanges rather than a set list of questions) with seventy-five job seekers, some of whom I interviewed more than half a dozen times over the three-year period, and nine of whom I reconnected with for follow-up interviews in 2009. (While I use the term *job seeker* for all of my interviewees, some individuals did have some form of employment at the time I interviewed them, including short-term or part-time positions in high tech or generally low-paid, low-status jobs in entirely unrelated fields. Yet these workers characterized themselves as unemployed, and therefore so do I, because they continued to actively search for work in, or related to, their former specialty at pay and status levels closer to those of their former positions.) I aimed for a diverse but representative sampling of Dallas job seekers. Although the presiding stereotype of laid-off tech workers in 2001 was of a twenty-something dot-commer who, like Icarus, had soared too high too fast and plummeted to what many saw as a deserved fate, most of these job seekers came from the decidedly more staid fields of telecommunications and computing. I interviewed men and women, twenty-somethings and sixty-somethings, whites, African Americans, native-born and immigrant Latinos, and Asian Americans of Indian, Pakistani, Chinese, and Japanese descent.[9] However, like the Dallas high-tech workforce itself, most interviewees were white men between the ages of thirty and fifty with at least a college degree. Most earned between $40,000 and $100,000 a year when employed, which by most estimates places them within the middle- or lower-upper classes. Few were born in Texas. About half were Republicans and half were Democrats, with a few Independents situated in between. All were extraordinarily generous with their time, candor, and insight.

By some accounts, although rarely their own, these laid-off high-tech workers were classic victims of economic globalization and free market ideology. As their former employers had warned them—usually explicitly—loyalty and security were no longer part of the social contract of employment nor, for that matter, were benefits, pensions, retirement accounts, full-time work schedules, or company-sponsored training. Their professional lives were instead destined to comprise a collection of part-time, short-term, usually contract positions, bridged by periods of unemployment, underemployment, and self-employment. Following their layoffs, many job seekers relied on limited unemployment benefits, fell into debt, accepted low-paid, low-status interim jobs, feared for their families' economic well-being, and experienced depression, self-doubt, and discouragement.

From another angle, however, jobless tech workers fit less neatly into the role of the sympathetic victim of impersonal and exploitive market forces. For one thing, tech job seekers rarely perceived themselves as victims of their former employers or of corporate capitalism more generally. (Unlike previous generations of laid-off white-collar workers, they did not blame themselves for their layoff either, at least not most of the time.) There were losers in this new economy, they believed, but the losers were not them. As they saw it, the losers were those outmoded men and women who failed to cast off the dependent mindset of the "organization man," who foolishly looked to paternalistic employers to provide them with job security and financial stability. In contrast, these workers saw themselves as "companies of one," entrepreneurial agents engaged in the constant labor of defining, improving, and marketing "the brand called you." Whether unemployed or working full time, they framed themselves not as professional failures or dependent employees but as savvy and self-reliant competitors in a market that, once it "corrects itself," would affirm and reward the value of their work through well-paid and high-status, if not necessarily secure, employment.

Ultimately, I argue, these workers were neither passive victims nor empowered free agents. How they saw the world, and the choices they made as they navigated through it, were the product of the historical and cultural context in which they lived. Understanding that context entails tracing out multiple, interwoven histories—intellectual, economic, and cultural; understanding how that context shaped the beliefs and behaviors of people living within it entailed listening to the people themselves.

As Emile Durkheim has argued, it is impossible to consider economic activity in isolation from moral beliefs because economic behavior is always imbued with a moral dimension.[10] Job seekers' model of how the world works and how they might best advance their interests therein, like all stories of how the world works, is a myth, not in the sense that it is false, but that it is made up, a symbolic way of conceptualizing society's moral order and situating oneself within it. I therefore set out to identify and understand this mythic constellation of beliefs and the individuals who espouse them. I trace the process by which job seekers draw on existing ideologies and discourses as well as on personal experience to construct a meaningful model of the world and their place in it. I consider how these beliefs shape individuals' everyday activities and experiences as they navigate prolonged unemployment and job searching, whether alone in their home offices, with their families at their kitchen tables, or amid swarms of fellow job seekers at job fairs and networking events. I also investigate the processes and channels by which these ideas are refined, communicated, and sustained over time through collective rituals and material realities. In short, I seek to paint a detailed picture of how white-collar U.S. workers live, how they feel, and how they think in the midst of professional and economic crisis.

This book builds on and engages with existing scholarship on white-collar workers in the United States, most vitally that of Katherine Newman and Kathryn Dudley, whose studies of economic crisis and downward mobility informed this project from its inception.[11] In many respects, I see this study as the "after" picture to Newman and Dudley's "before." Newman found that managers laid off in the 1980s were struggling to make sense of their professional experiences according to a cultural model of work and success that had for decades been crumbling under the weight of changing occupational patterns. Steeped in a managerial culture of meritocratic individualism that attributes professional failure or success to individual ability, these white-collar workers blamed only themselves when their jobs disappeared. When I began my own study of laid-off tech workers a quarter century later, insecurity had become the crowning feature of tech workers' professional lives. Although they shared their predecessors' strong faith in individual agency, tech workers laid off in the early 2000s saw the self-critical managers of the 1980s as textbook examples of how *not* to handle a layoff. In the 1990s, when Kathryn Dudley interviewed white-collar workers in Kenosha, Wisconsin, about the plant closings that were pushing their blue-collar neighbors into the unemployment lines, she found them unabashedly in favor of the closings, which they saw as a necessary byproduct of social and technological progress. Whether they would be so optimistic about economic change if it were their own jobs going offshore to foreign competitors seems an obvious question, one this study, undertaken nearly a decade later, is able to answer.

This study also stands squarely on the shoulders of the many ethnographic studies and cultural histories of work and U.S. culture that preceded it.[12] I am particularly indebted to those scholars whose research concerns the culture of high-tech work and workers, many of whose findings I reference throughout this book. Many of these studies, written at the height of the dot-com bubble, effectively capture the idealism and ideology of a new generation of workers fashioning the organizational structures and cultures they believed would be the future of work. My own project, started during the tech crisis of the early 2000s and completed during yet another, even fiercer economic downturn, is intended to engage with and expand on the important conversations those studies commenced.

I am also not the first scholar to take the ideologies of insecurely employed and unemployed professionals as my subject. Barbara Ehrenreich's undercover journey through the world of white-collar job seeking (including career coaching sessions, job fairs, networking events, job search seminars, and a professional makeover) identifies on a national level some of the same trends and tendencies I discuss in chapters 2–5.[13] Ehrenreich showcases the potentially soul-crushing absurdities of an industry designed to profit from the desperation of those at the mercy of a volatile labor market and increasingly demanding and inscrutable job search process. The structure of her research, which included brief stops in multiple states, demonstrates the ubiquity of the white-collar job seeking culture she and I describe. Yet this multisited approach precludes a more intimate portrait of individual job seekers, who come across as a somewhat monolithic and enigmatic group. In *The Corrosion of Character: The Personal Consequences of Work in the New Capitalism,* Richard Sennett also explores the toll that "flexible" employment takes on U.S. workers.[14]

He argues that the short-term, fragmented nature of modern work has stripped employees of the stability, autonomy, and sense of purpose that once undergirded their values and identities. Sennett's conclusions are persuasive and disturbing, but his account, which is presented as an extended philosophical essay, lacks the empirical evidence and ethnographic detail that prolonged fieldwork among a larger group can provide.

I intend to address this gap by bringing job seekers' own words and experiences to the center and elucidating their worldview in a manner that is both accurate and sympathetic, one that, as Clifford Geertz would say, "exposes their normalness without reducing their particularity."[15] Without giving way to easy critique or distant abstractions, I hope to go beyond simplistic assessments of these job seekers as unwitting dupes of the capitalist system; unsympathetic, overprivileged buffers getting their comeuppance; or valorous free agents prepared to claim their rightful place at the head of this new economy. Instead, I hope to present a fair portrait of men and women struggling to make sense of the changing world around them and to navigate that world's complexities in a manner that fills their savings accounts and their souls. Their experiences might also serve as glimpses of the future, if current economic and managerial trends continue. Many of the major changes shaping white-collar work today—rising frequency of job change, expanded use of outsourcing, offshoring, and part-time or contract workers, relative absence of labor unions, rapid rates of organizational and technological change, and prevalent self-employment and entrepreneurship—have long been central to the structure and culture of high-tech work. As these shifts spread outward into a majority of workplaces, tech workers' experiences and ideologies may serve as canaries in the mines of the U.S. workforce, rushing down the occupational paths that lie ahead in order to identify the possibilities and dangers that await.

***

In chapter 1, I provide a history of Dallas's high-technology industries, from their postwar origins in manufacturing, through the boom and bust of the computing, telecommunications, and dot-com industries, and into the post-9/11 recession and jobless recovery. In chapter 2, I follow Dallas-area job seekers through their layoffs and into the early stages of their job search, examining what appeared to me a surprising lack of anger and anxiety about their new predicament. It is in this chapter that I outline the ideology of career management, which represents a historic cultural shift in the mindset of white-collar U.S. workers toward employment, dependency, and security. Perhaps best described as neoliberalism for the organization man set (or the *Who Moved My Cheese?* crowd, to offer a more modern cultural reference), career management builds on a long history of management theory and American mythologies of meritocratic individualism and masculine agency.[16] It naturalizes the absence of secure, long-term employment, casts the resulting insecurity as an empowering alternative to dependence on a single employer, and prescribes explicitly individualistic, apolitical, pro-market means by which one can best position oneself to succeed in an increasingly global and competitive world.

In chapter 3, I examine how job seekers go about looking for work—their frustrations with online job searching; struggles with depression, isolation, and discouragement; and the specific strategies they employ for finding leads, marketing themselves to potential employers, and maintaining their self-esteem and positive outlook in the meantime. Networking is by far the most widely and enthusiastically endorsed job search method among unemployed tech workers. I offer a brief history of networking in chapter 4, both the old-fashioned "talk to your friends and family" approach and the more complicated and extensive system of organized networking events in which job seekers are brought together to swap leads and job search strategies. Through thick description of one particular networking event, I consider the role these groups play in buttressing job seekers' spirits, sense of community, and professional identity while also undermining opportunities for open critique and collective action. In chapter 5, I focus more explicitly on the material realities of joblessness. Although better positioned than many to withstand prolonged unemployment, these job seekers do face financial challenges, which they attempt to alleviate by cutting costs, depleting their savings, accumulating debt, and taking on low-paid interim jobs. Yet my central finding in this chapter is the hidden extent to which self-proclaimed flexible, entrepreneurial free agents depend on the steady income of an employed spouse to remain solvent while between positions. I then analyze the ways in which new ideologies of work and career have developed alongside the rise of the two-earner family and significant changes to traditional notions of marriage and masculinity. Although this reliance on spousal support functions in some respects as a buffer against the harsher material and emotional challenges of unemployment, it also has its costs, particularly for female job seekers, who are far less comfortable relying on spousal income than their male peers.

In the book's epilogue, I extend the story into 2009, with its skyrocketing unemployment rates and global financial crisis. I offer updates on the professional and personal statuses of the job seekers who populate the preceding chapters, exploring whether or how their beliefs have changed in the half decade since I first interviewed them, a full eight years after most of them first lost their jobs, and at a time when the market has failed, rather spectacularly, to correct itself as many of them had predicted. I ask their advice for a new cohort of unemployed workers (a group to which some of them once again belong), and invite their predictions as to what the future holds, for them, for their countrymen and -women, and for the economy that they had so vigorously believed would reward their allegiance.

1

Silicon Prairie

In January 1985, four hundred influential Dallasites gathered by invitation only to celebrate the opening of Infomart, a $97 million experiment in high-technology marketing. Following hors d'oeuvres of seasoned salmon in a brioche shell, caviar-topped potato slices, and mini leek and herb quiches, guests enjoyed a chilled chanterelle terrine with squid and pheasant mousse in a walnut and chives vinaigrette. The second course ushered in cream of artichoke hearts and lobster soup, followed by a palate-cleansing grapefruit sorbet. The veal entrée was followed by a winter salad of watercress, Belgian endive, and tomatoes, flavored with a simple vinaigrette of olive oil and lemon juice, and then a sumptuous dessert: a tulip-shaped cookie shell filled with chestnut mousse and chocolate garnish served alongside a white chocolate leaf and a chestnut-shaped truffle.[1]

This impressive French feast was just one of sixteen activities heralding Dallas's new "palace of information," a 1.6 million-square-foot building patterned after the Crystal Palace designed by Joseph Paxton (who was actually a gardener, not an architect) for the Great Exhibition of London in 1851. Paxton's one million-square-foot glass and iron Palace was designed to showcase products of the industrial age and further the Exhibition's goal of giving people "a living picture of the point of development at which all nations will be able to direct their future exertions."[2] Nearly a century and a half later, Dallas's Infomart was built to showcase the technological innovations of a new information age. Hoping to reflect both the architecture and the "spirit and forward-thinking purpose" of the original Crystal Palace, Infomart architect Martin Growald borrowed many structural details in designing its twentieth-century successor. Like the Crystal Palace, Infomart's metal and glass frame is decorated with delicate white cast-aluminum panels and built around central semi-circular vaults, both of which contribute to its greenhouse-like appearance. The building's interior also reflects elements of its predecessor, including an elaborate crystal fountain, English-red phone booths, and a central atrium (sans the original aviary). Even its wood floors bear a pattern identical to that of the original Crystal Palace.[3]

All that nineteenth-century charm, however, was really just a vessel for late twentieth-century technology. Infomart was designed as a trade mart for computers, a "high-tech bazaar" with seven floors of showrooms, exhibition space, lecture halls, and meeting rooms, all equipped with cutting-edge computing and telecommunications equipment.[4] This revolutionary application of the trade mart concept (concentrating multiple vendors in a single commercial location) to high-tech products and services was expected to draw over 350,000 visitors a year and to cement Dallas's position as a high-tech center worthy of national acclaim. In honor of Infomart's opening, Governor Mark White declared the week beginning January 21, 1985, Information Processing Week in Texas.[5]

From its inception, Infomart had its critics. Some took an aesthetic stand against the structure, describing its lacy white exterior as a "metal-and-glass wedding cake" and "a giant 1850s Mississippi side-wheeler about to bust loose from its moorings."[6] Others were more concerned about its fiscal viability; despite the pomp that accompanied its opening, Infomart opened with less than half of its available exhibition space filled. (It also turned out that many of its frequent visitors came not to shop for computers but to ride in the glass-walled elevators.) Over the next two decades, Infomart's prospects, and public perception thereof, waxed and waned. Although the space never achieved its intended goal—the computer mart

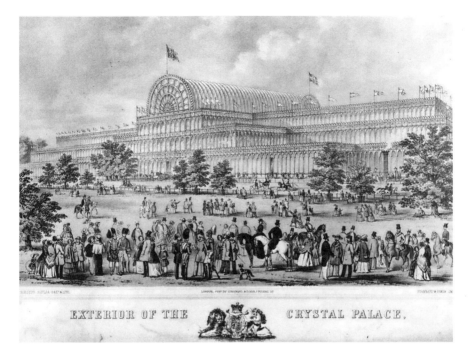

EXTERIOR OF THE   CRYSTAL PALACE,

Figure 1. The Crystal Palace. The original palace, built for the 1851 Great Exhibition of London, burned to the ground in 1936. Infomart has since been recognized by Great Britain's Parliament as its official successor. Hulton Archive/Getty Images.

concept was scrapped after only a few years—the story of how (and how much of) Infomart's space was in use at a given time intertwines with the broader history of Dallas's high-tech industries and the region's efforts to establish itself as a high-tech region on par with California's famed Silicon Valley. That story, however, begins much earlier, in a time when Infomart was not even a glimmer of glass and metal in Dallas's collective eye.

Until World War II, Dallas was a minor manufacturing center in the United States, specializing in food processing, apparel manufacturing, and printing and publishing. During World War II, Dallas and its neighboring city Fort Worth benefited from the booming wartime defense industry, which, due to some serious lobbying on the parts of Texas legislators Sam Rayburn and Lyndon Johnson (then Senate majority leader), brought numerous defense plants to the area. Companies were also drawn to Dallas's pro-business environment, with its low taxes, inexpensive land,

Figure 2. Infomart, modeled after the original Crystal Palace, stands just off a major freeway in downtown Dallas. Photograph by Nancy Windrow-Pearce.

cheap and largely un-unionized labor force, affordable cost of living, and abundant natural resources. Manufacturing was already the primary source of employment in Dallas County by the 1940s, but the number of manufacturers in the county more than tripled between 1947 and 1987. In 1949 alone, five new businesses opened each day, and thirteen new manufacturing plants opened every month. Many of those new ventures were concentrated in the computing and electronics industries. Companies such as Texas Instruments, originally an oil and gas exploration company, won sizable defense industry contracts and drew top engineering talent to the region. Such companies also spawned generations of spin-off companies, helping to grow Dallas into the nation's third-largest technology center by 1970.[7] The 1974 opening of the Dallas–Fort Worth International Airport, positioned roughly equidistant from New York, Los Angeles, Mexico City, and Toronto, strengthened the city's reputation as a national financial and business center and its attractiveness as a home for corporate headquarters.

Following the tendency of high-tech firms to develop in clusters (as evidenced by California's Silicon Valley, Boston's Route 128, and North Carolina's Research Triangle) the companies that sprung from or came to do business with Texas Instruments and other Dallas tech firms stuck close by their larger peers, many of whose headquarters were located in Richardson, a suburb north of Dallas.[8] Land was inexpensive and plentiful in Richardson, which soon became known as "The Electronics City," and the region proved a magnet for new ventures and corporate relocations. Although the area's high-tech roots lay in the manufacturing of computers and other upscale electronics, this clustering of companies, capital, and talent left Dallas well positioned to expand quickly into other high-tech fields as they emerged.

With the breakup of AT&T and the subsequent deregulation of the telecommunications industry in the early 1980s, Richardson found itself home to hundreds of start-up telecom companies looking to enter this new market (which opened further when the Telecommunications Act of 1996 allowed any communications business to compete in any market against any other). Most of these companies were pioneered by former employees of computing and communications companies already in the area and amply funded by venture capital. These firms organized themselves along a stretch of highway running from Dallas through Richardson and up into Plano, Richardson's neighbor to the north, later expanding to both the east and the west along perpendicular President George Bush Turnpike, forming a T shape. This region quickly earned the title "Telecom Corridor," and its rapid growth and speedy cornering of the telecom market soon garnered national attention. By 1989, the *Wall Street Journal* was calling Richardson one of the "Boom Towns of the 1990s." In 1992 the Telecom Corridor appeared on the cover of *Business Week* as one of "America's New Growth Regions," and that same year Richardson's Chamber of Commerce registered the moniker "Telecom Corridor" as its official trademark.[9] Still, Dallas leaders believed that their region was being overshadowed by other, more famous tech centers like Silicon Valley and Boston and yearned to establish Dallas as their equal, if not their better.

Although the Bureau of Labor Statistics had already named Dallas a leading center of high-tech employment the year before, in 1984 Dallas Mayor Starke Taylor created a twenty-six-member task force to evaluate the state of the city's high-tech situation.[10] Taylor's concern was well timed, as both the computing and semiconductor industries fell into a slump in 1985, leading to widespread layoffs and the closing of many smaller companies.[11] It was in this environment that Infomart opened its doors, and many attributed the building's failure to reach its projected occupancy of 100 percent by 1986 to the continuing shakeout from this downturn. Others blamed Infomart's shuffling start to flaws in the assumption that computers could be bought and sold in the same manner as clothing and furniture.[12] (Infomart was built within a larger complex known as Market Center, which already housed four large, architecturally nondescript buildings used as wholesale markets for, among other things, furniture and apparel.) In an attempt to woo a different market segment, Infomart executives ditched the one-stop-shopping model and refocused on providing services to companies and their customers, namely education on computer systems and software applications. This shift mirrored a larger one taking place in the high-tech industry. The United States, it was argued, was moving from an industrial economy based on manufacturing to a postindustrial "service/information economy."[13] In response, companies began to focus less on manufacturing and selling computer hardware and more on marketing and providing information technology (IT) services designed to solve business problems with customized technology. In telecommunications, the new craze was fiber-optic technology, which would vastly increase the capacity of the U.S. long-distance telephone system and allow users to transmit both voice and data faster and with less distortion than current microwave systems. Well placed to meet this new demand, Infomart's occupancy rose to just over 60 percent in 1988, fueled in great part by companies' need for access to the advanced fiber-optic network that ran beneath the building's patterned wood floors.

The new IT and telecommunications companies needed people in addition to bandwidth. High-tech employment grew more than twice as fast in Texas than in the nation as a whole from 1988 to 1994, and computer-related services surpassed manufacturing as the state's largest high-tech industry. The Dallas–Fort Worth area was home to much of that growth, accounting for over half of the state's high-tech jobs (and almost 80 percent of Texas's telecom jobs) in 1995.[14] The local supply of tech workers, extensive as it was, proved inadequate to meet the growing demand for skilled tech workers, and by the year 2000 Dallas was importing engineers and computer scientists from other countries to fill their payrolls.[15]

The spectacular rise of the Internet and the dot-com companies it birthed over the course of the 1990s has been chronicled extensively elsewhere.[16] Essentially, once the Internet morphed from a government-funded collection of networks that was free to the public into a privatized commercial enterprise, venture capital firms, many located in northern California, began pouring money into companies looking to make a profit selling, facilitating, or augmenting people's access to and use of the Internet. The apparently infinite supply of venture capital for high-tech start-ups and the phenomenal success of early dot-com IPOs (initial public offering, or a company's first sale of stock to the public) led many in the late 1990s to announce the birth of a "New Economy." Characterized by "a fundamentally altered industrial and occupational order, a dramatic trend toward globalization, and unprecedented levels of entrepreneurial dynamism and competition—all of which have been spurred to one degree or another by revolutionary advances in information technologies," this New Economy was one in which the old rules of economics were said to no longer apply.[17] A company could therefore be labeled successful even with no profits or identifiable source of future profits.

With old economic models for evaluating a company's current and potential future worth (such as the ratio of price to earnings) deemed obsolete, stock valuations became increasingly speculative (and, it has since been revealed, increasingly fraudulent). A nation of investors looking to boost their portfolios with hot Internet stocks often based their decisions on whether and what to buy or sell on media coverage that tended toward uncritical hype of both individual dot-com companies and the tenets of the New Economy.[18] Eager to take advantage of this speculative bubble, venture capitalists and executives rushed seedling start-ups to IPO while the market was bullish on all things Internet. Although Silicon Valley's existing technology infrastructure, ready pool of tech talent, extensive funding sources, and liberal, risk-inclined culture combined to make the region the United States' dot-com center, other regions—Dallas included—offered their own sizeable contributions to the growing Internet industry.

In January 1998, *D Magazine* (the *D* stands for Dallas) challenged Dallas entrepreneurs and investors to dive into the admittedly risky but potentially superlucrative world of dot-com start-ups.[19] The article alleged that Dallas, usually a hotbed of technological innovation and entrepreneurship, was revealing itself to be a laggard in the high-tech explosion because engineers and other tech workers were too comfortable in their secure, well-paid telecom jobs to take a risk on entrepreneurial ventures. Once Texas's tech center, Dallas was in danger of being surpassed by nearby

Austin, which, with its large, technologically inclined research university and Internet-friendly bohemian culture, had already established itself as a major player on the dot-com scene. Dallas techies were aware that their city's fledgling forays into the Internet business were heavily overshadowed by their trendier neighbor to the south and resented being cast as the slower and stodgier of the two cities. The article's author also feared that if Dallas remained overconcentrated in telecom it might suffer enormously should that industry experience a downturn like those in energy and banking that had crippled the inadequately diversified local economy just over a decade before. Such worries were relieved, at least temporarily, when only two years later, in 2000, *D Magazine* revised its assessment and proclaimed Dallas "the third coast of e-commerce."[20] The issue's cover recast Grant Wood's iconic *American Gothic* with two thirty-something, white dot-commers, complete with USB port and oversized geek chic glasses frames, Dallas skyline peeking up over the farmhouse roof. Not only were many of Dallas's more staid technology giants reportedly venturing into online enterprises, but a whole new cluster of small, innovative Internet firms was cropping up in a corridor of its own. "What a difference," the article read, "26 months can make."[21]

Deep Ellum, a neighborhood east of downtown Dallas, was founded as a "freedmen's town" by former slaves after the Civil War. The area, located on Elm Street just east of the rail yard, was called Deep Elm, but the heavy Southern drawls of its inhabitants revised its pronunciation to "Deep Ellum." Home at various points to the manufacturing of gin and Model Ts, Deep Ellum was best known as an entertainment center, particularly for African Americans. The neighborhood gained notoriety in the 1920s and 1930s as a destination of choice for Texas bluesmen like Blind Lemon Jefferson, Sam "Lightnin'" Hopkins, and Huddie "Leadbelly" Ledbetter, and as a favorite hangout of the bank-robbing duo Bonnie and Clyde. The area declined in the 1940s and 1950s due to a combination of the closing of the railroad depot and streetcar line and white flight to the suburbs. In 1969, the addition of an elevated freeway bisected Elm Street and eliminated the community's central block. (Less than twenty miles to the north, that same freeway serves as the central spine of the Telecom Corridor.) The area languished until the mid-1980s, when an influx of artists and nightclubs (encouraged by city planning and zoning authorities) revived the neighborhood, at least in the evening hours.[22]

Figure 3. "Silicon Prairie Stakes Its Claim." Cover from December 2000 *eDallas* supplement of *D Magazine*. Reproduced with permission of *D Magazine*.

Developers soon began buying up lots in Deep Ellum and converting them into lofts and office space designed to attract young people with a yen for the area's artsy, urban feel and inexpensive rents. These converted warehouses were particularly well suited to young companies looking to break into the Internet business, where large, open offices with modern design touches were thought to both facilitate and metaphorically represent the antihierarchical, social corporate cultures that had become the trademark of dot-com companies.[23] Deep Ellum represented not only an ideological and geographical alternative to the bland suburban office parks that housed most Dallas businesses, but the area's long history of jazz, vice, and urban strife appealed to dot-commers' bohemian, anti-establishment brand of capitalism.

One of Deep Ellum's first high-tech residents was dot-com entrepreneur Mark Cuban. In 1995, Cuban and his business partner rented a converted warehouse to house their start-up, AudioNet, which pioneered the streaming of audio and video data over the Internet. The large space also housed a full basketball court, reflecting both Cuban's love of the sport and the company's adherence to the idea that dot-com workspaces had to be fun as well as functional. Cuban's company, later renamed Broadcast.com, sold to Yahoo in 1999 for approximately $6 billion. Yahoo kept its Texas operations in Deep Ellum, moving into the red brick railroad buildings at the neighborhood's center. Broadcast.com's very public success and Cuban's high-profile persona as volatile local celebrity and eventual owner of the Dallas Mavericks basketball team only increased Deep Ellum's regional cache, and the neighborhood's name became shorthand for Dallas's dot-com scene. (Deep Ellum was variously referred to as the Content Corridor, the Dot.Com Corridor, and e-Commerce Street, but none of the nicknames stuck.) Dozens of Internet companies set up shop in the neighborhood's spacious old industrial buildings, most of which were newly renovated, wired for high-tech action, and positioned atop miles of high-capacity fiber-optic cables.[24] High-tech professional associations began to hold their meetings and social events in Deep Ellum's trendy bars and restaurants, and traditional brick-and-mortar firms moved their mixers and recruiting events to Deep Ellum to position themselves as new economy converts and scout fresh tech talent.

Not all of Dallas's tech start-ups sought out digs in trendy Deep Ellum. Many based themselves along the Telecom Corridor, often alongside or even inside the larger, established tech firms from which they had been recently spun off. Others moved into less glamorous suburban office malls, where their trendy modern workspaces and casual style of dress and leadership diverged sharply from those of their old economy neighbors. Still others were run from individual homes. Infomart also cashed in on the spoils of the Internet boom. Occupancy swelled from 64 percent of capacity in 1995 to almost 70 percent in 1997 and nearly 90 percent in 1999. The first-floor High Tech Café, billed as the nation's first "cyber bar," installed data jacks and power plugs beneath the salt and pepper shakers so patrons could use their computers and access the Internet while munching on "Megabyte chips" under light fixtures made from old computer monitors. In 1998, the Dallas Internet Society moved its monthly meeting to Infomart, cementing the building's—and Dallas's—successful entry into the Internet age.

Despite its notoriety, Deep Ellum and the rest of Dallas's dot-com scene never accounted for as many jobs or as much income as the city's larger computing and telecommunications companies, and Austin remained Texas's Internet hub, much to Dallas dot-com boosters' chagrin. That the city never placed all or even most of its technological (and financial) eggs in the Internet basket proved a double-edged sword for the Dallas economy. When the Internet bubble burst in 2000, Dallas was not nearly as hard hit as Austin and Silicon Valley, whose economies were by that point heavily dependent on an army of nimble (and mostly as yet unprofitable) Internet start-ups. Dallas's continued concentration in telecommunications and more traditional computing businesses might have effectively shielded Dallas from the fiscal and labor market repercussions of the dot-com crash had that event not been quickly followed by the one-two punch of a telecom fallout and nationwide recession.

Just as the spectacular rise of what is now referred to as the Internet or dot-com bubble was fueled by a number of factors, so was its downfall. April 14, 2000, earned the name "Black Friday" when it recorded the largest-ever points drop of both the Dow Jones Industrial Average (Dow) and the NASDAQ, but Internet stocks had been stumbling for months. Stocks dipped in January after Federal Reserve Chairman Alan Greenspan suggested an imminent interest rate hike and fell again in February when that quarter-point hike arrived. Still, the general feeling was that although the current market volatility was worrisome, the New Economy would prevail. In the background, however, the flow of venture capital into new and existing enterprises had slowed, and many companies, even those whose witty commercials during the Superbowl had so recently captivated a national audience, were swiftly running out of money. Investors had grown weary and wary of the constant parade of new IPOs, and it was slowly becoming apparent that many if not most Internet stocks were hugely overvalued. Even after Black Friday, however, many economists remained stubbornly optimistic that this downturn was a blip and not a bust.

Belying that optimism were the hundreds of Internet companies that began closing their doors or declaring bankruptcy as their stocks plummeted and their venture capital slowed or dried up in the early 2000s. At first, the damage appeared to be limited largely to Internet firms, but its repercussions soon spread to related areas of high tech. Years of overinvestment in information technology, particularly around apocalyptic predictions about the Year 2000 problem (Y2K), had already weakened demand for computer software and hardware. As the aftershocks of the dot-com crash rumbled in their direction, those industries quickly buckled, dragging the U.S. tech workforce down with them.

The telecommunications industry, in contrast, continued to flourish even as other tech industries crashed around it. Investment in telecom companies in 2000 was at least twenty times greater than investment in dot-com companies. Investors discomforted by the volatility and unproven nature of so-called new economy companies perceived telecom as a safer way to cash in on high-tech growth. The collapse of dot-com stocks actually prompted a surge of new investment in telecom, as many investors optimistically traded their shrinking shares of Internet stock for a piece of the telecom pie.[25]

In early 2000, as dot-com companies in nearby Deep Ellum failed by the dozen, Dallas telecom companies were offering engineering and computer science professors $5,000 for each new recruit they brought to the company.[26] Within two years, however, the situation had dramatically reversed itself; over $2 trillion of value in telecom stocks had disappeared, along with over half a million telecom jobs.

While the dot-com crash and the ripples it sent through the U.S. economy clearly undermined the telecom industry's stability, it was eventually toppled by problems all its own.[27] During the 1990s, it was often said that

Internet traffic was doubling every one hundred days, growing at a rate of more than ten times per year. Although growth slowed after 1997, when traffic only doubled each year, the tenfold-growth model continued to drive the development of telecommunications infrastructure, where fiber-optic cables were being laid at record speed to keep up with this supposedly astronomical demand. Telecom companies "dug up the nation's thorough-fares and dove to the ocean floor to lay millions of miles of fiber that, for the most part, would remain dark," because while all those miles of fiber were being laid to meet an as-yet-nonexistent demand, engineers were dramatically increasing how many signals each fiber could carry.[28] A fiber that in the early 1980s could carry only one signal could, by the late 1990s, carry eighty. This hugely expanded capacity meant that the existent infra-structure was more than capable of handling whatever demand was likely to arise, and the money (over $90 billion, much of it borrowed) and labor spent in laying and maintaining all that surplus capacity was wasted.[29] The telecom industry was already on shaky ground, then, when account-ing scandals at some of the nation's leading telecom companies, such as WorldCom and Global Crossing, combined to erode public confidence in the industry and shatter the value of its stocks, kicking off an industrywide downturn in the latter half of 2000.

By September 11, 2001, the U.S. economy was already in the midst of a recession, one that officially began a full six months earlier. After a decade of unprecedented, arguably unsustainable growth, particularly in high tech, and more than a year of a bear market, employment finally reached its peak in March 2001 and began declining. The terrorist attacks of September 11, as tragic as they were, simply "gave another sharp twist to the deflationary circle that had been buffeting the economy since the NASDAQ's collapse in March and April 2000," destroying whatever hope Americans, particularly the unemployed among them, may have held that a recovery was just around the corner.[30]

As the national economy collapsed around an already crippled high-tech industry, companies began laying off workers by the tens of thousands. Dot-coms, many of which had never established Human Resources depart-ments, were faulted for their inept handling of dismissals; some skipped layoff announcements altogether, leaving bewildered employees with no warning, no severance packages, and no idea what had just happened.[31] Telecoms usually conducted their downsizings more professionally, but the sheer mass of people losing their jobs in that industry, sometimes more than ten thousand in a single round of layoffs, drew national attention and critique. Prior to September 11, 2001, media coverage of the tech downturn focused primarily on Internet companies, particularly those whose on-paper fortunes had obscured serious flaws in their business models and financial footing. In these early months of the downturn, public response to dot-com layoffs and their victims tended toward scorn rather than sympathy.

On the one hand, investors were furious to see their portfolios shrink and frustrated that companies that had been sold to them as vanguards of the New Economy turned out to be depressingly vulnerable to the rules of the old. On the other hand, the country was gripped in a national bout of schadenfreude, as "spotting the next dot-com to turn up its toes had turned into a popular spectator sport."[32] *Fortune* began running a "Dot-com Deathwatch" column listing on cartoon tombstones the names of Internet companies that had filed for bankruptcy or ceased operations. Websites such as FuckedCompany.com and dotcomfailures.com offered similar tallies and gave points to users who accurately predicted the next company to go under. With hoodwinked investors playing the role of victim, laid-off dot-commers were left looking like villains, or at least accomplices, in the defrauding of a nation and the destruction of a once-solid economy.

The national mood shifted after the September 11, 2001, attacks on the United States, as blame for the tech industry's downfall switched from the shoulders of whippersnapper dot-commers to Middle Eastern terrorists. In addition, although the victims of Internet layoffs had been stereotyped as recent college grads with an overblown sense of entitlement and an artificially inflated net worth, as layoffs spread outward to other sectors of the tech industry and beyond, media coverage became decidedly less snide and more somber. (*Fortune*'s cartoonish dot-com graveyard, for instance, was replaced by a simple numerical tally of total jobs lost.)

It turns out, however, that even in the early days of the downturn, dot-commers accounted for a very small proportion of total jobs lost. Nearly 90,000 workers in the Internet economy lost their jobs from January 2000 to April 2001. That figure was dwarfed, however, by the over 2.2 million jobs lost in the overall economy during that same period. Even within high-tech, Internet-related positions accounted for only a fraction of jobs lost. By 2001, telecom had established itself as the unfortunate but undeniable frontrunner in high-tech job losses, and the industry continued to shed jobs steadily every year through 2010.[33]

Texas was already leading the nation in tech job losses before the telecom crisis hit.[34] Once telecom layoffs were added to the mix, the results were even more devastating, especially in Dallas: the city lost 10,000 high-tech jobs in the first six months of 2001, 7,000 of them in telecom. By the end of 2002, the Dallas area had lost 25,500 jobs, and by 2003 Dallas County had lost more jobs than any U.S. county besides Santa Clara County, the heart of Silicon Valley. By mid-2004, a full 19 percent of the nation's technology jobs had disappeared since the recession began in 2001. Dallas was even harder hit; losses there were closer to 30 percent, a full third higher than the national average.[35]

Dallas's unemployed workers, many of them middle-aged, middle-class, white-collar tech workers with long careers already behind them, found themselves looking for work in an exceedingly tight labor market. (This downturn saw a dramatic rise in the percentage of white-collar workers among the total unemployed, although blue-collar workers still accounted for the majority of the jobless.[36]) Several thousand job seekers began to regularly attend job fairs and networking events in Dallas even as corporate attendance and sponsorship of these events plummeted. Although each fiscal quarter saw optimistic claims that a recovery was just around the corner, when economic gains eventually did begin to appear they failed to bring about the predicted decrease in unemployment. The recession officially ended in November 2001, only one month after the terrorist attacks on the United States and long before most workers in this study lost their jobs, but mass layoffs and high unemployment continued unabated throughout 2002 and 2003. In what was later termed a "jobless recovery," a phrase that tech job seekers dubbed a frustrating oxymoron, productivity surged despite the vastly shrunken workforce because of companies' early investment in laborsaving information technology and the expanded workloads of remaining employees. Nearly two years into the official recovery, U.S. employment had actually decreased by over one million workers since the recession's end. Government tax cuts predicted to ease unemployment with a growth of 5.5 million jobs by the end of 2004 ultimately fell more than 3 million jobs short.[37] Amid what was then the worst hiring slump since the Great Depression, U.S. workers began to

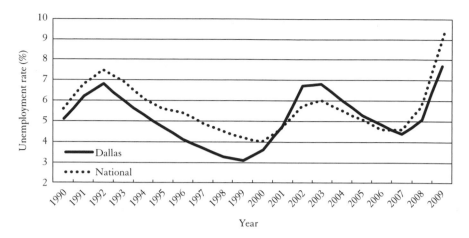

Figure 4. Unemployment rate in Dallas area vs. national average (not seasonally adjusted). The unemployment rate for Dallas and its tech-heavy suburbs, Plano and Irving, hovered slightly below the national average until mid-2001, when it began to surpass the national rate, due primarily to losses in technology-related sectors. In the more recent recession, Dallas's unemployment rate, while high relative to the previous two downturns, remained slightly below the national average. Data from U.S. Department of Labor, Bureau of Labor Statistics.

suspect that many of the jobs lost would not be coming back, at least not in the same industries and not any time soon.

Dallasites did not need to read the papers to know that the tech industry remained in a slump. They could simply look around them. The Deep Ellum neighborhood had never taken off as planned. At night the area teemed with more young club goers than ever, but by day its streets were filled with the detritus of the previous night's activities, and the crime rate was on the rise.[38] The increasing number of empty storefronts there did not necessarily reflect a tech-specific crisis, but they did stand as an apt metaphor for the city's disenchantment with the lure of dot-com prosperity. A local high-tech awards ceremony was canceled for fear of offending the thousands of Dallas tech workers laid off by the very companies it intended to honor, and the Dallas Internet Society stopped holding meetings in early 2003.

Along the Telecom Corridor, office vacancy rates more than doubled between 2000 and 2001, and in 2001, the Dallas metropolitan area was home to 2.86 million square feet of unoccupied office space. The situation worsened as the telecom slump continued, and by 2003 the city of Plano alone had more than 4.5 million square feet of empty office space, and office vacancies neared 30 percent regionwide.[39] Oddly enough, although Infomart was also home to a large number of telecom companies by the time the market crashed, its occupancy rates, although not unaffected, remained relatively high throughout the downturn. As telecom boomed over the late 1990s, Infomart had leased less "people space," or offices, and more storage space for telecom companies' massive switches and computer servers. Although dwindling funds or bankruptcy forced some occupants to vacate their Infomart offices and storerooms, most companies, even as they hemorrhaged workers by the thousands, still needed space for the massive equipment on which their businesses depended.

Infomart's resilience, then, stemmed from its timely divorcing of its own prospects from those of the Dallas labor force.[40] Although servers and switches remained business musts, individual workers did not. It is the stories of those individual workers, then, that truly convey the scale and scope of job loss and unemployment in Dallas and its high-tech industries.

2

A Company of One

Enrique Vivar knew his chances of being let go in the company's next round of layoffs were high. The projects he had been working on of late were, in his own words, "not horribly essential" to his team's bottom line. Still, said Enrique, a midlevel engineer and project manager, he continued to work hard, staying late and taking on additional responsibilities when asked. He averaged about fifty hours a week in the office, in addition to pursuing his Executive MBA on nights and weekends. He considered this a respectable work week, but knew his manager disagreed:

[My manager] said, "You need to work more, you need to work extra hours." I said, "Hey, I'm already working forty-five to fifty hours a week. I'm not even going out to lunch because we have conference calls with Pacific Time…and sometimes I'm leaving the office at 5:30 or 6:00 p.m. I get here at eight o'clock in the morning. I'm working fifty hours a week. I'm pursuing an MBA and I've got family too.…I had a small kid who's three years old at that time, a newborn, a wife who didn't work, and, you know, we don't have any family to help us, and I'm dealing with work, MBA, and family. I'm trying to juggle everything. So, I mean, I thought I was doing a good job, doing my work.

When he was called into his manager's office in October 2001 on the day after the pending layoff was announced, Enrique was disappointed but not particularly surprised.

Enrique is a cheerful, talkative man in his midthirties with dark, wavy hair and smiling brown eyes. Fluent in three languages, he peppered our discussions with vivid, insightful metaphors, comparing himself at various moments to a bear, a gardener, a prostitute, and a Ferrari. A native of Mexico who has lived in the United States for more than eighteen years, Enrique considers himself "fully bicultural," but frequently referenced his Latin-ness when explaining his personality and behavior. "Latins," he said, "are very warm. We've got to give twenty thousand hugs and kisses to say hello and another twenty thousand hugs and kisses to say goodbye.... We crack a joke every second." In this case, the stereotype fits. Enrique is charming and funny; his warmth and sincerity pervaded our interviews, particularly when conversation turned to his family, wife Anna and their children, three-year-old Maya and eight-month-old David.

At eighteen, Enrique moved to the United States from Mexico City to study engineering at UCLA. Upon graduating he returned to Mexico where he found a job with an engineering firm and was soon promoted to project manager. After five stressful but exciting years there, Enrique moved to a U.S. engineering and architectural firm, where he led an effort to lay 3,200 miles of fiber-optic cable in Mexico. Enrique was laid off in 1999 when that company disbanded its international division, but the firm's CEO immediately hired him to undertake a joint consulting venture, which dulled the sting of the layoff significantly. When that new company was not successful, Enrique, by then living in Dallas with his U.S.-born wife and their first child, started talking to employment recruiters, also known as headhunters. After a few near misses (he was offered a job but let go before he even began working there when the company instituted a hiring freeze), one of the recruiters he was working with called to tell Enrique that he had been offered a job, without even being interviewed, by a start-up telecommunications company; if he accepted, he would start the following week. Although he was concerned by the company's unorthodox hiring practices, Enrique had heard good things about the company's owner, who, he said, was "like the Bill Gates of telecommunications"; with no other offers on the table, he took the job. It did not start well.

> I got in there on a Monday and on Wednesday the person I reported to directly was [laid off and] escorted out.... There [were] no procedures, nobody would tell you what to do. It took me five weeks just to get voicemail. I was one of the very lucky ones to have a computer when I got there. There were people, it took them three weeks to get computers. I asked for a laptop because I could take my laptop to meetings, take the minutes and stuff like that.... It took them three months.

Although initially hired as a software developer on a contract basis, after a year Enrique was brought on full time and promoted to the position of project manager soon after.

As the telecommunications industry started its downward spiral, however, the company's business slowed and its stock plummeted. On a Monday morning in October, employees were told by conference call that there were going to be layoffs; employees who were losing their jobs would be informed by their managers over the coming week. Enrique got his call the next morning.

> So the next day I got there as usual at eight o'clock, and the manager calls me in and says, "I need to see you." And I said, "I don't want to see you." [*Laughs*] He knew that I knew, and so I just walked into his office, and he said, "I'm really sorry to tell you, but..." And what struck me as odd was that I really had a good relationship with my manager. I mean, we went to lunches together.... He called me into his office, gave me my papers, and said, "You know, this is nothing personal."

Like most of his laid-off peers, Enrique harbored no personal animosity for the manager who delivered the news—the two kept in touch for years after—nor for the company's executives. As he saw it, they were all victims of economic forces beyond any of their control. Yet while he believed that the decision to lay him off was beyond his immediate supervisor's control, Enrique still marveled that the man he lunched with, whom he considered a friend, was terminating him. As well, while the description of his layoff as "nothing personal" was intended to bolster and reassure Enrique, the impersonality of the layoff was what most disturbed him.

> I was able to go and say goodbye to some of my coworkers and friends, and I was escorted out within an hour. I got there at eight o'clock, he called me in at 8:10, and by 9:10 I was out of there. No [employee ID] badge, no nothing. Of course they had police officers making sure that safety was [maintained]. I knew that it was going to be that way. I had heard about it. I had seen it previously because we had had layoffs twice before. I had seen it. I knew that it was the way to do it, but I felt like a piece of furniture.

He understood the security protocol for layoffs—he had witnessed it before and agreed with its rationality—but the process stung nonetheless, highlighting as it did the uncomfortable similarities between himself and a discarded desk chair. Still, as he saw it, an employer's merit was determined more by how they handle layoffs than by whether they have them, and ultimately he thought his employer did a pretty good job.

Once he had been escorted out of the building, Enrique found himself unsure of where to go next.

> I was afraid to go home. It was a very tough time for me. But at the same time I knew I hadn't done anything [to cause] it....And at the same time I felt like I had done something wrong....Was it the MBA? Was it that talk with [my boss] about tak[ing] over more projects? Was it the fact that I wasn't working seventy hours a week? What is it, you know?

Enrique's waffling over how great a role his job performance and conduct played in the decision to let him go reveals a profound ambivalence, one I explore later in this chapter, over the extent to which individual employees determine their own professional fates. Despite his fears and financial concerns, however, Enrique was comforted by the fact that he had survived this experience before and would certainly make it through this time as well.

Like many other technology professionals who lost their jobs between 2000 and 2003, Enrique was no stranger to the layoff process. Only thirty-two, he had been laid off once before and had seen scores of friends and colleagues let go in similar downsizings, closings, and reorganizations. As a young man just out of college, Enrique expected to "take the company," a term he translates from his native Spanish as meaning to stay employed at one company for life. After his first layoff, his perspective on loyalty—both his and that of his employer—became more complicated.

> People are not loyal anymore. I'm very loyal to a company. I consider myself pretty loyal to a company, *if* they're nice to me. I really see that it's a give-and-take type of relationship. You want me to do something, you've got to pay me to do something. Things are changing—I've got to do these things, you've got to pay me. But if somebody else tells me to do the exact same thing and they pay me more, I'm going to go away....I have changed. I am a changed man. I'm not loyal to anyone. I'll sell my soul to anyone but the devil as long as the price is right.

In just a few sentences, Enrique's description of himself shifted from loyal employee to "pretty loyal" when treated well to a man for sale to the highest bidder.[1] Loyalty is a trait he valued highly, but not one he saw as part of a revised (some would say dismantled) social contract between employer and employee. That Enrique's ambivalent attitude toward loyalty was shared by many of his white-collar contemporaries has been attributed by Richard Sennett to the character-corroding nature of modern employment.[2] Yet Enrique had not given up on loyalty completely; it mattered a great deal to him in his relationships outside of work. He spoke often of how fortunate he was to have a handful of loyal, longtime friends who supported him throughout his layoff and job search.

> I have some friends...they're actually David's godparents, and they did something which I think is very touching. He [David's godfather] was out of work when I had a job at [the telecom start-up]. And I kept on saying, "Come on" [in an encouraging tone]. I talked to him twice a week, three times a week, and said, "You're going to keep on going." Well, the cards turned, and I was the one laid off. And all of a sudden out of the blue I get this care package. It's [covered in] happy faces, and I open it up and there is candy and stuff like that and I open up the card and there were forty dollars. Two twenties. And [the card] said, "Go out with the family, have dinner on us, and the candy is to sweeten your life." I mean, that was, I'm the type of guy that hardly cries, but I shed a tear because somebody is really interested in you, somebody cares for you, and the fact is that you don't expect things like that. You do not expect things like that. So once that happens you really know that there's a place for you in life.

The value Enrique placed on loyalty in his long-term personal relationships stands in sharp contrast to his avowed mercenary attitude toward employment. Enrique did, however, take great pride in the quality of his work and had developed strong relationships with coworkers and clients that he retained long after leaving a job. Although he believed that he worked hard for his employer, Enrique saw it as a marriage of convenience, not commitment. The company had its best interests in mind just as he had his. As he put it, "I'm not going to be married to any company. If somebody comes and says, 'Here, we'll double your salary or [give you a] 50 percent increase in your salary,' heck, you know, the bear dances for money. Remember that."[3] When Enrique compared himself to a dancing bear, he pointed to the absurdity of conceptualizing the relationship between employer and employee as one buttressed by love or loyalty. The bear might love his trainer, and the trainer might return his affection, but when the music starts, the bear dances because his next meal depends on it. The foundation of every employment contract is the exchange of labor for money, as Enrique and his peers exhort every U.S. worker to remember.

This has not always been the case. For much of the twentieth century in the United States, loyalty was a highly valued part of the employment contract; loyal employees were recognized and rewarded, and workers sought out and stayed with companies that promised a secure, familial workplace. It was a time when the bear, in theory, at least, danced for money *and* for love. Yet, as Enrique noted, times have changed, and it was not employees like him who changed them.

The term *layoff* once referred to a temporary interruption in one's job. During lean periods, workers were let go with the understanding that they would be rehired as soon as business picked up. In the 1970s and 1980s, however, layoffs in the United States became more frequent, more permanent, and more likely to occur in prosperous companies following the new "lean and mean" management ethos. Attributed to a mélange of forces, including automation, deindustrialization, business cycles, and cost cutting, often achieved by sending jobs overseas, these layoffs initially affected mostly blue-collar workers. During these decades, most laid-off blue-collar workers were as shocked as they were angry. Many felt betrayed by companies to which they had dedicated years of hard work, companies they had believed in, even loved. Works such as Kathryn Dudley's *The End of the Line,* Dimitra Doukas's *Worked Over,* June Nash's *From Tank Town to*

High Tech, and Michael Moore's documentary film *Roger and Me* vividly express the personal and communal trauma wrought by these mass layoffs and plant closings.[4] Yet just as layoffs were becoming a predictable, if by no means welcome, part of blue-collar working life, corporations found a new group of unsuspecting workers to upend.

White-collar workers have accounted for a steadily increasing proportion of total U.S. job losses since the 1980s.[5] Each of the last four recessions, the durations of which are designated by the National Bureau of Economic Research as 1981–1982, 1990–1991, 2001, and 2007–2009,[6] has affected a higher percentage of white-collar workers than the last.[7] Even in the prosperous years sandwiched between those turbulent periods, white-collar jobs were increasingly insecure due to the rising emphasis on "flexible"— easily hirable and fire-able—labor (a trend heartily embraced by high-tech firms), the availability of inexpensive white-collar laborers abroad, and the financial pressures of quarterly reporting.[8]

Although they had seen their blue-collar countrymen and -women suffer through widespread layoffs in preceding decades, most white-collar workers were unprepared when the tide of layoffs swept in their direction. Those same white-collar workers had often been less than sympathetic to manufacturing workers who lost their jobs in mass layoffs or plants closings. Many used the logic of social Darwinism to fault their newly unemployed blue-collar neighbors for failing to adapt to a changing economy. By not educating themselves in preparation for the postindustrial future, for example, displaced autoworkers were said to have brought their fate upon themselves. They had "fallen to their 'natural' level in the capitalist world economy" while white-collar professionals had risen to theirs.[9]

Interestingly enough, white-collar workers blindsided by layoffs in the 1980s were similarly uncharitable to themselves when attributing blame for their own downward mobility.[10] Caught up as they were in the managerial world's ideology of meritocratic individualism, which equates professional failure with personal shortcomings, displaced managers often experienced their layoffs as evidence of their own inadequacy. Even in the midst of self-blame, however, laid-off white-collar workers in the 1980s joined their blue-collar peers in raging at employers they believed had betrayed them. They had worked hard, been loyal, had "taken the company," as Enrique would say, and yet they found themselves receiving pink slips instead of promotions.

In many respects, high-tech workers laid off in the early 2000s felt and behaved similarly to white-collar workers laid off two decades before. They were surprised and angry, frustrated and scared. Some blamed themselves; some blamed the economy. Some, although fewer than might be expected, blamed their employers for mismanaging the company or for laying off the wrong people. But almost no tech workers I spoke with criticized their employers for disloyalty or for not providing cradle-to-grave employment, which marks a significant change from the managerial culture of the 1980s, where protection from layoffs was supposed to be merit's reward. Modern-day tech workers no longer expected a company to provide such things.

Forty-seven-year-old Phil Wright had worked in high technology for twenty-five years when I interviewed him in 2002. His career spanned half a dozen states, twice as many subfields (many of which did not exist when he began his career in 1977), and companies large, small, and downright tiny. Although Phil's employment history hardly fit the traditional career narrative of steady progress up a corporate ladder, it is the sort of narrative one hears over and over again when talking with U.S. workers today. The average U.S. worker now changes jobs at least ten times over the course of a career, and workers in the high-tech hub of Silicon Valley twice as many as that. The careers of young workers will likely only push those numbers higher; the average thirty-two-year-old in 2000 had already worked for nine different companies.[11] Although Phil never planned to have such a varied career, it turns out to have suited him.

> Once I know a subject... when it gets to the point of just turning the crank and making things happen, it's not a lot of interest to me. I've always said that I'm very stable in my personal life. My wife and I have been married for twenty-seven years. But on my business life, you know, I'm a little more erratic. I'm a huge risk-taker on the business side of things.

Since his previous layoff, in June 2001 when the e-commerce company he worked for closed down, Phil said with a smile, "I've been doing everything I can not to find a job." Instead, he had become an independent consultant for start-up companies, helping entrepreneurs get their businesses off the ground. His income depended on those firms receiving funding, and at the time we spoke he had yet to make a dime. The couple was living off their savings, and Phil's wife, who had been taking a break from her career in sales, was considering returning to work to help pay the bills. Despite such concerns, Phil was enjoying himself and was optimistic that the work he had put in would eventually pay off.

Phil's willingness to embark on a risky, uncertain career as a start-up consultant is in part a product of his personality. It is also, however, a corollary of his broader understanding of contemporary employment, in which, he argued, all work is risky, and all jobs are by definition temporary.

> During the eighties, companies realized they don't have any loyalty to their employees anymore. During the nineties, employees realized they don't have any loyalty to their companies anymore. And now, I think, any employment is based on a need and a skill. You know, very much on a contractual basis. If a company has a need for my skills and I can supply that to them, they hire me. When that need is over with, when they don't need me anymore, sure, I'm terminated. And I was just having, I'll say a discussion but it was really an argument with good, good friends of ours over the weekend, and they're still thinking in that old mode. And that old mode doesn't exist anymore. They're saying, "Oh, but it's so terrible to have people working at a company twenty years and then they lay them off." Yeah, [obviously it is terrible]. What's your point? I don't know any company, where it's in their charter, where it's in their goal as a company, to provide employment to people. You know, it's just not there. They're in business to provide a service or a product. They're not in business to hire people.

If, as Phil believed, risk and impermanence are intrinsic components of the "new mode" of employment, setting out on one's own, as he had, is not all that more risky than trying to live out one's career at a single employer.[12] Even those who were far less enthusiastic risk-takers than Phil agreed with him that loyalty is the hallmark of a bygone era.[13] Some workers preferred this matter-of-fact transaction to the paternalistic work relationships of yore, while others remembered (or imagined) fondly an era of employment security and an expansive corporate welfare system. Yet whether suspicious of or nostalgic for that bygone era, nearly all agreed that the days of corporate loyalty are over. Long gone, and likely for good.[14]

For some, this changed attitude toward layoffs and insecure employment was born out of personal, often painful, experience. Mike Barnard, a fast-talking, white, native Texan approaching his fiftieth birthday, lost his job in late September 2001 when the large media company he worked for halted their expansion into new telecommunication technologies and disbanded Mike's entire department. Mike did not initially plan to work in high tech. As an undergraduate at the University of Texas at Austin, he planned to be a doctor. After realizing "that memorizing phonebook-sized tomes wasn't for me," he switched his major to Radio, TV, and Film. Upon graduating he worked in television production, primarily making corporate training and marketing videos. Then sometime in the late 1980s he read a book called *The Media Lab* about "the convergence of computing along with text and motion media," which he immediately saw as the future of his field: "I thought, you know, this is where my career is going to be going, following whatever this convergence thing leads to."[15] From that point on, in a variety of positions—some full-time corporate jobs, some freelance gigs, once at a company he founded with a friend—Mike explored the interrelationship of media production and emerging technologies—first laser discs, then CD-ROMs, then online streaming media. It was his curiosity about where the future of media technologies might be headed that led him to his previous position, which involved helping a relatively traditional media company transition into the Internet age. Until, that is, the funding for the new venture ran out.

This was not the first time Mike had lost a job, and he suspected it would not be the last. Despite his frustration watching a department he built from scratch vanish in the post-9/11 economic panic, Mike's most recent layoff was much easier than those that preceded it:

> The first time you get laid off, you're like, "Oh my god. What have I done wrong? Obviously I've done something wrong." And it happens a couple of times for various reasons and you go, "You know, I didn't do anything, and not only that, this is a bump in the road. Something else will pop up." And sure enough it always does.

Losing a job, Mike joked, gets easier with practice, and today's workers are getting far more practice at it than they would like. Nearly 60 percent of job seekers in this study had been laid off more than once.[16] Despite high tech's reputation as a uniquely volatile industry, this figure is not far from that of the U.S. population at large. Over half of all families have experienced at least one layoff, and nearly one-fifth of U.S. workers were laid off in the previous three years alone.[17]

Job seekers' attitudes to layoffs are also shaped by their perceptions of the economic climate in which their layoffs and job searches took place. Nearly 80 percent of laid-off technology workers in the Dallas–Fort Worth area cited the condition of the U.S. economy as the primary reason for their job loss.[18] Job seekers tended to view their former employers not as enemies or betrayers, but as fellow victims of economic forces beyond the company's control. Amit Mehta, a slim, soft-spoken thirty-year-old from northern India, had lived in the United States for nearly ten years when I interviewed him in 2002. Amit lost his job as a revenue analyst at an airline software company in Dallas a few months after the terrorist attacks of September 11, 2001. Although this was his first layoff—and from his first job out of graduate school—Amit was matter of fact about his departure from the company:

> After September 11th...in order to maintain the stock price [as profits dropped across the airline industry], the only way that seemed fit was to cut costs and the only way to cut costs at that point was...to let go of people. And so after that we had a 10 percent reduction in workforce and my job was eliminated.

Amit's description of events framed his layoff not as a tragic tale of failure or betrayal but as a sound managerial decision in the face of declining profits. He still used the term *we* when referring to the company from which he was let go, a subtle indicator of how profoundly he had internalized the company's point of view. In characterizing layoffs as the unavoidable and appropriate response to lagging profits, Amit relieved himself and his former employer of responsibility for any pain caused by those layoffs. Instead, they were both at the mercy of broader forces, in this case the devastating aftermath of 9/11. The attacks of September 11, 2001, were so dramatic and intimately tied to job seekers' images of the downturn and their job loss that occasionally even those who lost their jobs before September 11 cited the attacks as one of the factors behind their layoff.

Job seekers usually described 9/11 as one element of a perfect storm of crises of the early 2000s—the dot-com crash, Enron scandal, implosion of the telecommunications industry, and the national recession that followed. The factor job seekers referenced most often to explain their job loss and difficulty finding reemployment, however, was the economy—which they described as "sick," "soft," "down," and "in the tank." As Andrew Ross found in his research among dot-com employees in New York, "the market was perceived as an unchallenged authority that was somehow denying the company permission to succeed, and very little could be done about it."[19] When Enrique Vivar explained, "I just feel that the economy isn't strong enough to give me a job," for instance, I asked him what it was that had made the economy that way, and he offered a laundry list of factors.

> It's a lot of things, Carrie. I feel that there was a lack of leadership in terms of when the [contested 2000] presidential election occurred; there was a lack of trust in the system. Hey, the system is not working, we can't elect a president. There's the [end of the] telecom era, there's a lack of confidence in the accounting rules that we have, there's a lack of confidence in how we're doing business. You know, the Enron case…MCI, WorldCom. It's a lack of confidence in are we going to go to war, are we not going to go to war? September 11th. It's just everything altogether. Think of how bad it's been the last year and a half. All the events that have led us to today. The fall of the dot-coms, the fall of the telecoms, the fall of Enron, bad accounting at WorldCom, at Qwest, at all of these companies, September 11th, war with Iraq, terrorism with Al Qaeda, a crazy guy in DC shooting people.

To a degree, these public and incontrovertible crises allowed job seekers to look beyond themselves and their employers when they sought to place blame for their current situations. That is not to say job seekers never experienced self-doubt (as discussed in chapter 3), but the belief that they are looking for work in a time of great social and economic crisis shaped how job seekers experienced and understood individual job loss. When corporations close entire departments and lay off as much as 70 percent of their workforce in a single day, it is difficult to argue that employees are being selected for termination on the grounds of personal shortcomings. And as tens of thousands of highly qualified applicants flooded an already weak labor market, even the most strident individualists in the tech workforce came to believe that certain forces and events were beyond one's control, that bad layoffs can indeed happen to good people.

For some workers, this normalization of job loss occurred gradually over the course of a career. Other job seekers, particularly those in the first decades of their professional life, never expected a career characterized by anything other than frequent job change. The "organization man" model of employment has never been a reality for Americans in their twenties and thirties—not for them, not for their peers, and rarely for their parents. By the close of the twentieth century, most young people entering the job market were familiar with the prevalence of layoffs and held no expectation of lifelong employment.[20] As one Dallas career counselor explained:

> The new generation has a different perspective, because they no longer have the influence that you go to school and go to a corporation and they'll take care of you. That definitely has been ingrained to the next generation. The corporation will not be taking care of you.

No interviewee espoused this view as clearly and as fervently as Daniel Klein, a twenty-eight-year-old software developer. Raised in southern California by two serial entrepreneurs, Daniel took a while to settle on a major, complete college, and find his way into the field of high tech. At the height of the Internet craze, Daniel found himself working at one of the most lauded dot-com consulting firms of the era. He enjoyed the firm's inclusive, if at times all-consuming, corporate culture, and became close friends with a number of coworkers. He was disappointed to be among the six hundred employees let go in the company's first round of layoffs in early 2001 (the company closed down a year and a half later) but not surprised or angry: "You can't be angry," he said, "at a company that is just trying to cut its losses." Seizing the opportunity to live closer to his long-distance girlfriend, Natalie (whose own layoff is discussed in chapter 5), Daniel moved from San Francisco to Dallas to work for a more stable, if decidedly less sexy, software firm specializing in health care management.

In his first two years there, Daniel was promoted twice, and became one of the company's youngest managers. As much as he enjoyed the stability and upward mobility of his new job, Daniel made no assumptions about his future there and was critical of coworkers who did:

> I think some employees sometimes complain that their career growth isn't managed here [at his current company]. That always annoys me because I feel like, you guys aren't children. You need to manage your own careers. We can help you, but if you don't take responsibility for your career growth then you're hurting yourself. Why should a company have to do that for you?...People say, "Well, I gave the company ten years, blah blah blah

blah blah." Look, they paid you for those ten years, so I think you're even, you know?

To Daniel, the very ideas of corporate loyalty and company-sponsored professional development were not just outdated but ridiculous. He saw no logical reason why corporations would perform those functions for employees, or why employees would expect them to. More specifically, Daniel cast himself as the reasonable adult, in contrast to coworkers who, "like children," adopt an attitude of dependence toward their employer. This framing of secure employment as a form of childish dependence represents a significant shift from previous models of white-collar work. It allowed Daniel to adopt a posture of self-reliance that shored up his threatened masculinity and professional identity but relinquished any ground from which he might launch a critique of his former employer or the broader system of increasingly insecure employment. In addition, while Daniel was quick to dismiss others' belief that they are entitled to a job as an illusion, he failed to recognize the extent to which his own "independence" was equally illusory; at least for the time being, he, as much as they, depended on his employer for his livelihood.

In his advice for his coworkers—"manage your own careers"—Daniel articulated a belief expressed, with varying degrees of fervor, by every job seeker I interviewed: that the key to professional success today lies not in loyalty but in well-planned autonomy. This philosophy, encapsulated by the phrase "career management," served simultaneously as a mental model of work and the labor market, a set of behavioral guidelines, and a badge of identification for its loyal adherents. While the high-technology workforce of Dallas did not invent this ideology (I trace its origins later in this chapter), nor are they its only adherents, it was an integral, even defining aspect of how they conceptualized themselves, the employment relationship, and the nature of professional success.

At core, *career management* entails seeing oneself not as an employee, even when traditionally employed, but as an independent entrepreneur, as, in the words of one job seeker, "a company of one." Mike Barnard described this new attitude toward employment, one he thought all workers needed to adopt if they wanted to protect themselves against job insecurity:

We're not going to go back to the sixties or seventies or whatever in terms of the job market, so I think people are going to have to start changing their view on their jobs.... You need to be able to look at your job now as tempo-rary and evolving. Learning is the new labor.[21] That's what it is. It's being able to go and look at your job as evolving, look at yourself as an indepen-dent contractor, more as an independent contractor and less as an employee. Think of what it is that you can offer as opposed to [asking,] "What do you want me to do?" Be more proactive at what it is that you're trying to do. [That is] where the answers really lie.... Going out and looking for a job, it's a sucker's game. You'll keep it as long as they want to let you have it. That's easy to say. A lot of people are more than happy to go and do the nine-to-five gig and go home and not worry about it, but they are liable to be a victim. They will be victimized because they allow themselves to be.

Like Daniel, Mike positioned himself as an independent forward thinker against the foil of the "suckers" and "victims" who perceive job security as a possibility, let alone a right. The claim of heroic self-reliance is again used to establish a masculine agency, while victimhood is defined not by losing a job or experiencing professional or financial hardship but by the very act of seeking secure employment.

Peter Dumond, a white former chief technology officer who looks much younger than his thirty-eight years, something he says has served him well in the youth-obsessed culture of high tech, argued that career managers[22] are simply responding to a changed labor market in which there is no lon-ger much practical difference between a so-called permanent position and a temporary contract job:

I think everybody's going to turn into [a contractor]. I think this [recent spate of layoffs] is going to further kill the thought of lifetime employ-ment.... Most people now are only staying two years at a job. It used to be, three years ago, five years was the average. Back before the early nineties people were staying twenty years. Their whole lives. [Most people stay] two years now. What's the difference between two years at a company and tak-ing a one-year contract? One year. And in some cases, you just take a second contract and you've extended that to two years.

According to Peter and his fellow job seekers, many of whom had al-ready worked as contractors at some point in their career, if your job is no more secure or long-term than a contract position, it makes sense that you should think and behave like a contractor, conceptualizing each job as just one in a long string of temporary contract positions.[23] The ideal career manager cannot, as they see it, allow him or herself to be lulled into a false sense of security. Each position is simply preparation for the next, an opportunity to hone and expand your skills, ideally while performing satisfying, high-quality work. A career is no longer the linear progression up a predetermined corporate ladder. Instead, it is something to be actively pieced together from an assortment of part-time and contract positions, so-called permanent jobs, periods of self-employment, and, inevitably, occasional unemployment. Even while employed, career managers must stay abreast of industry trends and keep their skills and professional degrees and certifications relentlessly up to date, a daunting and often expensive task considering the rapid rate of technological change in most high-tech professions. Career managers must assemble and maintain active networks of personal and professional contacts to whom they can turn for information, job leads, and additional contacts.[24] They must remain constantly aware of labor market trends, such as what skills are in demand, what industries are in decline, and which appear likely to grow in the future. A career manager's most important connection, then, is not to an individual employer, but to his or her professional network and to the labor market itself.[25] Accordingly, employability has become the new measure of security for career managers, taking priority over actual employment.[26]

The logic of career management provides these workers with a narrative for themselves and their careers that does not depend on old patterns of upward mobility. It is a narrative that is by no means unique to these job seekers, but one that increasingly characterizes how white-collar workers across the country think and talk about themselves and their careers. Much of career management's distinctiveness stems from its explicit rejection of previous ways of thinking about loyalty, security, and the social contract of employment, particularly those espoused by the organization men of the postwar era and the meritocratic individualists of the 1980s. Organization men followed the Calvinist tradition of seeing hard work and self-sacrifice as the key to occupational success. Today's white-collar workers argue that being a loyal employee, or even a talented employee, is not enough to guarantee success in today's hypercompetitive economy.

Career management also revises the tenets of meritocratic individualism to reflect the changed realities of the professional labor market, which it frames as both natural and inalterable. Blending together the Protestant work ethic and the all-American lure of entrepreneurship, career managers see themselves as entitled to prosperity not so much on the basis of their technical skills (although they pride themselves on those as well) but on their willingness to take responsibility for upgrading and marketing those skills. This new narrative frames the insecure nature of contemporary employment as a means through which workers accumulate a varied and valuable portfolio of skills that will ensure their future prosperity. Erving Goffman argues that a person's self-image and framework for evaluating oneself and others, what Goffman terms a "moral career," changes over one's life course.[27] At each point, the individual's image of his own past, present, and future is constructed in such a way as to explain his current situation, usually in a favorable light. Career managers' professional narratives therefore construct unemployment as neither anomaly nor tragedy, but as just another component of the varied career they have been actively culling over the course of their professional lives.

As is clear from the quotations above, the narrative of the autonomous, flexible company of one depends to a great extent on the foil of the naïve, dependent corporate victim who is still playing loyal employee in a world where such a role is not only unrewarded but actively scorned. In contrast, career managers emphasize their independence and unwillingness to trust in employers' largesse. Career management thus provides a narrative that celebrates rather than stigmatizes job seekers' unsteady employment records and associates job loss not with failure but with self-reliance and a willingness to do whatever it takes to succeed.

In adopting an ethos that celebrates self-determination above all else, even prosperity, white-collar career managers situate themselves as the latest incarnation of a distinctly American tradition. Kathryn Dudley, writing about Midwestern farmers in the 1980s, argues:

> Independence and self-reliance are the qualities of character traditionally thought to guarantee success in U.S. society. Not the kind of "success" associated with conspicuous consumption or the excessive display of material wealth, but the moral achievement associated with being "your own boss." It is not for the comforts or pleasures of a moneyed life that the self-reliant strive, but the wherewithal to be beholden to no one. The freedom to call your own shots, take your own risks, and rise or fall on your own merits is, to the independent-minded, the only brass ring worth reaching for.[28]

What tech workers and farmers share—along with actors, athletes, and musicians, all of whom have been found to espouse a similar view toward professional autonomy—is the experience of working in a volatile industry, one in which neither employment nor prosperity is guaranteed by any entity larger than one's self.[29] Amid the insecurity inherent in the fast-paced, innovation-fueled world of high tech, workers espouse a worldview modeled after America's origin myth of self-reliant pioneers fending for themselves in a risky environment where job security is something you create yourself rather than something gifted from above. (One online job board catering to contract workers claims to "reflect the 'spirit' of workforce pioneers who are leaving the corporate world to become independent professionals."[30]) The unemployed worker is refashioned into a frontier-like, self-sufficient career manager who, in the words of one job seeker, "takes control of [his or her] own destiny." The high-technology industry may be notoriously volatile and insecure, but if current trends continue, this perspective is likely to become more the norm than the exception for U.S. workers.[31]

Career managers frame themselves as savvy pragmatists pioneering new strategies for navigating an increasingly insecure world. They are in good, or at least plentiful, company; a 2003 survey found that over half of adult workers in the United States are confident in their ability to earn a stable income outside of conventional work structures.[32] Yet tracing the origins and development of the ideology of career management belies the sense one sometimes gets from talking with job seekers that theirs is a philosophy forged by a grassroots movement of professionals. Career managers did not invent this ideology, nor are they alone in espousing it. Instead, the idea that workers must function as companies of one has its roots in management culture and is intimately connected to a decades-long corporate campaign to "prevent emotional commitments to the firm, and make sure that employees, when shown the door, will not seek the window instead."[33]

Ironically, in the early twentieth century, corporations fought doggedly to instill the very mindset they now urge employees to shed. In the late 1800s, when self-employment was the ideal for middle-class white men in the United States, companies had to convince employees that a career within a corporation was a legitimate and sufficiently masculine option for ambitious, talented young men. To this end, employers started offering employees insurance, pensions, and other benefits under a budding system of welfare capitalism. To foster employee loyalty, they popularized the image of the corporation as a family and developed internal promotion systems that promised advancement and prestige to enterprising employees, allowing every young clerk to believe that he too might someday run the company.[34] Their tactics worked, creating generations of white-collar employees who not only embraced but felt entitled to lifelong corporate employment and the accompanying benefits.

The transition from encouraging loyalty to aggressively discouraging it was a gradual one for corporate America. When, in 1976, management expert Douglas T. Hall encouraged employees to proactively manage their own "protean careers," he was revolutionizing the very notion of what constituted a career.[35] At that time, most companies employed entire Human Resources departments to usher employees into, up through, and sometimes out of the organization. As Hall saw it, replacing institutionalized promotion tracks with individualized career trajectories would empower workers and create mutually beneficial partnerships between employer and employee. The language Hall and subsequent management experts used to characterize this new attitude to work and mobility is essentially identical to that of the job seekers quoted above. Employees were urged to "act as their own bosses and to behave as if they are running their own little businesses within the larger concern," as the welfare capitalist's "imagery of love and marriage [was] replaced by an imagery of temporary, short-term affairs or one-night stands."[36] When Enrique declares he is "not going to be married to any company," he is not so much rejecting a proffered proposal as mirroring the attitude most employers now encourage.

Although career management was initially offered as a strategy for improving performance and increasing job satisfaction within a particular firm, it was a short step from urging employees to act like empowered entrepreneurs within the corporation to asking them to act similarly on their way out. Many companies now inform employees upon hiring that they have no intention of providing lifelong employment.[37] In a particularly direct example, a sign posted on a bulletin board at a downsizing manufacturing plant read:

We can't promise you how long we'll be in business.
We can't promise you that we won't be bought by another company.

We can't promise that there'll be room for promotion.
We can't promise that your job will exist until you reach retirement age.
We can't promise that the money will be available for your pension.
We can't expect your undying loyalty and we aren't sure we want it.[38]

Such blunt disclaimers are, however, relatively rare. More often, the message comes cloaked in the familiar language of self-empowerment, as when an executive explains, "To give my employees job security would be to disempower them and relieve them of the responsibility that they need to feel for their own success."[39] Corporate endorsements of career management are now reinforced through other cultural outlets targeting the U.S. middle-class, including career advice manuals, self-help books, business school curriculum, and mainstream media coverage of job loss and unemployment.[40] This rhetorical reframing of insecurity neatly transfers the burden of maintaining the social contract squarely onto the shoulders of the individual worker, who is expected not only to bear that burden but to welcome it as an opportunity for self-reliance.

Although it would be an overstatement to say that the job seekers I met welcomed that burden (few, for instance, employ the emphatically pro-insecurity rhetoric of "free agenteers"[41]), they have in effect consented to shoulder it. The language they employ to describe their approach to work and career draws directly on the discourse of impermanence, autonomy, and responsibility espoused by corporate employers. This should come as no surprise, since most job seekers were once managers themselves, and as such have had ample exposure to managerial culture and vernacular. Yet it calls into question what, exactly, it means for a job seeker to declare him- or herself a company of one. It is too simplistic to suggest that in parroting managerial ideologies of autonomy and impermanence career managers are unwitting dupes of a rigged system. Despite the sometimes valiant tone with which they announced their independence, and the near-evangelical ardor with which they suggested others do likewise, career managers were well aware that insecure employment was foisted on them rather than forged by them. And yet it is equally clear that in embracing individual responsibility, job seekers have internalized the logic of the corporation at the expense of other ways of seeing the world.

For example, despite the presumptions of neoclassical economics, corporations and individual employees are not equivalent entities. Regardless of how vehemently job seekers proclaim that employment is a contract entered into by equals, in which either side is free to walk away should that relationship lose its appeal, employers retain the upper hand unless employees are as capable of finding quality reemployment as companies are of finding new workers to replace them. In a tight labor market, this is not the case. Yet in a culture that extols the virtues of individualism it is sometimes difficult to recognize the agency of entities larger than individuals.

The acceptance that layoffs are common, for instance, and not the fault of any one person or company, intertwines with job seekers' belief that there is little if anything they can do to stop layoffs from happening. Looking to the courts, the government, your union, or the generosity of employers to protect you, job seekers from across the political spectrum said, is a fool's errand. (Job seekers in this study, most of whom are not native Texans, were split relatively evenly between the Republican and Democratic parties; a small group of independents and self-proclaimed libertarians situated themselves as political centrists.) As Mike Barnard opined:

> I think that the people that are doing the work need to be a little less naïve, and . . . view themselves as business people and not as somebody who's joining some community. You're not joining a community when you go to work. That's not to say you can't have friendships and so forth, but the community ultimately is autocratic. It's run from the top. The reality is you really don't have a say. You may not like that they're going to lay you off, but can you do anything about it? Not really. And all the labor laws and stuff like that, they really don't make that much difference if you're fifty-years years old and you've been working at [a large stable company] for twenty-three years and they decide to lay you off. The reality is that they can do this.

In his disinterest in and skepticism of efforts to combat professional insecurity with "labor laws and stuff like that," Mike embodies what Henry Giroux has identified as the "culture of antipolitics" in the United States today which "dismisses as futile both the discourse of critique and the call for social transformation."[42] As everyday life has become increasingly corporatized, Giroux argues, people have lost sight of possible alternatives to the status quo, replacing social values with market values and turning away from collective or institutional solutions to social problems. This perspective is perhaps best encapsulated by the job seeker in his late fifties who told me, "I'm not naïve enough to think that I can change the world on my own, and I'm not going to sacrifice myself in a lost cause. I've been there. I went through the sixties. Beat your head against the wall all you get is a bloody scalp. I don't need that."

For most job seekers, this lack of faith in collective action was coupled with disdain for those who do pursue or suggest organized responses to economic crisis. This attitude was evident when I spoke with job seekers in 2004 about the practice of *offshoring,* or sending work overseas to lower-cost locations.[43] Although the country at large was said to be erupting into a "blaze of anti-outsourcing activism," the job seekers I spoke with exhibited no such inclination.[44]

The stir over offshoring that surfaced during the 2004 presidential primaries did not occur because offshoring was a new or unusual phenomenon. For decades, U.S. manufacturers of everything from cars to shoes to children's toys have been relocating factories across national borders and outsourcing production to foreign firms in pursuit of lower taxes, lenient regulations, and cheaper labor and facilities. The new controversy was sparked by the expansion of the offshoring trend to include operations that are highly paid and require advanced training, particularly those in the high-technology industry. This shift belied the palliative promises that have long been used to justify and promote sending jobs abroad; namely, that the "good jobs"—those requiring education and advanced skills—would always remain at home.

Although their own jobs were some of those now heading overseas, job seekers were remarkably consistent in applying the logic of career management to the global labor market. Mike Barnard's first exposure to offshoring took place in the late 1990s when, as he described, his employer discovered that Indian engineers would work for a third of the money the company was spending on "very high-end, high-dollar engineering talent" in the United States. More recently, on a contract job his team sent their raw data to "some group in Singapore who would go and mush it up into a report" overnight. As Mike saw it, these companies were right to engage in a lucrative and increasingly necessary business practice:

> I think the reality is that with basically instantaneous global telecommunications in place pretty much anywhere, everything being digital, you cannot…remain competitive in anything involving information technology

without at least considering outsourcing as an option.... This whole new economy thing, regardless [of what people want or do], it's going to come. It's going to come because we're seeing it and we're seeing it in transparent borders. We're seeing it in stuff like NAFTA [North American Free Trade Agreement] or whatever. We're seeing it. We're not going to go back to the way we were before, and what we're feeling is pain as we're having to realign ourselves. And the United States has to become part of the global economy and [ask ourselves] if we're going to remain competitive, what do we have to do? We've got to be better marketers. We've got to do smarter things about our business. And when you're dealing with what you can do as an individual, [you] have to start looking at yourself as part of that new economy as well.

In Mike's conceptualization, the appropriate response to global competition is just career management writ onto an international scale. Where others might see the culmination of highly contentious, politically nuanced historical trajectories around industrialization, immigration, globalization, and neoliberalism, Mike saw only individuals (individual nations, individual corporations, individual workers), each responsible for making the best of a situation that was, in Mike's view, beyond their control.[45]

In their commitment to participation in the global economy and disdain for what they perceive as protectionist measures designed to artificially buffer the United States and its workers from the harsher aspects of competition, high-tech workers—and other professionals, managers, and highly trained technical workers—have been accused of slowly seceding from the nations in which they dwell.[46] This privileged class of workers, some fear, feel little connection to either their country or their fellow citizens, and in the face of social problems on the national or global level will withdraw "into their own private habitats, enclaves with security guards if need be."[47] It is true that the workers I spoke with did not feel a nationalist impulse to keep jobs on U.S. soil, and they believed their economic well-being was closely tied to larger global forces. Yet these workers cared deeply about the status of the United States on the global playing field. They saw their enthusiastic participation in the global economy not as rejection of their country but as an effort on its behalf. From their perspective, if anyone is withdrawing into selfish isolationism it is those who refuse to evolve with the times and improve their own skills, preferring instead to erect trade barriers these job seekers believe will work against the United States, artificially isolating it from the global fray and preventing it from assuming its rightful role as the leader of the global tech scene. Not only will each individual be better off when they take responsibility for their own career, the argument goes, but a community of self-reliant workers armed with the latest capabilities and committed to the industries of the future, rather than the past, is best positioned to usher the United States into this new century of global competition.

In their discussions of offshoring, job seekers once again invoked the foil of the willing victim, looking for security in an insecure world. Those who believe companies cannot or should not be able to send jobs overseas were said to suffer from the same delusion as workers who think companies owe them secure, long-term employment. According to Alex Brodsky, the information architect-cum-waiter from the introduction,

> The people who are pissing and moaning about the fact that their job got moved someplace else, those people's problems would exist whether it moved someplace else or whether they got fired or whether they got downsized, they would have the same set of problems.... My response to them is do what you've got to do. I'm really sorry that you can't sit in your cube and get $60,000, $65,000, $70,000, $80,000 a year for writing code because there's a guy who can probably do it better than you and do it faster than you and do it for one-tenth your salary. That part of it is irrelevant. Everybody needs to understand that there's no gold watch anymore. You're not going to go to work for a company and get your pension. You have to be prepared.

The career manager's "solution" to offshoring is not to oppose it ("pissing and moaning" about jobs going overseas "is not going to get you hired any quicker," according to Alex), but to manage your career in the direction that will, at least in theory, best shield you from displacement by foreign competition. In this, career managers invoked once again the language of empowerment, and took upon themselves responsibility for maintaining their employability. They are not, they insisted, victims of the capitalist system. They are willing and conscious participants in that system, each a little capitalist enterprise that stands to gain much more from fully participating in the global economy than from fighting a rearguard campaign against it.

There was a certain self-righteousness in job seekers' endorsement of offshoring. They prided themselves on having adjusted to the economic system, and could be harsh in their assessment of those who ask that the system adjust itself to them. (Important parallels can be drawn here to white-collar workers' critiques of labor unions, and to the disdain U.S. farmers who held onto their farms throughout the 1980's farm crisis expressed toward farmers who rallied against foreclosures.[48] The difference here is that unemployed career managers can hardly be framed as the beneficiaries of the system they endorse.) Enrique Vivar, for instance, attributed the instinct to protest offshoring or ask for corporate or government assistance as born of Americans' inflated sense of entitlement:

> I think in the states we want to earn a lot of money for very little effort. That was the seventies, that was the eighties, and maybe the beginning of the nineties, but times have changed. You know, let me put it to you this way. Why don't [people who are protesting offshoring] go to school one day in the afternoon or two days in the afternoon after work? Why don't they get training, additional training? Oh no, the company's got to pay for it. How many people do you know that invest in themselves so that they can retain their jobs? Is the company supposed to do that or [is] the individual? You want to retain your job, train yourself.

Enrique was offended by the suggestion that things like career advancement and financial security should come naturally, that they should be taken as rights rather than hard-won privileges. His own job loss and unemployment were difficult, he admitted, but as he saw it the difference between him and his anti-offshoring peers was that he was willing to do what it took to improve his own situation:

> I went through an MBA and I had two kids and I was unemployed and I was looking for a job all at the same time. And yeah, it was tough, but if you don't invest [you won't get ahead]. And I'm right now looking at what do I need to do to get reaccredited as a PMP [project management professional], I don't want to lose my accreditation as a PMP. I need to go to school too. I need to take some classes. You need to invest time in yourself. And some people would argue with me. Well, what about family? When is family important? Well, that's one thing. You want to live in the states and you want to live the American Dream, you have to pay a price. There's a price to pay.

It was his willingness to pay that price, Enrique believed, that identified him as a successful career manager and allowed him to shore up his sense of

himself as a manly doer, as opposed to a lazy dependent. On those exhausting days when hours of job searching earned him not a single lead or interview, he was not failing at career management but proving his mettle at it.

Alex Brodsky shared Enrique's pride in having done what he needed to
do to get by. He also shared Enrique's frustration with people who look to
the government for help in their time of need:

> [It's] not so much that it's the government, I just don't feel like anybody
> owes anybody anything. I'm a believer in luck, and I'm a believer in karma.
> But think back about a lot of folks that you know who always seem to have
> the worst luck. There always seems to be this correlation between people
> who don't seem to keep their ducks in a row and a high level of bad luck.
> Granted, I had a lot of bad luck, but I guess the difference is I refused to
> continue having it as much as possible because I didn't dwell so much on
> what happened to me as what I did about it. So just keep getting up, dusting
> yourself off, and going forward, because the minute you don't, you're done.
> You might as well just lay down and die. So I look to myself. I guess I never
> looked to the government. I never expected the government to provide any
> programs, never expected the government to have any kind of further mech-
> anism in place that might see me get employed any sooner. The government
> has really been off the radar for me as far as that goes. I guess that's where it
> comes back to what I was saying before about just what human beings are
> willing and not willing to do. Nobody wants to shovel shit, but they pay you
> for it, and you may have to until something better comes along. I guess for
> anybody who thinks that gainful employment of any kind is below them, I
> guess I don't have a lot of time or sympathy for them.

For Alex, it all came back to doing what you have to do, so long, of
course, as what you have to do does not entail making any demands of
corporations, the government, or your fellow citizens. Alex did receive
government-funded unemployment benefits—as, for that matter, did
Enrique. (Only one interviewee, twenty-five-year-old telecom engineer
Luke Helgesen, who had moved back in with his parents following his
layoff, refused to take his unemployment benefits, which he saw as "too
socialist.") Because those benefits are part of the status quo economic system, however, Enrique and Alex saw them as natural or normal forms
of aid, in contrast to the additional or enhanced (and therefore illegiti-
mate) assistance for which disgruntled protestors are lobbying, such as

protection against layoffs or prohibitions against offshoring. That existing unemployment benefits are themselves the hard-won product of decades of collective labor organizing did not figure into their assessment.

Tech workers' faith in individual achievement clearly shaped their attitudes toward political intervention in economic affairs. Most job seekers were doggedly opposed to government programs or regulations they believed would hinder the system of competition that was, in their view, the foundation of the modern business world. In reality, few Americans, career managers included, espouse a truly laissez-faire approach to the economy—"Even people...who consider themselves minimalists when it comes to government regulations...actually expect the government to regulate the economy and protect [certain] interests," such as environmental quality, worker safety, and the minimum wage.[49] That most people claim to support an unfettered market while accepting many forms of fetter as natural and even necessary demonstrates the extent to which the debate over free market ideology is less about principle than about politics and self-perception. Some tech workers, for instance (although not Enrique), did support government initiatives they believed would help workers achieve their full competitive potential: subsidized education and training, extended unemployment benefits to cover transitional periods, and a revamped educational system that teaches students the tools of career management rather than preparing them for a model of employment that no longer exists. Those same workers often opposed programs or protective legislation that would impose restrictions on corporations or the labor market and, as they saw it, stifle competitiveness and discourage workers from advancing their own professional interests through individual initiative.

Job seekers' attitudes toward health insurance exemplify their conviction that the market is the most effective and efficient mechanism for solving social ills. The health insurance options available in the early 2000s were, in my informants' opinions, woefully ill-suited to meet the needs of career managers, employed or not. (This was prior to the health care reforms signed into law by President Obama in March 2010, provisions of which were intended to improve unemployed Americans' access to affordable health care.) U.S. white-collar workers have traditionally received their health insurance from their employers, leaving unemployed, self-employed, or contract workers to choose between the equally unattractive options of going without insurance or purchasing expensive individual coverage. Under the Consolidated

Omnibus Budget Reconciliation Act (COBRA) of 1985, eligible terminated employees and their families have access to group health coverage for a limited period, but even this coverage is prohibitively expensive for most job seekers. Despite their frustrations with the obviously outmoded system of linking health insurance to corporate employment, tech workers showed little interest in pushing for better or more flexible coverage through political means. Instead, they expressed an almost-unanimous confidence that the insurance industry would eventually change on its own to accommodate the needs of an increasingly mobile workforce.

Multiple job seekers were confident that independent insurance companies would, due to the profit motive, eventually close the gap in providing affordable insurance to the unemployed. Peter Dumond, for instance, argued that coverage options would proliferate as insurance companies competed for a growing market of self-employed, insecurely employed, or otherwise uninsured workers:

> I think you're going to see more companies that offer more insurance pools [for] people. I think there's going to be more cafeteria-type stuff where you get to pick [which plans or benefits you want]. I think that employees are just going to want to have their own thing and carry it all the way through and not have to deal with one employer. I think that is something that is going to happen. It isn't around now, but I think that type of stuff is going to happen.

Other job seekers offered their own scenarios as to what the future of the health insurance industry might be, but all agreed that health insurance would become increasingly centered on the individual rather than the employer. Hindsight has revealed these predictions to be false, at least in the sense that by 2010 corporate initiatives had not resulted in less expensive health insurance for the unemployed. The significance of job seekers' assumptions that the market would ultimately solve their problems, however, lies not in their accuracy but in the vehemence with which they were asserted. And it was not just affordable health care job seekers believed the market would provide. They predicted similar changes in how people managed their retirement accounts and pension funds, which mobile workers need to be able to carry from one job to another.[50] They also foresaw significant changes to the structure of unemployment benefits, which often discouraged tech job seekers from taking interim and contract jobs, as they lost their benefits if their income rose above a certain (arguably low) income level. Such changes, they believed, would occur because they make economic sense, not because any group or agency struggled to make them happen. Thus even when they believed deeply in a cause, like expanding the availability of affordable non–employment-based health care and insurance, job seekers saw no need for political action because they were convinced that the invisible hand of the market was already working behind the scenes on their behalf.

The whole premise of career management is that because corporations are no longer looking out for their employees, a worker's best chance at security and prosperity is to rely on individual skills and planning. Looking to the government as a substitute patron would just re-create the situation of dependence and vulnerability that tech workers were so eager to condemn and avoid. It would also undermine the ethos of career management and the traditions of individualism and entrepreneurship on which it stands.

The emotional salve such proclamations of empowered individualism engender is evident. In an unstable world, the belief that you are the master of your own destiny is an intoxicating one. So too is the certainty that you are nobody's victim, nobody's dupe, nobody's interchangeable employee. Yet maintaining that identity comes at some cost. Unemployment is not easy, not even for the most dedicated career managers. As much as they extol the benefits of their flexible, autonomous approach to work, job seekers encountered many of the same pressures and problems as did laid-off white-collar workers in previous generations. As career management's own founder, Douglas Hall, observes:

> Now that I can see the "protean career" up close I can see both sides—the upside you just mentioned [that people will see that the locus of control for their career is in themselves] and the not so positive elements. It can certainly be very stressful, when people suddenly find themselves out of [a] job.... In the face of all the adaptation people need to make, it is really hard to maintain your sense of identity, of who you are.[51]

Assuming responsibility for events and outcomes that are objectively beyond the control of any one person is an exhausting task. So, too, is preserving a sense of self, and self-esteem, in an unstable world.

Considering the amount of emotional labor involved in maintaining and presenting an image of oneself as a confident, self-reliant career manager, it makes sense to question whether career management might be, when it comes down to it, just words. An earlier study suggests that managers who adopted the rhetoric of autonomy were just donning "ideologically correct garb [in] conducting themselves in public as agents of entrepreneurial zeal."[52] It is true that in many professional settings and at most events where the unemployed gather, publicly rejecting the logic of career management could result in discomfort, social and professional isolation, and even censure. (I consider one such occasion in chapter 4.) Adopting the rhetoric of career management and presenting oneself as a company of one might therefore be less a matter of deeply felt identity than strategic cultural performance. There are indeed moments when interviewees diverged from career management's party line to reveal more ambivalent attitudes toward insecurity, autonomy, and unemployment. These instances demonstrate important fissures and inconsistencies within job seekers' worldviews, and I endeavor to make sense of them when they occur, but they do not belie the extent to which job seekers had internalized and were attempting to live according to the entrepreneurial ideals they espoused.

Job seekers' self-presentations and the opinions they set forth were remarkably consistent over long periods of time (up to eight years) and across diverse contexts, including one-on-one interviews, casual conversations alone and in groups, and as observed at a range of networking and job search events. Such consistency would be unlikely, if not impossible, were these displays merely a matter of posturing or performed reluctantly under duress. This is not to say that coercion and posturing played no role in job seekers' self-presentations (both are discussed in subsequent chapters), but that they alone cannot explain why job seekers adopt and cleave to the rhetoric of career management.

In addition to what job seekers said, what they did on an everyday basis—how they looked for work, organized their days, managed their money, and interacted with others—reflected a deep and enduring faith in the career management ideology and its concomitant behavioral guidelines. To explore this connection between job seekers' actual lives and the worldview they espoused, in the following chapters I set about documenting how they navigated the realities, both mundane and abstract, of daily life as a company of one.

3

The Hardest Job You'll Ever Have

Keith Hartmann, forty-four, specializes in helping U.S. technology companies expand into the Japanese market, and he believes he was born to do the work he does.

> You know, my whole purpose in life is to work between the United States and Japan....I'm half Japanese, and growing up, my father was in the military and my parents did not understand each other very well. My father did not understand Japan. He was with the generation of Americans that thought that Japan was a third-world country, so Japan was never talked about in positive terms. There were a lot of cultural issues that I watched growing up, and almost all of their conflicts were based on cultural ignorance of each other. And so what I've done is taken that childhood traumatic experience [*chuckles*], and now I find myself working with Japanese and American companies and making sure that they work together. Forcing them to look at the issues and resolve them and go on.

In college, Keith initially wanted to be a doctor, and he put himself through school working full time as an orderly in a hospital emergency room. He eventually switched majors, ultimately earning a bachelor of arts degree in Asian Languages. Because he believed that "with a Japanese degree you can't do anything," Keith went on to get his master of business administration (MBA) with a specialization in International Business. During the 1980s and 1990s, he worked for a series of large companies looking to expand into Asian markets. For the last fourteen years, he has worked almost exclusively in high tech, focusing on sales and development in international markets. Keith has been married for twenty years and has three teenaged children.

Three years before I met him in 2001, at the encouragement of many friends who were themselves entrepreneurs, Keith left a corporate position to open up his own business as an independent consultant. His wife, who was not working outside the home at that time, handled the accounting. Keith quickly found a number of relatively long-term contracts, including one with his former employer, but working on a contract basis had its pros and cons.[1]

> In the corporate environment they have [an] IT [information technology department], they have all sorts of support personnel to help you. You just go to work and you do what you're supposed to do. As an independent contractor, if the PC breaks I have to take it down and do everything myself. On the other hand, as a consultant I have charged between $1,000 and $2,000 a day. And so at that kind of rate I only had to work three days a week. And so I had lots of free time. I could go to all my kids' stuff. It gave me a lot of flexibility I didn't have as a corporate employee.

As Keith saw it, the increased risk and logistical challenges of running his own business were compensated for by the personal flexibility that came with setting his own schedule and the financial benefits of consulting (offset somewhat by the absence of employment benefits such as health care and retirement accounts).

After two years running his own consultancy, Keith was approached by an acquaintance who was the chairman of an international company and invited to run the company's Asia Pacific operations. Tiring of the stresses of self-employment and excited about a new opportunity, Keith took the job. In November 2000, after just five weeks there, the company's venture capital was cut off, the expansion project halted, and Keith was laid off. Although the layoff was unexpected, it left Keith in a position not dissimilar to the one he had been in during his previous two years as an independent contractor. Keith said he has been "looking for work" since November 2000, but he also worked as a paid consultant during that time. These states are not mutually exclusive; consultants are always, in a sense, looking for work. This ambiguity undergirds the complexity of what, exactly, constitutes employment (and unemployment, for that matter) within the framework of career management.

Work and identity are indisputably tethered for U.S. workers (especially, it has been argued, for men, although I complicate that assumption in chapter 5). It is the destabilization of identity that results from job loss, most scholars agree, that prompts the many emotional and psychological problems traditionally associated with unemployment, particularly for white-collar workers.[2] As Katherine Newman argues, "downwardly mobile managers are left hanging and socially isolated with no stable sense of who they are. Trained to see identity as a matter of occupation, yet unable to claim a place in the business culture they came from, they remain socially disabled and suspended in time."[3] Newman compares this state of lacking a fixed professional identity to existing in a liminal or "in-between" state. Managers lose their cultural identity and social status when they lose their job, and unemployment is the uncomfortable and anomalous transitional state they occupy until successfully reemployed. The stigma of unemployment, she argues, stems from the need to maintain clear boundaries between cultural categories like the deservingly employed and the shiftless unemployed.[4] Yet what happens when the binary opposition that undergirds those moral judgments is itself blurred, when the line between unemployment and employment becomes increasingly difficult to trace?

According to the tenets of career management, all work is temporary, and a career is culled together through a variety of positions—short term and long, full time and part time, entrepreneurial and working for someone else. Like Keith, many job seekers earned money in various ways following their layoffs—sometimes using their professional skills, sometimes not—while still describing themselves as unemployed and looking for work. Although I discuss the material challenges of unemployment and the nature of the interim jobs tech workers hold in chapter 5, this chapter considers what job seekers' days looked and felt like, and how they managed their time and their emotions as their job searches wore on.

For Keith Hartmann, the primary difficulty of unemployment was not financial.

> We had a lot of savings, and we had it in safe investments, so our money didn't crash, our investments didn't crash along with everything else. So we are just living off of my retirement.... We don't live lavishly. We have a nice home but we don't drive new cars. We both have eight-year-old cars. But we have a lot of savings and that will take us for, I don't know, I could probably live for another eight years if I had to. But who wants to do that?

Their relative financial security notwithstanding, Keith and his wife had their worries, which they tried their best not to pass along to the kids.

> We don't fret about it in front of the kids. The kids know I'm out of work, but it's my responsibility to have an income, not theirs. So I don't want to talk about it too much. They know I'm looking. They know I don't have a job. But other than that I don't think their lives have changed.

Despite Keith and his wife's best efforts to shield their children from the stresses of his unemployment, the entire family was affected by it, as Keith's later comments revealed:

> We've gone through two Christmases now and they've not been big. The kids have never said anything. In fact this past Christmas we gave the girls paper and said write a Christmas list, and my littlest one wrote, "I only want dad to get a job. That's all I want."

As he repeated his daughter's wish, Keith's words became choked with emotion and his eyes welled with tears. Clearly, his being out of work had affected his daughters; their lives had changed, even if only in small ways. In that touching moment, Keith's confident self-presentation faltered, and when he began to speak again, it was to describe what he saw as the worst thing about unemployment, which concerned neither his children nor his finances, but his very function in life:

> The biggest thing for me, the biggest negative factor for this job search has been a feeling of not belonging to anything. I used to always either go to my own work or go to a company to work. I'd have a place, I'd have a function

in life, and now I'm just kind of floating around. I feel like I don't have a
purpose. The purpose is to find a job. But I don't belong to anything, and
that's a very strong feeling of detachment, I guess.

Despite the identity-bolstering ideology of career management, being
out of work presented tech workers with many of the same challenges faced
by previous generations of laid-off managers. At times they felt isolated, un-
valued, and without purpose. Career managers identify themselves strongly
with the work they do and their ability to be remunerated for it, although
not necessarily in a single, long-term job. Keith, for instance, said he felt
he was contributing to something when he worked as a consultant, even
though the entities to which he was contributing changed with time. He did
not have a single employer whose long-term success could be used to measure the fruits of his commitment, but he felt that the work he did had value
and that he, in turn, had a purpose in life. Now, with no professional function, Keith was not sure where his value lay, or if he had any value at all.

True to career management form, however, when unemployment challenged his identity and sense of self-worth, Keith sought out explicitly individual solutions.

[When I was consulting,] I was contributing to something. I was helping
somebody get somewhere. And now I can alleviate that feeling by volunteering. I find that volunteering helps. And I've been doing a lot of that....I'm
the volunteer interpreter for the [local] police department. If they have a
wreck or something that involves a Japanese person in the middle of the
night [with whom] they need to communicate, they have my number so
they'll call me. And I'm just trying to stay busy. And I'm trying to make
sure that at least some of this activity may turn into something that will lead
me to a job, but it's not always that way. You know, a lot of the job-seeking
places[5] will tell you, quit concentrating on yourself. Concentrate on helping others. Through your helping others something good will come back to
you, and I think that's true. So I count all of these things. And I've just become involved in the White Rock Lake Clean-Up Club. And I don't think
that will help me directly. I might meet somebody, but I'm doing that just
because it's an activity and I get to meet people.

Assisting the police and cleaning up his community served multiple purposes for Keith. It kept him busy, connected him to people, and allowed

him to do some good in the world. In addition, when he said he "might meet somebody" while cleaning up the lake, Keith meant someone who might offer him a job or otherwise assist him in his search.

Many job seekers practiced a more direct form of volunteering as job search strategy. Risk taker Phil Wright, from the previous chapter, described himself as unemployed despite working many hours a week as an unpaid consultant to start-up companies. He had not yet received any money for this work, but was certain he would when those companies received funding, a percentage of which was pledged to him. Phil was not the only person to gamble that working for free would ultimately pay off financially. Many job seekers engaged in volunteer work with the hope that it would turn into a paid position, either full-time or contract. A number of web designers offered their services for free to friends, small businesses, and local nonprofit organizations in the hope that their work would get them noticed and lead to paid design work. One woman, a PhD-physicist-turned-programmer, volunteered for a few months assisting an entrepreneur who was looking to start a business streaming video online. Her initial hope was that a position would materialize for her at his firm should it receive venture capital funding, a goal shared by the half dozen other tech workers helping out on the project. After working about ten hours a week for a few months, she realized that the target market for the company's digital technology was going to be the pornography industry, and she decided to donate her services to her daughter's school website instead. Others had more successful experiences with this strategy and eventually received pay and, occasionally, job offers from the organizations for which they volunteered.

Volunteering offered benefits for job seekers that extended beyond the financial. As much as they saw layoffs as inevitable, these tech workers by no means dismissed the emotional impact that losing a job can have. They said that job loss is common, that it is relatively expected, and that it gets easier with time, but they never said it doesn't hurt, at least for a little bit. To describe their emotions following a layoff, many tech workers referenced Elisabeth Kübler-Ross's stages of death and dying—shock and denial, anger, bargaining, depression, and acceptance.[6] For tech job seekers, as for Kübler-Ross, the endpoint of these stages was not happiness at the event that precipitated the process, but acceptance. Job seekers may never be thrilled to be laid off, but they saw acceptance as an admirable and attainable goal. Even as they moved through these emotions, tech workers described them as "natural," "typical," and "predictable." One young job seeker said of his layoff:

> It did have an impact on me when I first discovered that it was me. I asked, "Why me?" Of course, the natural question. But they had to make decisions. I guess at some point you just accept it and move on.

Enrique Vivar echoed this perspective:

> When you're laid off, [you ask yourself] what is it that I did to deserve this? Why was I pinpointed? Why was I singled out? Was it something I said? Something I didn't do? Some skills that I didn't have? And you can't go about living saying, Oh yeah, it was the skill sets that I didn't have. I didn't have the language or I didn't know how to do this. It's just you were in the wrong place at the wrong time. That's it. You need to move on.

For previous generations of laid-off workers, "Why me?" was often a question that consumed them, that cut to the core of their identity and undermined their sense of self. For tech workers in the 2000s, "Why me?" was a legitimate question, but one that a good career manager should push quickly aside in the process of moving on with his or her job search.

Job seekers expressed a similar attitude to the challenges of prolonged unemployment, something they experienced at record rates. The average duration of unemployment has risen significantly over the previous forty years, from just under ten weeks in 1970, to nearly twenty in 2003, to more than twenty-four weeks in 2009.[7] During the recession of the early 2000s, white-collar workers were increasingly overrepresented among the long-term unemployed, belying long-held presumptions that their skills, education, and backgrounds would shield them from prolonged unemployment.[8] White-collar workers accounted for approximately 30 percent of those unemployed more than twenty-seven weeks in 2003 (in the 2007–2009 recession that figure rose to nearly half).[9] Technology workers faced even darker prospects; in 2003 they accounted for a full third of those unemployed six months or more in the United States.[10] In that same year, North Texas technology workers spent an average of 13.6 months, not weeks, out of work following a layoff, nearly three times the national average.[11]

The negative impacts of job loss, particularly depression, discouragement, and isolation, are generally exacerbated by prolonged unemployment.[12]

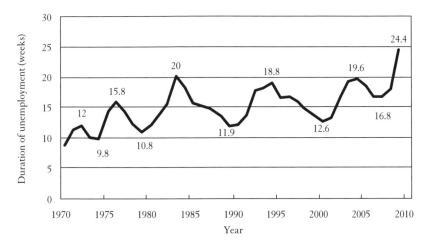

Figure 5. Average unemployment duration (in weeks). Unemployed Americans spent an average of fewer than ten weeks looking for work in 1970; that figure rose to nearly twenty-five weeks in the 2007–2009 recession. Data from U.S. Department of Labor, Bureau of Labor Statistics.

Indeed, many tech workers reported experiencing periods of depression during their time out of work, something they tended to discuss quite matter-of-factly. Ed Donnelly, a fifty-eight-year-old job seeker whose story I detail in chapter 5, described the challenge of staying emotionally upbeat as he headed into his third year of unemployment:

> It's been what, three years now? And [*Ed pauses for a long moment*], my wife has been under treatment for depression for many years now. It's purely clinical, and whatever the chemicals are that cause depression, she got them. Now I'm under treatment for depression too. [Seeing] the same counselor, and taking some of the same drugs. I'm not nearly on as heavy a drug dose as she is, but in my case, it's mostly environmental. Being out of work. And if I can get a decent job, I'll probably be able to drop the treatment. But until then, keeping my attitude up is a real challenge.

Luke Helgesen, a much younger job seeker just short of his thirtieth birthday, described his own brief encounter with postlayoff depression:

> [You] hit that stage in [your] job search, the depression stage. I don't know what to call it. I know I hit that. That was about two weeks, three weeks, four weeks. I didn't keep a calendar. [*Laughs*] Maybe I should have. And

then once I was like, Aw, I've got to get out doing something, and [my mood] picked back up. I don't know if [other] people went into that malaise [for] longer than I [did] or what the deal was, their situation was. I don't know.

On one level, these frank disclosures demonstrate the cultural normalization of mental health concerns such as depression in recent decades. Such conditions, and the various means used to treat them such as therapy and antidepressant medications, have lost much of their stigma in the contemporary United States. Thus to admit depression carries little of the sting it might have for previous generations of laid-off (especially male) workers.

Job seekers' belief that depression is a normal response to job loss and unemployment also emboldened them to talk openly about their private struggles. As Keith Hartmann said, speaking more broadly about his layoff and the challenges that have followed: "I would be willing to discuss any of this anywhere. I don't think that my situation is because I've done something bad. It's not really a reflection of me so much as it is a reflection of society and the economic climate now." Instead of denying that he experienced depression and frustration, Keith, who eventually spent twenty-two weeks looking for work, focused on what he could do to alleviate those feelings when they arose. For one thing, he started working out regularly, a common practice among job seekers, many of whom said they had never been as fit and healthy as they became after losing their jobs. One marketing executive lost over twenty pounds in his first year of job seeking; another led aerobics and yoga classes in return for a free gym membership; and Keith competed in two local triathlons. All three of these job seekers made a point of mentioning that regular exercise has the added benefit of combating depression.

In addition to elevating job seekers' moods, activities such as volunteering and exercise also added structure to what could be a frustratingly unstructured period. The loss of a job strips away the foundation of a worker's daily life. In the absence of a prescribed schedule and defined work role, the rules and responsibilities that once ordered tech workers' days suddenly disappeared. Despite the common plea of working men and women for an escape from the fetters of those very rules and roles, in reality, this collapse of routine is rarely relaxing or liberating. As Keith explained:

Once you've lost your job, you lose a lot of structure in your life. It's good for people to develop a schedule where they do this a certain time of day

and they do that a certain time of day, and keep [to] it. It gives you a sense
of regularity that without [which] you feel like you're on vacation or something. You don't know when to wake up. You stay up all night watching
TV and stuff.

Once he realized this, Keith stopped "staring at the computer all day" and
set about reintroducing structure to his days and drawing rigid temporal,
spatial, and conceptual boundaries between home and work—the work of
job seeking, that is.

Tech job seekers often said that looking for a new job *was* their new
job. They also said it was the hardest job they had ever had. Rather than
conceiving of unemployment as the absence of employment, job seekers
saw unemployment, or job seeking more specifically, as just another form
of work. To buttress their perception of job seeking as a job in itself, unemployed white-collar workers created a system of looking for work that
shared the form if not the function of professional employment. According to Katherine Newman, "The tools we use to make meaning out of an
unexpected event are those bequeathed to us by our culture."[13] In shaping
a new model of unemployment, job seekers drew directly on the model of
paid, full-time employment, thus imbuing the work of job seeking with
the same moral value traditionally reserved for work that commands salaries or wages.

To this end, job seekers tried to re-create in their unemployment the
rhythms of the office. Some insisted on leaving home to do their search,
using the public library or a resource room for the unemployed (which
many cities and nonprofits offer) to check e-mail, search job boards, revise their resume, or research potential employers. For job seekers who
conducted their search from home, the commute lasted only a few short
steps from the kitchen to the home office. Although many job seekers enjoyed the extra time being out of work allowed them to spend with their
families, like most people who work from home, they often implemented
a system of rules to buffer their workday activities from the domestic life
taking place just outside the office door. One project manager looking to
start his own company, for example, posted a sign outside his home office
door that reads "Daddy is at work" or, when flipped over, "Daddy is at
home." Daddy was, of course, technically at home regardless of which side
of the sign was on display, but his wife and children understood that being
"at work" meant being inaccessible despite being only a few feet away. Job

seekers also swore by dressing professionally, even at home, as this made them feel more professional, strengthening their perception of themselves not as out of work, but as busy at work in this new job of job seeking.

Yet when Keith Hartmann talked about needing to "stop staring at the computer all day," he was referencing more than just the need for structure and activity. He was laying out his ideas about the best way to go about looking for work. As noted above, job seekers felt an acute need to fight off depression and despair while unemployed; most important, they felt an acute need to find a job, and they were almost unanimous in how they initially went about doing that.

After taking a month off over the holidays, when he believed companies would not be hiring anyway, Keith started his job search on January 2, 2001.

> I submitted my resume to a job opening I found on the web and within four hours the company called me. I thought, hey, you know, this is not that difficult. And it turns out they didn't make me an offer and I never got any offers after that. But I spent from January to April, four months, looking on the Internet every day. Doing searches, and I couldn't get people to respond. Or someone would call once and they'd say I want to talk to you further and I could never reach them again. It was the most bizarre thing. I didn't understand it.

Online job boards were an obvious starting point for freshly unemployed tech workers like Keith, who naturally sought a high-tech solution to the problem of unemployment. When first launched in the early 1990s, online job search engines provided a unique opportunity for quick and easy access to millions of potential employers. The sites were touted as a tool to "level the playing field" between employer and employee by allowing both sides access to external market information when making decisions about compensation and employment.[14] At that point, simply placing your resume online distinguished you as a tech-savvy candidate to potential employers. As the popularity of sites like Monster.com and HotJobs.com grew—in 2004 four million Americans looked for work online each day—the allure of the online job market diminished significantly, as did its capacity to mark users as technologically advanced.[15] (By 2009, submitting a resume on paper rather than by e-mail had become "laughably passé, at least in some circles," and the bar for evidence of technological know-how had been raised above online resume submission to include participation on social networking sites, maintaining a blog, and eschewing "outdated" e-mail providers.[16])

Even technologically savvy job seekers like Keith were quickly dispirited by their experience of online job hunting. This is not surprising, as studies have found that fewer than 10 percent of people actually find their jobs through the web.[17] Job seekers' initial excitement at finding dozens if not hundreds of openings that suit their skills and interests quickly faded when scores of e-mailed resumes failed to elicit a single response. Peter Dumond, the youthful thirty-eight-year-old job seeker quoted in chapter 2, described his response to the experience:

> I'm pulling my hair out. It's very frustrating because for the longest time nobody would reply. And it's like, guys, at least have the courtesy to reply. You send a resume in for an offered advertisement through the website. Back when I was an engineer, I'd get a card in the mail. The traditional, "Thank you for your resume. You're being reviewed." Just an acknowledgment. [In fourteen months] I've gotten four electronic but two physical cards as acknowledgment that I've submitted a resume. It's like guys, just acknowledge me. I know that you can do that. It doesn't cost you a thing.

This lack of response, of acknowledgment, even, was the most frustrating aspect of online job searching for tech professionals. Job boards were likened to "black holes" by job seekers who felt that any response, even a negative one, would be preferable to dismissive silence. One job seeker commented that he would rather receive an e-mail saying, "No job for you, asshole. We would never, ever, ever hire you," than get no reply at all. This lack of response cuts so deeply because it pulls at the edges of career managers' belief in their status vis-à-vis corporations. When corporations fail to offer even the slightest professional consideration to a job applicant, they belie job seekers' perception that the individual and the corporation are on equal footing in the professional arena. Each job seeker may see him- or herself as the CEO of a company of one, but the CEO of IBM does not see each applicant that way nor does even the most junior member of the company's HR department, who neglects to send even a "thanks, but no thanks" e-mail in response to the job seeker's excruciatingly crafted resume.

Despite their frustrations, job seekers knew that the sheer number of applicants competing for jobs posted online had a lot to do with companies' failure to respond. For most employers, it is impossible to look through, let alone acknowledge, every resume that comes in. More to the point, and why online job boards have turned out to be far more of a boon for employers than employees, companies have access to tens of thousands of qualified candidates and can afford to dismiss all but those few applicants who perfectly match the position's skills and salary requirements.

Having learned how job boards work through experience, most job seekers employed strategies to game the system of online job searching. For example, most companies use filtering programs to sort through submitted resumes. Matches are usually presented to employers in chronological order, with the most recently submitted resume first, so some job seekers resubmitted their resume each day to keep it nearer the top of the pile. (Tellingly, members of online dating services use the same trick to keep their profiles at the top of searches for potential mates.) Filters are set to search resumes for certain keywords, such as "MBA," "C++ Programmer," or "health care," depending on the position and ideal candidate. The more keywords a job seeker has on his or her resume, the higher he or she will appear on the company's list of suitable candidates; not enough keywords, and the application is deleted. Job seekers I met reported dusting their resumes with keywords even when those terms did not reflect their own experience. An applicant who knows that a hiring company wants a candidate with a PhD in computer science, for example, might add the phrase, "Considering pursuing a PhD in Computer Science," so that his resume would be read as a match by the company's search program. Job seekers assumed that by the time their trick was discovered their resume would have been seen by an actual person, which put them well ahead of the filtered-out competition. Like assembly line workers who develop and exchange "tricks of the trade" to exert at least a small amount of control over their work and set themselves apart as someone with special skills,[18] job seekers proudly shared tactics for besting a system they saw as a barrier between them and hiring companies.

Job seekers' tweaking of their resumes to match the ever-changing parameters of employer preferences reflects the complicated impression management required of twenty-first-century job seekers. Individuals looking for work are expected to modify their self-presentation for every audience, constantly repositioning themselves and their work in slight but significant ways. A decade or so earlier, to present themselves to hiring companies, job seekers needed a good suit and a stack of identical resumes run off at Kinko's. Thanks to technological advances in word processing and online communication, job seekers of the early 2000s could modify their resumes in response to each potential employer's specific needs and priorities. Most job seekers in this study had at least three separate resumes, each geared to a different kind of position, which they used as templates when tailoring their resume even further for a specific job. (For instance, a programmer with management experience might have one resume emphasizing her technical skills for programming jobs, another geared toward managerial positions, and a third presenting herself as an independent consultant for hire.) These advances allowed greater flexibility in self-presentation, potentially broadening the sorts of jobs for which one might be considered. As argued in Erving Goffman's classic *The Presentation of Self in Everyday Life,* this constant impression management leads to the replacement of a constant sense of self with a "cosmopolitan" self that can be easily adapted to different situations. This constant adaptation places a new burden on job seekers, for whom the work of self-presentation now has no end.[19]

Enrique Vivar, for instance, was plagued by the fear that his resume, despite innumerable revisions and feedback from friends, MBA classmates, headhunters, fellow job seekers, and his wife, was flawed and preventing him from getting interviews.

> I had to rewrite my resume. I had it more or less written, but I didn't think it was that great. At the same time I started looking for some contract work and stuff like that. A bunch of friends said, "Well, you've been on the construction side of it, so why don't you send me your construction resume?" So I had to make a construction resume. There were three different areas that I could focus on. One was IT [information technology], the other one was construction, and the other one is business development in Latin America. So I had to do three types of resumes. That took me a while.

When we spoke again six months later, Enrique was concerned that his resume still needed work:

> It's kind of like you plant your seeds and you wait for the corn to grow. Right now I've planted a lot of seeds...but at the same time I haven't seen the fruits of that hard work, fruits of the hard labor. The one thing is, I don't

know, maybe my resume didn't work. I went to the career center [at the university where he received his MBA], they checked it out, and then I gave it to somebody else, and they said it stinks, and then I rewrote it and gave it to somebody else and he says it stinks. I mean, I have people rewriting it for me. I've gone every single route with my resume short of hiring a professional to write my resume. And every time I give it to someone new he says it stinks. I guess what I'm trying to think of is that it's like a piece of art. Some people are going to say I love it, and some people are going to say, "That's a piece of junk." So I don't know. At this point it kind of undermines your confidence too on what your writing abilities are. And I am just frustrated, and that's the only bog, when I think, in hindsight, I should have gone and hired someone and paid $350–$400 to get my resume done professionally and then this wouldn't have happened.[20]

Although intellectually he recognized the impossibility of achieving the "perfect" resume, Enrique could not shake the nagging feeling that such a resume, were it to exist, could have landed him a job months earlier. With so little control over the job search process, it becomes far too easy for job seekers to agonize over those details that they can, or at least believe they can, control.

Another job seeker related a similar experience with his business card. According to these tech workers, a current business card—not one from a previous job with new numbers scribbled on the back—was a job-hunting necessity. Those who lacked up-to-date business cards were often dismissed by other job seekers as unprofessional and unprepared. As with resumes, job seekers frequently carried a collection of varying business cards featuring slightly different titles or information, usually purchased at little cost from copy shops or online printers. The exchange and critique of cards was something of a ritual among job seekers, as I learned when I first began my fieldwork with what I believed to be quite professional-looking home-printed business cards. Upon receiving that card, multiple job seekers helpfully suggested that I visit a particular website where one could purchase 250 cards for just the price of shipping. Such sites offered a variety of layouts, fonts, and graphics, creating yet another opportunity for job seekers to agonize over how to best represent themselves on paper. I was chatting one day with a man I had met several times when he proffered his business card. I declined, saying he had already given me his card, but he insisted, although the contact information on it was identical to that on the first card. His card featured a large spherical graphic in the top left corner, and on the new card he had changed the sphere from red to green. He had done so, he explained earnestly, because he had come to suspect that the red orb was reminiscent of a stop light, and might be subconsciously discouraging potential employers from contacting him. By changing the color, he hoped, he was giving employers "the green light" to hire him.

Job seekers' constant awareness of and concern about their self-presentation reflected how deeply they had internalized a sense of themselves as the marketing departments of their own companies of one.[21] They comfortably referred to their resumes and business cards as "marketing materials" and to themselves as "bundles of skills" to be showcased to potential customers.[22] I witnessed eerily similar scenes at numerous gatherings of job seekers. A speaker at the front of the room—sometimes a small meeting room, other times a huge auditorium—asked the audience, made up of people from a variety of fields, to raise their hands if they were in sales. A few hands moved skyward. The speaker then chided the group, saying, "Every hand in this room should be raised. You are all in sales, and what you're selling is yourself." Taking this logic to its extreme, one group of unemployed tech workers tried to auction themselves off on eBay.[23] As angst-ridden discussions of resumes and business cards revealed, to be engaged in the constant work of marketing oneself, particularly when no one appears to be buying, requires a great deal of emotional labor.[24] For job seekers, whether this perspective was psychologically taxing was beside the point. As with other aspects of career management, it was, they believed, the only reasonable and productive way to see and conduct oneself in the labor market.

The question of how job seekers went about marketing themselves draws us back to the image of Keith Hartmann, sitting in front of his computer, isolated and discouraged by the experience of online job hunting. Keeping busy and structuring their days around the rhythms of paid employment helped job seekers feel more productive and engaged and less depressed and discouraged, but what they ultimately wanted was to feel less *unemployed*. The boundary between employment and unemployment may have been decidedly blurrier for this generation of tech workers, but it had not disappeared entirely. Keith might make money contracting; Phil might say he is unemployed while consulting for start-ups twenty hours a week; the sign on the door might say that Daddy is at work. Ultimately, despite their rhetoric, job seekers were looking for more profitable, steadier work in one form or another, and whether or not they achieved that objective remained the ultimate measure of how well they performed the work of looking for work. The path to that goal was often a long one, however, and as they traversed it job seekers found other, less absolute yardsticks by which to measure their worth.

4

Rituals of Unemployment

Tech workers often described their evolving approach to job searching as a progression out of the darkness and into the light. After months holed up at home, searching online all hours of the day and night, rarely venturing away from the muted glow of the computer screen, most job seekers made a conscious decision to try something else. At the urging of friends, colleagues, and job search professionals, they stopped web surfing and started networking, moving out of the house and into the light of day.

The term *networking* encompasses a wide range of activities. The first, in the more traditional notion of networking, involves communicating with people already known to you, whether intimately or remotely. Most laid-off tech workers' first act as job seekers, even before they started searching the job boards, was to reach out to their established personal and professional networks. The day after he was laid off, Enrique Vivar started e-mailing his friends and associates.

I contacted a bunch of friends that I had. Said, hey, you know, this happened. I actually...sent a broadcast e-mail to the entire group [his MBA class] saying that I no longer worked for [that company], and that any e-mail [should be sent] to my personal e-mail. And of course I got seventeen phone calls within the hour. "Oh, I'm so sorry. Is there anything I can do for you?" So I felt like there was a lot of support from my MBA group.

The postlayoff mass e-mail was something of a custom among tech workers. Usually as soon as they arrived home from work after hearing the news, job seekers sent a message to their entire address book—friends, family, current and former business associates—informing them of their new circumstances, updating their contact information, outlining the sort of job they were now seeking, and asking for any potentially useful leads or contacts. Previous studies have suggested that white-collar workers are uncomfortable reaching out to the people they know for assistance, professional or otherwise, while unemployed.[1] For these tech workers, the lessening stigma of unemployment, coupled with the less personal medium of e-mail, made it easier to broadcast the news immediately and in one fell swoop, rather than having to make dozens of potentially awkward phone calls. Job seekers were also confident that letting as many people as possible know about their plight—and therefore be on the lookout for possible openings—was the most effective way to land a new job, and the research backed them up on this.

Social psychologist Stanley Milgram is best known for his experiments in which subjects willingly administered what they believed to be lethal doses of electric shock to other research subjects even as those subjects (actually actors) screamed and begged for mercy.[2] Six years after that infamous project, in 1967, Milgram conducted a very different study, this one utilizing chain letters instead of mock electrocution, in which he claimed that any two people in the world can be connected through a string of acquaintances on average only six people long.[3] Milgram's study was later proved to have serious conceptual and methodological flaws, but the concept of "six degrees of separation" has lived on, both in popular culture, as the title of a Will Smith movie and the model for the parlor game "the six degrees of Kevin Bacon" (the goal of which is to connect any actor to Kevin Bacon through six or fewer other actors with whom they have appeared in movies), and as the foundation for subsequent research on social networks.

Reaffirming the power of networks through less spurious research, in 1973 sociologist Mark Granovetter studied the interactions that lead professional, technical, and managerial workers to new positions, concluding that social contacts are crucial in connecting people and jobs.[4] (Granovetter does not use the term *networking,* which was not popularized until the 1980s.) His findings dealt a critical blow to the then-popular idea that economic and social spheres were growing more independent, and that social contacts should therefore play an increasingly insignificant role in economic processes like matching people to jobs. Subsequent research supports Granovetter's conclusions; statistics vary somewhat, but most sources find that between 80 and 95 percent of jobs are found through networking.[5] Ironically, even the *Guide to Internet Searching* counsels job seekers that, "Your very best tool for finding jobs is through networking."[6]

Granovetter overturned another popular assumption when he found that although people with strong connections to an individual are more likely to offer their assistance, people with weak ties to the individual—defined as someone they see only "occasionally" or "rarely"—are most likely to yield information that leads to a new job, as people with strong ties between them are more likely to know the same people and have access to similar information. This counterintuitive finding—that the closer two people are, the less likely they are to help each other find work—has multiple implications for job seekers. First, it suggests that those whose work histories bring them into brief contact with a large number of people, as was the case for highly mobile tech workers, are better positioned to find work than individuals with close personal ties to a smaller number of contacts. Second, it justifies job seekers' devout reliance on another form of networking, one designed to capitalize on the strength of weak ties, the roots of which can be traced to early governmental efforts to assist the unemployed.

The United States has offered employment services since 1907. Initially organized through the U.S. Bureau of Immigration and Naturalization and intended solely for new immigrants, these programs were inherited by the newly created Labor Department in 1913 and expanded (later, under the U.S. Employment Service) to serve the general unemployed and job-seeking public.[7] Such programs tended to focus on unskilled, semi-skilled, and blue-collar workers. Efforts were made to expand the Service's programs to job-seeking professionals following World War II, but public employment services never caught on with professional job seekers.[8] Instead, a more popular forum among professional and white-collar workers was the job search club, which appears to have originated in 1939 with the founding of the Forty Plus Club, a New York–based nonprofit cooperative to assist executives, managers, and professionals over the age of forty in their career transitions.[9] Highly praised for their efficacy (job clubs have been found to improve a job seekers' chance at successful reemployment by a full 15 percent[10]), job clubs proliferated over the 1980s as white-collar layoffs became increasingly common. Some narrowed their focus to subsections of the unemployed populace, targeting a particular industry (technology, banking, health care), job function (marketing, sales, accounting), or demographic group (women, Indian Americans, entrepreneurs). Although they differ in their form and priorities, job clubs generally provide unemployed managers with career counseling, office space, access to computer and communications equipment, and the opportunity to network with current and former members.

This final component of the job club model—networking with other members—is the most controversial. Studies of unemployment since the Great Depression have dismissed job seekers' tendency to associate with other unemployed people as psychologically comforting but ultimately unproductive; working people, it is presumed, are better positioned to offer job search assistance than are nonworking people.[11] Job clubs turn this presumption on its head, built as they are around the assumption that job seekers can help each other find jobs by supporting one another and sharing leads and advice. In contrast to Granovetter's model, this form of organized networking is not intended to capitalize on existing relationships but to expand one's network, and therefore one's chances of getting a job, through the deliberate accumulation of new contacts, many of whom are themselves unemployed.

By 2001, tech job seekers in any major U.S. city could choose between hundreds of events intended to support and assist job seekers. Although many of these groups loosely followed the job club model, the proliferation of home offices, personal computers, widespread Internet access, and cell phones in the U.S. middle-class had decreased job seekers' need for the physical space and technological resources job clubs once supplied. A few organizations still offered these services, but most had narrowed their focus to providing career and job-seeking advice and networking opportunities. Reflecting this new emphasis, the term *job club* has fallen from use, replaced in most cases by the terms *networking group* or *networking event,* even when the group or event offers services other than networking as well, such as career counseling, resume revision, inspirational speakers, opportunities to connect with hiring companies, or lectures on industry trends.

A handful of Dallas networking events were offered by city or county governments, and a few were run by small, for-profit businesses or career services firms. Following the tradition established in their earlier years, the government-sponsored events tended to be dismissed by tech workers as too low-level, offering resources primarily for minimum-wage jobs (as I discuss in chapter 5, tech job seekers sometimes take such jobs, but they rarely need government assistance to find them). Networking and job search events that charged sizeable membership or event fees were also treated dismissively by job seekers. Most were out of job seekers' price range; in her undercover stint as a white-collar job seeker, Barbara Ehrenreich encountered $600 job-seeking boot camps, $200-an-hour career coaches, $250 "image management" makeovers, and $100 resume revision services.[12] More important, the tech job seekers I spoke with were skeptical that pricey programs offer anything measurably different than what they received for free, or almost free, at local nonprofit events and organizations.

There were hundreds of job search and networking events in Dallas alone, many of which formed in response to the downturns in the mid-1980s (banking and real estate) and early 1990s (computing). Some organizations were founded for the specific purpose of assisting job seekers, while others entered that market reluctantly. In the last half of the 1990s, networking events in the high-technology industry (often originated by professional associations) served as social spaces for techies, matchmaking forums for ambitious entrepreneurs and eager venture capitalists, and recruiting opportunities for companies looking to poach new talent from competitors.[13] Networking events—whether billed as happy hours or lecture series—became central to the structure of high-tech recruiting and deal making. As the market turned southward, it is no surprise that unemployed high-tech workers saw these gatherings as natural forums in which to advance their job search. Some groups disagreed, and actually raised their entry fees to discourage the tides of job seekers, who were allegedly scaring away employed attendees with their constant self-promoting and requests for leads. Other organizations changed with the

times, repurposing themselves to meet the needs of their now mostly unemployed constituents by converting events that once served as rendez-
vous points for venture capitalists and start-ups into weekly or monthly
networking events and high-tech job fairs.

The most popular networking events in Dallas, however, were run not
by professional associations nor by for-profit groups like Forty Plus but by
local churches. The involvement of religious institutions in assisting the unemployed, financially and spiritually, is by no means novel. In his 1982 review of job search literature, Stephen Mangum noted that many authors of
commercial job search literature tend to be overtly religious, and that much
of the literature emphasizes both the will of God and a humanistic commitment to the goodness of mankind and the intrinsic value of meaningful
work.[14] Churches have traditionally played a central role in maintaining
local social services infrastructures, particularly since the Reagan administration's conferral of responsibility for the administration of social and
health services to state and local governments and the 1996 passage of welfare reform legislation.[15] In times of high unemployment, the provision of
church-sponsored services to the unemployed seems a natural extension of
this role. By 2002, roughly a quarter of all U.S. churches offered job search
programs, a trend that has continued into the more recent recession.[16]

The concept of church-sponsored professional networking opportunities might seem unorthodox in some communities, but in Dallas the cou-
pling of church and job seeking raised nary an eyebrow. Texas leads the
nation in the number of churches and church members, and around the
time of my study over 95 percent of Texans reported having some religious
affiliation.[17] (A city whose inhabitants' religiosity is matched only by their
consumerism, Dallas is rumored to have more churches and more malls
per capita than any other city in the United States.[18]) Fueling the apho-
rism that in Texas bigger is always better, in recent years Dallas has seen
an explosion of Protestant "megachurches" with congregations in the tens
of thousands and sanctuaries whose seating capacities rival that of some
football stadiums.[19] Thanks to their huge congregations, excellent funding, and flocks of willing and able volunteers, these megachurches, many
of whose campuses include schools, fitness facilities, ballroom-style audi-
toriums, and restaurant-quality kitchens, now provide services that range
far beyond the spiritual, including sports teams, soup kitchens, educational
speakers, and, of course, job search and networking events.

In form and function, church-sponsored networking events are not that different than those led by secular organizations. Although held in church buildings, these events are open to job seekers of any or no religion, and only occasionally reference religious themes overtly, usually in a brief, nondenominational closing prayer. Most tech job seekers in this study, like most Dallasites, were themselves churchgoers, and were neither surprised by nor uncomfortable with groups' religious affiliations. Some job seekers, as I will describe in a moment, saw God and religion as integral components of their job search and the value system that guided it. Others, whether nonbelievers or unaffiliated with a particular church or religion, simply ignored that their networking took place (sometimes literally) between the pews. The few objections I heard to interjections of religiosity into otherwise professional events came only as a result of direct questioning on the subject; in these few cases, it was not the expression of religious belief that bothered attendees, some of whom were churchgoers themselves, but the commitment of scarce meeting time to nonessential activities. Time spent praying left less time for networking.

Although nearly every job seeker I met attended multiple networking events over the course of a week—and sometimes over the course of a day—some groups were more popular than others, inspiring loyal attendance week after week, month after month, even year after year. One of these was TechNet, a weekly meeting for job seekers in software-related industries. Like many events, TechNet offered job seekers advice, encouragement, and contacts; ultimately, though, TechNet served a far greater and more complicated role in job seekers' lives, bolstering their professional self-image while reinforcing specific ideas about the optimistic, individualistic shape that self-image should take.

***

At a quarter to eight on a Monday morning in the spring of 2002, cars and trucks began to fill the vast parking lot of a suburban church. Attendees, who paid a ten-dollar monthly membership fee to attend these weekly events, trickled in and arranged themselves in the plastic and metal chairs situated around the small tables that filled the otherwise bare meeting room. Many held white and green cups of coffee purchased at one of the nine Starbucks locations within ten miles of the church. Although TechNet

is open to job seekers of all ages and levels working in fields loosely related to software and programming, most of the forty or so attendees were
white men between thirty and sixty, roughly reflecting the demographics
of Dallas networking events and the field of high technology in general.
Women and ethnic minorities—Hispanics, Asian Americans, and, least
common, African Americans—made up a small but noticeable minority
at most events, approximately 20 and 15 percent respectively. (Exceptions
are those events specifically geared toward women or racial minorities;
there are many of the former in Dallas, which tend to draw women of all
ages, but only a few of the latter, most commonly for Indian Americans.)
Despite their small numbers—and despite studies suggesting that minority groups, including women, are at a disadvantage in networking[20]—not
one Dallas job seeker reported experiencing gender or racial discrimination at organized networking events, although some did believe they faced
such discrimination from hiring companies. At TechNet, almost all members had college degrees, and two-thirds held a graduate degree, usually in
computing-related fields or business administration.

Some first-time attendees sat alone, self-consciously absorbed in reading the newspaper, checking cell phone messages, or ruffling through fold-
ers or briefcases. Most members, however, quickly coalesced into groups of
two, three, or more to chat and catch up on the week's events. The world of
high-tech networking in Dallas was small but densely populated. Despite
the vast number of networking and job search events held each week, individuals tended to run in the same circles. If you met someone at one event
you were likely to run into him or her again, whether at another meeting
of that group or another like it. Word of mouth was a powerful force in
these circles. Networkers liked to plug their favorite events to other job
seekers they met, and many networking events circulated information
about other events in the area. The same people who made it to a happy
hour for unemployed software engineers one week, for example, were
likely to unintentionally meet up again at a breakfast lecture on high-tech
entrepreneurship the next week. This tendency was exacerbated for this
particular group, as every meeting included the dissemination of a calendar of upcoming tech- and job-related events in the area, making it all the
more likely that attendees of one event would cross paths at future events.

A few minutes after eight, the group's volunteer leader, Will Ericsson,
called the meeting to order with a few light-hearted introductory comments.

As attendees continued to trickle in, with a dry-erase pen Will filled one panel of the whiteboard with a calendar of upcoming events, some from a list he prepared, others shouted out by the crowd as he worked his way through the days of the week. The week's options included a half dozen regular events that are announced every week (in case a newcomer has not yet heard about them), four job fairs, a happy hour for tech workers, a free financial planning session ("If you haven't looked at your financial position yet," Will said, "you need to do that today"), and a professional meeting for the Association of Information Technology Professionals (AITP). The AITP event, which was held at a Dallas hotel, was recommended as "one of the best out there," but it included dinner and cost $30. Few job seekers were willing or able to pay that much, but one attendee revealed his trick for avoiding that charge. He goes for the predinner networking, then waits in the lobby until dinner is over, at which point he returns for the job fair portion of the event (where job seekers are able to meet directly with representatives of hiring companies, recruiters, and the occasional career counseling firm promoting their services). Will complimented the man on his cleverness, suggested others heed this money-saving advice, and moved on to the next portion of the morning.

I first noticed Will in the early autumn of 2001 when I began attending events focused on the high-technology industry and its workforce. White and in his late-forties, Will is of average height and slim build, with wiry glasses and short brown hair speckled with gray. At that event (and every event thereafter) he wore pressed slacks and a conservatively striped button-down shirt, clean but worn brown loafers, and no tie. Had he not born an uncanny resemblance to a college friend of mine, I might not have noticed him at all. Will seemed at ease in the crowd—particularly in contrast to those job seekers who came to network but ended up shyly hovering at the edge of the room, waiting to be approached. He exuded both comfort and confidence and clearly knew a number of people in the crowd, including the speakers slated for the morning's panel on the status of venture capital funds in the Dallas–Forth Worth area. Will and I did not formally meet that morning, but I noticed him again the next week at a networking breakfast sponsored by a trio of local tech associations and again at a happy hour intended for casual socializing between techies. By shared event number four, Will and I were nodding greetings to one another in passing but had still not officially met. Finally, at an early morning lecture on the promising field of biotechnology, I approached him to say hello.

I learned that Will had been laid off almost a year before from a large Dallas-based electronics and aviation firm where he spent over twenty years working his way up to a senior management position. Nearing fifty, he found himself unemployed for the first time in his adult life.

> I was at [that firm] for twenty-two years, and so somewhere in there you tend to think you're going to be there until you retire. I had the expectation of retiring at fifty-five. I'm going to be fifty this year. Over the past six or seven years I started to say, "Well, it looks like I'll be able to retire from this place." I had kind of gotten complacent in that area. I don't think when I entered the workforce I had that expectation, but it just evolved that way.

His unexpected layoff and thus-far unsuccessful job search had prompted Will to replace his former expectations of employment, which were in essence those of the organization man, with career management's model of all work as temporary and all employees as contractors.

> This search has led me to believe that any engagement is temporary....I am beginning to believe the experts that say we are all temporary workers, and you should consider yourself as contract labor. It's going to be interesting to see how the business environment changes. Because I think it is changing. In some industries it's probably more so than others. I can see the company will have a small, very small core of its family jewels if you will, its secret sauce. This is what we're about, but then everybody else is contract labor. Some of it's short term, some of it's long term, but it's all contracted. And when they don't need that particular skill or they think you're outdated, they'll change you out for somebody different. I can see that happening and being the way of the future. When, I can't say. But I can see that happening.

Will did not, however, come to this revised way of thinking about employment on his own. He experienced a range of negative emotions following his layoff, and, he now believed, had been going about his job search in a wrong-headed and ineffective manner.

> [Since my layoff] I pretty well have gone through all the responses, the normal grief process, if you will. Not expecting it, some of that disbelief and

shock that goes on. Then the flurry of activity, thinking I'm doing the right thing to get back into the game. I really didn't understand the job search process until I got into some of the workshops. I probably would still be clueless if I hadn't.

The cure for his "cluelessness," as he saw it, came about a month into Will's job search when an unemployed friend brought Will, who is a devout Christian, to the Career Transition Ministry at a local megachurch. (For this researcher, it was at times difficult to keep straight the various church-sponsored career programs in and around Dallas, which at that time also included CareerCare, Career Connection, Career Solutions, and Career Outreach.) At that event he learned of a free twelve-week workshop series in which a jokey, energetic minister who is popular among Dallas job seekers offers "advice, encouragement, and contacts" to anyone going through a "job change," and it was at one of those workshops that a tablemate told Will about TechNet.

Although networking did not come naturally to Will—"It needs to be more of an inbred skill," he said, "and I'm not really that good at it, but I'm working on it"—he was soon invited to lead the group, an opportunity that Will saw as divinely inspired.

> Well, God always has a way of asking me twice, and that's how I know it's really something I need to do. And I had been asked to lead this group last September or so. And I said no. But then [the woman] who had been leading this one discovered she was just out of it in terms of her job search. The group was keeping her from her search. So she asked me, and that's when I knew I needed to do this.

That God "asked him twice" was certainly an important motivator in Will's decision to lead the group, but that was not his only reason for taking on the role.

> I call myself a leader, well, if I don't step up and lead, it doesn't really demonstrate that talent. I recognized that the group needed somebody willing to lead it. It's very interesting. There have been several people that walked through here and claim they're leaders, but are not really willing to take that challenge.... Again, it's how we can help somebody. I think that's how we demonstrate that we're not just takers. That we find some small way to

help somebody else in their search....I take great joy in seeing people landing. And being the facilitator, at least I am one of the first people that sees
it. I am just thrilled when somebody lands....For myself, part of it is, I recognize that the job *will* happen. It is going to come along at the right time.
I have very strong faith that it will happen in the right time. The other side
is I try and keep giving. I find that the more I give, the less I deal with myself in terms of the dwelling and that aspect of it. So I try and give a lot to
other seekers. I take great pleasure in leading this focus group and helping keep them focused. And when I see that they don't have a focus, saying,
"You need a focus." And you've heard me, I'm pretty hard on them at times.
I'm saying, "You want a job? You better figure it out, because we can't help
you [if you don't]." And sometimes, somebody wants some one-on-one help,
either on a resume or just trying to figure out where are they going or a
sounding board. I'm happy to do that occasionally. I try to stay out of the depression by helping others. And it works, pretty much.

As Will explains in this extended quotation, he had multiple, overlapping
motivations for leading the group. It allowed him to help other people,
particularly novice networkers, something his Christian faith compelled
him to do. It had the added benefits of warding off Will's own occasional
depression and doubts and helping him get by until that "right time"
when his own new job would appear. Serving as TechNet's volunteer facilitator also allowed Will to demonstrate his talent as a leader, show-
casing the very managerial and organizational skills he hoped would
eventually land him in a new executive position. Furthermore, assuming a position of authority within the networking groups enabled Will, a
former executive, to re-create the status position he once held within the
corporate world.

A majority of job seekers were not at the executive level (most were
midlevel managers), but executives and senior managers accounted for a
disproportionate number of event leaders, resume reviewers, and other
authoritatively positioned volunteers, suggesting that these individuals
gravitated toward roles that resembled those they held in the workplace.
This reality does not diminish the genuinely useful guidance and assistance
these volunteers offered to other job seekers. It does, however, help to explain the benefits, in addition to a feeling of goodwill, that high-level professionals reaped from participating in these events. Taking up positions of
authority within networking groups allowed high-ranking professionals

to showcase and sharpen their managerial skills and to preserve a sense of themselves as valued leaders effectively managing their charges.

Will's authoritative position at TechNet granted him a platform from which to broadcast his emphatic views on the importance of networking to any successful job search, something many new job seekers, he worried, failed to recognize.

> I'm always hearing [about people] just applying through the web. I don't think they get it. Now, I can understand it's hard to network, it's uncomfortable to network, cause I hate that as much as anybody....I'm not convinced that they understand what networking is about and what it's good for.

Yet even Will, who spent much of every Monday meeting trying to keep the sometimes unwieldy group focused on the business at hand, recognized that the group offered attendees other benefits that had nothing to do with landing a job.

> There's a big advantage to [groups like TechNet]. Whoever's idea it is had a great vision with [these] groups. One, it lets you get with like-minded people in a group that, while you may not get any job leads, you at least get that like-minded support. There's a lot of support in this group....If there's somebody that has a problem, they can just throw that out to the group and they will get an answer. They'll get an answer. It's also a way of getting energized whatever time of the week that you do your group. We used to meet on Tuesday afternoons, and I could just feel that surge of energy on Tuesday afternoon. Now we meet on Monday morning and I can feel that surge of energy Monday morning. At least for me personally. I've got to believe the others have a similar experience. It's literally like a support group, and a networking group, all these rolled into one.

As Will described it, the group's provision of information and job-seeking support was seamlessly intertwined with the community and emotional support it offered attendees. Although Will might have been dismayed to hear it, for some job seekers, the emotional support they received there, not the job-seeking advice or the networking opportunities, was the primary, if not sole, reason they continued attending meetings.

In private moments, many regular attendees admitted they had little faith or evidence that the group was helping their job search. Although they did not say so in front of the group or its leader, they questioned Tech-Net's core assumption that other job seekers were well placed to offer them good leads. Keith Hartmann, for instance, found networking events to be "a mixed bag":

> I find that most of the networking events that I'm going to are attended by other people who are out of work....I noticed it from the very beginning, but I always thought that even people who were not employed would have connections that they could give me. I just figured, people kept saying, "You never know. Just go to them. Just go to them." So I was just going to everything I could. It was at the end of the year that I thought, you know, what is the definition of insanity? Doing the same thing over and over and expecting different results? So, the beginning of this year I've been making a big push to do more things outside of that job seeker community....I'm getting out and just not going to any event where I think that half of the people will be unemployed people looking for jobs.

Unlike Keith, most job seekers continued to attend these groups even after they dismissed them as ineffective job search tools, frankly explaining that they enjoyed the group's camaraderie and found the meetings motivating if not productive in a more tangible way. As much as they cleaved to individualist principles, job seekers looked to one another for moral support and affirmation of shared identities, and they were rarely disappointed.

Some of those who found new jobs actually missed the solidarity and support they found in networking groups. Although the weekly networking sessions he attended did not help him land his new job, which he applied for online, Luke Helgesen, a matter-of-fact engineer in his midtwenties, surprised me by saying, a year after he'd found a job, that he missed the group intensely: "Networking is very, very good for fellowship....I really miss that, the people I was hanging out with on Monday mornings. So I don't think I'm going to do anything radical because of that [a joking reference to quitting his job so that he could go back to his networking group], but I do miss seeing them on a weekly basis." Luke's comments, and the experiences of others like him, reverse the typical presumption that individuals are stripped of their professional community when they lose a job and provided with a new one when reemployed. In today's short-term, contract-based work world, it might even be that the relationships established between jobs prove more significant and enduring than those fostered on the job.

A portion of every TechNet meeting was dedicated to capitalizing on, and in the process reinforcing, these reciprocal and comradely relationships between participants. After the week's calendar was laid out, Will invited attendees to offer up specific questions to the group, something they needed advice on or an obstacle they encountered in their quest for work. A large white-haired man in a striped dress shirt called out, "I got a major road-block out of the way last week. I got my daughter married last weekend." After the hearty applause died down, a quiet blonde woman in her forties said she had recently stumbled over an interview question that she had not been prepared to answer. "What do you say," she asked the group, "when they ask, 'What have you been doing for the last X number of months?'" A number of attendees took turns weighing in, suggesting she highlight her networking activities, professional events she had attended, volunteering she had done, or any classes taken or technical certifications received. Will added that in interviews he "takes credit for" the unpaid work he has been doing at a local venture capital firm that helps early-stage start-up companies get off the ground. An older, pony-tailed male programmer loudly suggested from the back of the room, "Tell them anything you've been doing that shows you're still fully engaged and on top of things."

Another attendee asked how to go about applying for the thirteen-week extension of unemployment benefits that had just been offered under George W. Bush's Job Creation and Worker Assistance Act of 2002. Several people chimed in, and a consensus quickly emerged that submitting an online application was far preferable to suffering the long lines at the local unemployment office.

A young Indian programmer then asked the group whether anyone in the crowd had been asked by a potential employer to take a Java proficiency test (Java is a software programming language). In a flurry of simultaneous responses, job seekers confirmed that they had taken similar tests. Apparently, multiple testing companies, all equally despised by job seekers, administer these exams on behalf of hiring companies, promising to assess "skills, knowledge, personality, and more."[21] An energetic and somewhat disheveled software designer and developer named Miguel loudly said of these tests, "All of them suck. They are wrong. The questions they provide you are wrong, and the answers are wrong. They are taken completely out of context." Numerous attendees agreed and offered comical examples (comical to other programmers at least) of poorly phrased questions and blatantly wrong answers that were marked correct. Mocking test writers' stupidity and lack of hands-on experience, attendees shared a happy moment of communal self-righteousness, celebrating and reaffirming their know-how, laughing at the expense of the very companies that refused to hire them. The young programmer who initially asked the question suggested, "What I'm hearing, for us technical people, they don't care who you are. They just want you to get ten out of ten questions right." As heads nodded around the room, Will said, "So you have to answer the questions wrong as required," and received another round of nodding heads. He continued, "I know you think, 'I'm a purist, and that's stupid.' But it's what you have to do." He then asked for volunteers to start collecting examples of the sorts of questions they were being asked and posting them to the group's online discussion board. A few attendees, including Miguel, agreed to kick off the online discussion. A brief debate then picked up over whether it was worth it to point out errors in the test to the hiring manager. The group was of two minds on this; some worried they would come off as abrasive or overly direct; others believed the hiring manager might think, "Hey, this guy not only got a passing score, but he knows more than the test does!"

As the chatter died down, Will called the group to attention. "Before we begin introductions, I've got four people I know who landed last week." He proceeded to name four former attendees, three men and a woman, who had found full-time employment; two in Dallas, one four hours south in Houston, and a fourth who "took her search national" and ended up in Arkansas. The group offered the four their congratulations in absentia with cheers, whistles, and energetic applause.

Will then prepared the group for "introductions," the activity that consumed the bulk of each hour-long meeting. Pointing to an easel at the front of the room, Will explained for the benefit of newcomers that each attendee would now deliver their self-introduction or *commercial,* a term that reaffirms the tendency to frame job seekers as companies or objects to be marketed rather than laborers. Designed to last between thirty and sixty seconds, these self-promotional spiels, sometimes called elevator speeches, are intended to convey the basics of one's professional experience and job search objectives in a concise and polished manner. As with their resumes and business cards, job seekers were expected to prepare multiple versions of their commercial tailored to different audiences. At TechNet, the standard commercial included, in the order listed on the oversized pad of paper: name, title and job function, target companies, geographic preference, and a positive for the week. Will was emphatic that each attendee cover each of these categories, explaining their job title and what exactly they do, what companies they are currently researching or trying to get a job at, where they hope to work (both how far they would be willing to commute and whether and to where they might relocate), and something good that happened to them over the past week. A fuller picture of what you're looking for, Will explained, makes it easier for your fellow attendees to offer useful contacts, leads, and advice.

Starting with first-time attendees and then snaking around the room, each member introduced him- or herself.

I'm a software tester, looking for a full-time or contract position in Dallas. My positive is that I think the market is getting better. I have a lot more leads this week than in the last three or four weeks. [white male, midforties]

I'm a software engineer with a specialty in COBOL [common business-oriented language programming]. I'm looking for something in Dallas, North Dallas. My highlight is that this networking group has definitely refocused my job hunt. There's a lot of good information here. [white male, early fifties]

I'm a web designer and developer. I want to stay near Dallas or Plano because that's where my husband works, and right now he's the one with a job. My positive is the Hewlett-Packard merger that's going to go through so my husband can keep his job. [white female, late forties]

I'm in mainframe computing, hoping to find some leads at MSNBC. I had some good positives for the week. I met a recruiter at [another networking event], and Will took a hammer to my resume [*smiles at Will*], and it looks a lot better. [white male, late forties]

I'm a computer janitor—I fix systems. SMU [Southern Methodist University] is one of my targets this week. As an employee of SMU you are free to take any of their classes. If you're a janitor at SMU, you can take any classes, so I could do that and take courses. That might be the best career path for me, but I've applied for an IT position there. My positive? I had jury duty. [*Laughs*] [white male, early forties]

I do Java programming. I'm definitely not tied to staying in telecom, since it's pretty depressed right now. I had spring break and was able to spend a lot of time with my kids and my wife too. [Asian male, midthirties]

I'm a software engineer with ten years' experience. I was looking to stay in Dallas, but I'm ready to move. I've lived here all my life, and I'm ready to move. My positive is that I've been out of work for a while, and getting involved with this group has really lifted my spirits. [white male, late thirties]

I'm a business analyst, used to be at JPMorgan Chase, and I also do mainframes. My target is Greyhound, and my geographic preference, I have none. My family is committed to moving wherever it takes. My positive for the week is that early this morning I got an e-mail from a friend who submitted my resume to a company in Detroit, so we've got our fingers crossed. [white male, midfifties]

I'm a software developer, have been for seventeen years. I've been a web developer onsite for five years, and I'm thinking about going for some [new] certifications. My positive is at my softball game I hit my first home run. Took me forty-nine years [*applause all around*]. [white male, early forties]

And so it continued around the room. Some commercials garnered laughs, others sympathetic groans. Will often reminded speakers that they needed to identify target companies in order to focus their search, but most people continued to skip that part of their commercial. Occasionally an attendee responded to someone else's commercial with the name of a contact or a piece of information (lamenting that a target company just instituted a hiring freeze, for instance, or that a firm in that industry just announced a new opening). On these occasions, the excitement of the individual offering the lead was palpable; despite Will's frequent remonstrations to save such information for the informal networking period at the end of each meeting, the person with the lead usually blurted out the information in front of the entire group before the next introduction began. Usually, the proffered information could easily have been e-mailed or discussed in a one-on-one conversation, and many job seekers did use these methods. Yet the pleasure of delivering the lead personally in front of a roomful of witnesses was undeniable, particularly as it situated a job seeker publicly as both benevolent and "in the know." (At some events, although not TechNet, time was allotted for individuals to announce new leads they had learned of, even though those same leads were posted online or in the meeting hall immediately following the meeting. One group even recorded how many leads each member brought to the group and awarded a prize to the "winner" at the end of each month.)

Like most networking events, TechNet's model was predicated on the belief that job seekers not only *can* help each other find jobs, but that they *will*. There is, as others have also noted, a certain irony to the extent to which career managers who pride themselves on their autonomy rely so heavily on their peers.[22] Only through cooperative behavior, the building and sharing of individual networks in the interest of creating an enormous collective network of information and contacts, will any single member benefit from participation in the group. Those who aid others in their searches are therefore believed to ultimately benefit themselves as well, on both karmic and pragmatic levels. Like Will and Keith, they feel better about themselves for having helped another job seeker. Every person you know who finds a new job also becomes one more employed person with a strong incentive—based in gratitude as well as convenient access to a large pool of skilled candidates—to bring fellow job seekers into their new company.

Yet the reciprocity of networking is slightly more complicated than this pragmatic model suggests. By sharing leads and publicizing upcoming events and job fairs, individual TechNet members actually increased the competition they would face at such events, subjugating at least their short-term self-interest for the good of their peers and the group as a whole. Rather than hoarding leads and information, however, most job seekers leapt at every opportunity to pass along pertinent information or useful contacts. This paradoxical commitment to mutuality and altruism among a group of people fiercely committed to an individualistic worldview of themselves and the labor market supports the idea that communities can be founded on, rather than threatened by, shared individualistic principles.[23] It also highlights the extent to which TechNet and other networking groups served multiple functions for job seekers, some of which had little to nothing to do with finding work.

TechNet's highly ritualized structure offered job seekers ample opportunities to publicly revise and assert their professional identities. As I noted above, by assuming positions of authority, executives like Will reasserted corporate hierarchy in a group that presented itself as one of equals. As well, during the question-and-answer period, experienced job seekers publicly established themselves as experts on the high-tech industry, labor market, and job search process. But it was in the delivery of well-rehearsed commercials that TechNet's critical role in reaffirming job seekers' professional identities was most apparent. When networkers recited their commercial each week, the point was not just to advertise their abilities and objectives to others, most of whom had heard the same job seeker make the same announcement each week for months; it was also to reaffirm job seekers' own perception of themselves as professionals. Each commercial was an opportunity to broadcast a professional identity—Senior Telecommunications Executive, Java Programmer, Project Manager—in the absence of a paid position or official title.[24] In their self-descriptions, tech workers also listed job functions (information architect, database administrator), certifications (project management professional, Microsoft certified information technology professional), and programming languages (COBOL, Java, C++) that make little sense to industry outsiders, but within a group of technology experts stood as clearly staked claims to a status grounded in expert knowledge and industry experience. These commercials, and the resumes and business cards that are their written equivalent, are, to paraphrase Clifford Geertz, the stories that job seekers tell themselves about themselves, and networking events serve as weekly rituals of identity maintenance in which to revise and retell those stories to a captive and supportive audience.[25]

That TechNet meetings resemble—in their structure, attendee demographics, and bland environs—the sort of team meetings and workshops that take place every day across the corporate United States is itself significant. Anthropologist Linda Layne has suggested that one way to lessen the stigma and isolation of unemployment might be to create "rituals of unemployment" modeled after rituals of retirement.[26] Layne is right that supportive rituals could play an important role in easing the stress and isolation of unemployment. As Bronislaw Malinowski argues, people take comfort in predictability and routine, which might explain why TechNet meetings follow such a rigid, unvarying structure.[27] Yet in suggesting retirement parties as prototypes for such rituals, Layne fails to recognize that the unemployed do not want to feel retired; they want to feel employed.[28] The rituals they have chosen to emulate are those of the business world, as are the identities they ritually reinforce week after week in their commercials.

The weekly recitation of commercials did not always proceed as planned. Sometimes a commercial garnered a broader response, provoking a quick discussion about the future of a target company, or the logic of getting a particular certification, or whether prospects for employment in a certain field are improving or declining. When such tangents arose, Will usually shepherded the group back on track, cutting off conversation and moving along to the next introduction. This Monday morning, the most provocative introduction, and the response it garnered, revealed TechNet's role in reinforcing a particular ideology and negating other, alternative ways of looking at the world.

In addition to identifying their comforting aspects, Malinowski contends that rituals reinforce socially approved attitudes and maintain social unity.[29] Within TechNet, this function was performed by the required "positive of the week" that concludes each individual's commercial. As evidenced above, job seekers' positives could be either professional ("I got an interview") or personal ("I hit a home run"); either type elicited warm congratulations, and sometimes applause, from the group. Occasionally, however, a job seeker denied having a positive for the week, as was the case with Martin, a handsome Asian American man in his midthirties. When it was his time to speak, Martin stood beside the brown laminated table in his crisp Oxford cloth shirt, his hair perfectly combed, and said in a voice heavy with resignation:

> I've been out of work for six months. I have two kids, my wife doesn't work. I got laid off from [a large telecommunications firm], along with a few other thousands of people. I spent the first months with my family, which was too much. When I stay at home, it's easy to get depressed. I had two interviews [two months ago], and none since then. Things are getting rough. I don't see a light at the end of the tunnel. I know it's there, but I don't know how long the tunnel is. I have a family to support. I use headhunters, I've networked. I have six months of savings left, but I'm below average with interviews. [TechNet members generally agreed that one interview a month was a respectable average.] None last month, none this month, yet.

Martin finished speaking and began to sit. Will reminded him that he had not offered a positive for the week. "I guess," Martin said, still mid-sit, one arm pressed against the table to support himself, "I guess I don't have a positive this week." Immediately, Will rejoined, "Of course you do," and other members began to offer Martin suggestions for his positive. "I'm sure some good things have happened this week, you just don't remember them right now," Peter Dumond offered encouragingly. "You're still married, right? You said you have a wife, and she's still beside you. That's a positive," called out a heavyset white man across the room. "And you're here with us, which is a good thing," added the woman sitting next to Martin, looking at him expectantly. "And hey," Miguel joked from the back, "next week has got to be better than this one, right?" "See," said Will. "It's all how you look at things. Come talk to me after and we'll figure out how to get your search back on track." And the group moved on to the next commercial.

Rather than acknowledge Martin's feelings as normal and legitimate, for many job seekers in the room that day had told me of similar moments of despair and struggles with depression, the group glossed over his obvious suffering and amended his introduction themselves so that it would conform to the norms of the group.[30] Group members were not unsympathetic to Martin; a number of people sought him out after the meeting to offer their business cards, volunteer to help revise his resume, or suggest companies and contacts he might want to follow up on. Will was not wrong, nor overly idealistic, when he framed TechNet as a support group. Job seekers discussed even the harshest, most personal aspects of job loss and unemployment—depression, discouragement, embarrassment, financial crisis, marital strife—with one another in more private conversations, whether during the informal networking period of the event or in discussions they had outside the group (some members saw each other socially, in addition to crossing paths at various events).

Yet the public response to this decidedly uncommercial commercial reveals the community's ideological boundaries and points to the ritual significance this performative portion of the meeting had for attendees. TechNet is modeled after a corporate meeting, and its tenets are those of career management, with its unbridled optimism and faith in the individual and the future. Negativity, self-pity, or unrestrained emotion threaten to erode those foundations. By refusing to follow the prescribed ritual, Martin rendered the mechanisms of that ritual briefly visible, revealing the emotional labor that goes into maintaining the identity of the good job seeker, the ever-positive career manager. This work is similar to that required of the employee in the absence of secure employment.

For those managers and professionals occupying the lower levels of the corporation, a good deal of emotional labor these days goes into articulating their autonomy and vaulted, take-charge initiative in the face of obvious but unmentionable constraints.... Yet, offstage, as in times past, these same employees are quite able to construct themselves rather differently—as relatively powerless subjects buffeted by larger forces, unable to take control of their own destinies or pack their own parachutes.[31]

The difference here is that job seekers were not performing this identity for would-be employers but for each other. Others have faulted job search clubs for imposing on attendees "a unified vision of what's wrong with the economy and how people can individually transcend problems that are rooted in structural and institutional transformation."[32] Certainly, TechNet shared this tendency to privilege individual agency over collective response. Attendees shared leads, advice, and many a good laugh, but at no point did they suggest working together to alter the landscape of the current labor market or protest their position within it. In the one meeting where professional unions were raised as a possible response to widespread unemployment, group members themselves quickly dismissed that possibility, joking that "we all know how well unions work these days." As in job seekers' discussions of globalization (see chapter 2), the weak labor market and scarcity of secure, long-term jobs were presumed to be natural, unavoidable conditions rather than the result of political or social trajectories that might be altered or opposed through collective action. Yet, unlike most groups that have been criticized for delegitimizing collective action and setting job seekers up for downward mobility, TechNet was run not by a paid counselor but by fellow job seekers. In addition, many job seekers who did not participate in organized networking used the same language of branding and marketing to describe their job search, and they exhibited the same individualism, optimism, and faith in the market as did diehard networkers.

Groups such as TechNet were not the sole proprietors or disseminators of this worldview. The ideas and behaviors they endorsed can be found in college classrooms, newspaper columns, and best-selling self-help books about mice chasing cheese. These groups are microcosms in which the norms and boundaries of the larger culture are concentrated for the benefit of those who have not yet come to them on their own or who seek reaffirmation in an intentional community of peers. If the groups' leaders were aggressive in transmitting those values, it was not because they wanted to indoctrinate their charges but because they so wholeheartedly believed that this was the best way to help them.

Three months after the meeting in which Martin confessed his lack of a positive for the week, Will sent the following e-mail to the group:

To: TechNet Mailing List
Date: Wed 6/14/2002
Subject: landing

My friends,

I began to think I would never write this message, but after 13 months of unemployment, I HAVE LANDED!

I want to thank each of you that have given encouragement through the months, and especially those that have dug deep into their networks and given contacts into my target companies. I have landed as a senior system engineer, leading a proposal effort. This is a 3-month contract to hire position at [an aeronautical engineering company]. My contact came thru a man that had been in TechNet, who landed there about two months ago.

I have turned over my co-facilitation role in the focus group to a fine man, who is committed to encouraging each of you in your search. James O'Hara is ready to help you in any way he can. James's email is [...] and telephone [...]. I encourage you to help him too.

The goal for each of us is the same, to obtain meaningful employment as quickly as possible.

Take a little time to help your fellow. Don't stop networking just because you land, but continue to help those next to you. You never know how that little action may become a blessing down the road. As I can help, feel free to contact me. And let me know when and where you land—I'd like to keep your contact information current, and celebrate with you on that great occasion.

Will Ericsson

Man Enough to Let My Wife Support Me

In discussing the challenges job seekers face, I have thus far focused primarily on emotional and professional hardships, but jobless tech workers also face very real material challenges.[1] Few of the job seekers I met were in danger of losing their homes or being unable to feed or clothe their families, but most had to dramatically alter their former lifestyle. Enrique Vivar and his wife, Anna, for instance, starting scaling back the day he lost his job.

The day that I was laid off I was like, okay, what can I cut? What costs can I chop? And it was like okay, cable goes out. Should I cut the DSL line that we have at home? No, I need the Internet connection. Car and cell phone, my wife's cell phone goes out. No more sparkling water, no more eating out. Stuff like that. You take a lot of things for granted. You work for them, but you take them for granted. They're gone. And to date I had $14,000 saved 'cause we were going to buy a new car for Anna. We *were* going to. To date I've spent the $14,000, and I've already started borrowing money from family. Because it's been, well, [from my layoff in] October to now it's been four and a half months.... We have about $50,000 in savings. My IRA and 401k plans altogether are about $40,000. I don't want to touch that. I would rather borrow from friends and family, because family will not charge me for interest. At this point. So, financially wise I'm not that afraid. I know that I'll get a lot of support from either my family or her family.

After Enrique had been out of work for more than a year, to help make ends meet, Anna, who had left her executive sales position when Maya was born five years prior, decided to go back to work. She found a part-time position working about thirty hours a week for a children's clothing store. Between Enrique's unemployment benefits and Anna's $7.50 an hour, they were able to cover the mortgage and part of their monthly expenses.

The Vivars' ability to weather the loss of Enrique's income depended to a great extent on their privileged class and educational status, something they shared with most other job seekers in this study. All but one job seeker had a bachelor's degree; some held advanced degrees in fields such as engineering, physics, computer science, and business administration. Their prelayoff annual incomes ranged from approximately $40,000 to $100,000, with a few high-end outliers among former executives. Solidly positioned in the middle- and upper classes, these job seekers had access to financial and professional resources rarely available to people in less profitable fields. Most had enough savings to carry them through a few months of unemployment, and all had access to lines of credit, although taking advantage of this option presented risks of its own.[2] Like Enrique, many also had the option of relying on loans from family or friends. Tech workers were far more likely to avail themselves of personal loans than previous generations of middle-class job seekers have been, in part, perhaps, because in the midst of a recession and widespread layoffs neither they nor their families saw their unemployment as an embarrassing secret to be kept from friends and family.[3]

Eight months later, Enrique was still looking for a position in high tech and searching for more creative ways to trim his family's budget even further.

We've done a couple of garage sales. We don't go out to dinner anymore. At all. I don't think we've gone out to dinner since a month, two months, three months ago. You start putting off a lot of the things that need maintenance in the house. Like the window shade in Maya's room is broken, and it's got a big piece of tape. Before it was like a no-brainer. Car maintenance, for example, that's starting to be put off. I know that my car needs an oil change, and I'm going to wait another 2,000 miles.... What else? It's funny, because you start questioning things that are needed, like David's dental appointment is coming up, and I said, "Well, how much is it?" [Anna] said between $120 and $150. Hmm? Could we put it off another month, two months? Is it going to really affect the way his teeth are? ...I haven't purchased anything for me. Like, if I have to eat at a Wendy's, I really question that. It's $4 that I could use now. It's $4, whereas, before, it was, "ehhh." [*Shrugs, as if to say that in the past, he would not have thought twice about such a small expense*]...Oh, the other thing is the YMCA. We applied for financial aid at the YMCA. So. I mean, I stopped asking my family for money, so we just got into credit card debt, which is the worst thing we can do, but after three months the family is starting also to get on your back.

By that point, Anna had taken on another job working a few hours a week as a receptionist at a small doctor's office. After his unemployment benefits ran out (even with Bush's thirteen-week extension), Enrique, too, found part-time work unloading trucks at an upscale furniture store on the 5 a.m. shift. "It's a job," he said, raising both hands in the air in a shrug. "Gets me out of the house, keeps my mind a little bit clear, makes me feel like I'm doing something worthwhile."

Enrique was hoping to get more hours at the store as the holiday season approached and had also started teaching Spanish at an adult education center a few nights a week. Unloading trucks in the wee hours of the morning and working retail at the mall are significant steps down the pay and status scale from Enrique's and Anna's former jobs. Such downward slippage was common among Dallas job seekers, many of whom found similarly low-paid positions outside their professional fields, including scooping ice cream, stocking drugstore shelves, selling home electronics, waiting tables, and delivering flowers. A flurry of radio and newspaper stories in 2002 and 2003 documented similar cases across the country—the telecom engineer with an MBA working for the U.S. Postal Service, the dot-com golden boy selling khakis at the Gap, the Ivy Leaguer driving a forklift.[4] The tone of such stories ranged from sympathy to schadenfreude. Almost none of them acknowledged that unemployed tech workers were fortunate to have landed jobs to which many Americans can only aspire.

Tech workers' socioeconomic class, higher education, and professional experience functioned as social capital that gained them relatively easy access to jobs that, although at lower wages and status than they were accustomed to, allowed them to maintain a downscaled but decidedly middle-class existence.

Job seekers referred to these jobs as "interim" positions, and most planned to quit immediately upon finding full-time work, or adequately paid contract or part-time work, in high tech. Rather than conceptualizing these jobs as evidence of their long-term downward mobility or descent into a lower occupational class, job seekers, particularly men, instead prided themselves on doing "whatever it takes" to support themselves and their families until they landed a better job. Several male job seekers who had not yet taken an interim job forcefully asserted that, were they in real need, they would not let foolish pride dissuade them from taking a lower-status job. Temporary downward mobility was thereby presented as a "manly flaw," similar to the claim that one is "too virile to be satisfied with just one woman."[5] In this case, rather than explaining their descent down the professional ladder as emasculating, male job seekers framed themselves as *too* manly and responsible not to take the low-status job. One young software salesman, a father of two whose wife was a full-time homemaker, said as we sat sipping tea in a Starbucks, "I don't have an issue if I had to go work in the mall for a few months, if I had to go work at Neiman Marcus or work here at Starbucks to make ends meet. Not a big deal. I don't have a problem with that." (He eventually did take a part-time job selling jewelry at a friend's store in the mall. One day a former coworker came in with his wife to shop for jewelry. It turned out that the wife's software consulting firm was looking for a new salesman; she put his name forward and he was hired full time three weeks later.) In this reframing of downward mobility, to accept a position that might be seen as "below them" in terms of pay and required education demonstrates job seekers' commitment to providing for their families.

Family provision took other forms as well. In addition to juggling four part-time jobs between them, Enrique and Anna also had to deal with child care for their two young children. Since Anna started working at the children's store, Enrique had assumed primary responsibility for Maya and David. His new role as homemaker and caregiver had given him a new appreciation for the role Anna had played for the previous five years.

A friend of mine told me, you are the only person I know that has gone from a full-time job to a full-time job without pay. And it's true. It's really frustrating. You know, um, I understand my wife now. And that's one thing that has brought us together, is the fact that she's been you know sort of providing for us and I've been taking care of the kids and it's a tough job. I didn't understand how tough it was until I had to do it. Cause she complained to me a lot about it. [Anna would say] "Oh, when you come home later than 5:30 I'm just miserable. The last three hours of the day are so tough for me." At the end of the day, she would just sit on the couch and just lay and do nothing. I was like, "Hey why don't you help me clean the kitchen?" "I'm too tired. Why don't you do it?" So we would have a lot of fights about that, and I didn't understand why. Now I understand why. Like this morning, I left and the kitchen was a mess. I'm sorry, I don't care.

CL: Have you enjoyed spending the time with the kids?

Oh, it's been great. That I wouldn't change for anything in the world.... My brother is just going to become a dad in September, and I told him, you do not understand the joy of being a father until you are a father. As a matter of fact, that quote was from my dad. And they made a book of when I was a baby. My mom and my dad made an album, and one of the things that my dad wrote in the book was, "Son, you will never understand what being a dad is until you have your own kid." And when my son was born in September of '98, he gave me the book. I opened it and I read the quote and I was crying. I was crying. Cause it is true. It is true.

This new arrangement had its drawbacks. Enrique found himself with little time to continue his job search, and tensions arose between him and Anna.

My time is devoted to just working or taking care of the children. I don't have much time to network. So I feel that I'm losing focus on my job search because I don't have the time to do that, which makes me wonder, now how am I going to find a good job? ... I'm frustrated. I'm much more than frustrated. I'm depressed to a point that we're seeing a counselor. And she asked, do you need any medication? It's not as bad as needing medication, but I have my good days and my bad days. I got the outstanding achievement award from my MBA class because I've always kept a positive attitude, and I believe that I am a very positive and optimistic-type individual. But it has gotten to the point where it's really dragging me down. What can

I do? Hey, am I that stupid that I can't find a job? At the same time you start to ponder all these things. Is my resume good enough? Am I good enough? Do I speak the language good enough? What am I going to do a year from now? And at the same time you say, well, eventually the market is going to open up. But the way the market is going, I don't think it's going to open up until probably the end of next year, maybe. Who knows.

Enrique was able to maintain a sense of himself as a valued professional when regularly participating in groups like TechNet, continually revamping his resume, and actively looking for high-tech work. That identity became more difficult to maintain in the absence of interaction with potential hiring companies and fellow professionals. Although he valued his time with the children and was glad to be bringing in money through part-time work, depression and self-criticism plagued Enrique, and his ability to externalize blame for his layoff and prolonged unemployment—that it was the fault of an ailing economy, the dot-com crash, the telecommunications downturn, 9/11—faltered.

Continuing financial concerns—the couple had borrowed money from both Anna's and Enrique's parents and built up significant credit card debt—heightened tensions in their marriage, especially when Anna's mother arrived for an extended visit. According to Enrique, his mother-in-law "started getting on my case about not getting a job" and wrongfully accused him of holding out for a high-level executive position out of pride, which he says was not the case. To make matters worse, Enrique was in the midst of studying for an exam that, if he passed, would earn him project management professional (PMP) certification, a credential he believed would serve him well on the job market.

So it was just a couple of days before my exam. I was really stressed out. . . . She [his mother-in-law] just got me at a very bad time, so I ended up telling her, "Look, this is who I am. If you like it, fine. If not, it's not a marriage for convenience, you know, where I'm going to provide and she's going to care for the kids. It's a marriage for love, and if you feel that your daughter is doing something else, fine, be that way, but there's the door." I didn't tell her, "there's the door," but pretty much it was very well understood. We had a shouting match and stuff like that. And then I walked out of the house and I tried to talk to Anna and Anna sided with her mom, which created a lot more pain in me. . . . And so that's one of the reasons we're in counseling. The other reason is we're very stressed out.

His mother-in-law's suggestion that Enrique himself was to blame for his continued unemployment—because he was overlooking lower-status jobs in hopes of landing an executive position—challenged not only his masculinity and ability to provide for his family (topics I will return to in a moment), but his sense of himself as an excellent job seeker in a depressed market. Although his mother-in-law's visit was eventually cut short, her words (and Anna's refusal to refute them) struck a blow to Enrique's sense of self, demonstrating once again how central a role external validation plays in maintaining the image of one's self as an effective career manager and how fragile that image can be when challenged.

Anna was exhausted, too, torn between supporting Enrique and expressing her own fears and frustrations.

> You know, it's very frustrating. The other night I kind of vented at Enrique, which was a horrible thing to do. An "I don't feel like you're ever going to get a job" kind of thing. Which is completely unfair, because of course he's trying and he's frustrated beyond belief. For me it's just frightening, and the worst part is this feeling like there's nothing we can do. We've hit every contact we have. Some more than once. At some point you want go to a party and be able to just talk to your friends and not say, hey can you get us an interview? And as a wife, I almost feel like I can have no other feelings other than to be supportive. I'm not allowed to be afraid. I'm not allowed to say, "What's wrong? [*Laughs*] Why aren't you getting a job?" I mean of course it's not fair to him for me to say that, but sometimes I feel like that and feel like I'm not allowed to feel that.

Neither Enrique nor Anna envisioned theirs as a marriage in which the husband serves as sole provider to a dependent wife and kids. Theirs is an egalitarian, mutually supportive marriage between two well-educated professionals, one of whom consciously chose to give up her executive career for the good of the family, at least until both children reach school age. Despite this, Enrique felt the pressure to provide, particularly under the critical eye of his more traditional mother-in-law. For her part, Anna said she wanted to be a supportive and understanding wife, but the financial and social stresses of Enrique's continued unemployment wore on her as well, creating a gap between the ideal wife she would like to be and the way she actually felt and acted.

Anna had considered going back to work full time, but that too was an imperfect solution.

> Honestly, it's one of those catch-22 situations. If I return to the workforce full time, we'll be left in a bind. He has to stay home to watch the kids when I'm working. And any job that I'm going to find is going to be 8 to 5, which is when he can make contacts with potential employers....So we're still kind of putting it off and saying, no, he's the one who really needs to find the work, and I'm not going to go out and find full-time work....I would go back to work, but my earning potential is significantly less than his is. He has ten years of concurrent work experience with an MBA. [*Laughs*] I have ten years of work experience five years ago. So it's a big gap in my resume, which would definitely cut down on the amount that I would be able to earn....I'm really sorry that I took off the years that I did, that I didn't stay current in my field so that I would have a resume to fall back on to say, "Hey, you can hire me because I've done this and this and this, and it wasn't in the eighties." [*Laughs*] Because I feel really helpless right now. I feel like there's really nothing I can do. Because the amount of money I'd be able to make going back into the workforce isn't sufficient to justify me being in the workforce. And I look down the road and that gets even scarier. At what point do I go back? It's kind of frightening if he doesn't get a good job.

Just as at his lowest moments Enrique worried that the decisions he had made were responsible for his current situation, Anna questioned her own role in shaping the family's predicament. She left the workforce because she believed it would be the best thing for her children and herself:

> I actually hadn't planned to stay home with my first child, but I had an executive position and I was finding that I couldn't do my job well and I couldn't be a good mom trying to do both. I felt like I was pulled, things weren't getting done at work. I felt that someone else was raising my child. And I really was completely unhappy.

Yet that decision, which for the most part worked well until Enrique's layoff, had coupled with structural and cultural biases against working mothers to reduce her earning potential.[6] She felt helpless as a professional because her time out of work had derailed her career and helpless as a wife because she felt unable to provide Enrique with unconditional emotional support.

There are those who suggest that, despite these challenges, Enrique and Anna were better off than many couples in similar situations because Anna made that initial decision to leave her job. The authors of *The Two Income Trap: Why Middle-Class Mothers and Fathers Are Going Broke* argue that couples in which both parents are employed full time are less prepared to respond to events like job loss.[7] In a crisis, couples like the Vivars can opt to send the stay-at-home parent, usually the wife, into the workforce to make up for lost income. When both partners are already working, the family loses that cushion. In addition, to maintain a middle-class lifestyle, most dual-earner families have already increased their standard of living to a degree that two incomes are required to meet basic expenses—mortgage and car payments, insurance, educational expenses—that cannot quickly be "cut" in tight financial times. The "two-income trap," then, is that once a family comes to rely on two incomes, financial setbacks are more likely to end in bankruptcy and foreclosure.

The experience of Dallas job seekers who were, even prior to their layoff, members of dual-income couples, however, suggests a more complicated interpretation of the ways in which depending on two careers to maintain one family shapes the experience of job loss and prolonged unemployment. On a material level, the presence of a working spouse's income cushioned the financial implications of job loss for many families. On a cultural level, the ways job seekers talked about their marriages and responsibilities reflected a decidedly new perspective on male and female gender roles—and on the nature of dependence and autonomy—within both the family and labor force. Perhaps most surprising, shifts around gender, family, and work seem to have had very different implications for male and female job seekers, further destabilizing traditional models of how middle-class men and women respond to job loss and unemployment.

Just over half of laid-off tech workers in the greater Dallas area had a working spouse at the time of their job loss, which corresponds closely to the nation as a whole, in which more than half of all married couples include two full-time earners.[8] The forces that have compelled the rise of dual-earner couples have been well documented if ardently debated. (Such couples are also commonly called "dual-career" or "two-earner.") Different accounts emphasize different parts of the equation, but the general consensus is that the rising cost of living has coincided with the dismantling of barriers against married middle-class women's workforce participation to create a situation in which most middle-class U.S. households either need or prefer to have two full-time incomes. The proliferation of dual-earner couples, like any cultural phenomenon, cannot be identified in any simple way as good or bad, beneficial or detrimental. Clearly, the introduction of the working spouse and the financial safety net she or he represents presents certain complications to the model of the self-reliant career manager. Yet determining exactly how belonging to a dual-earner couple reshapes the structure and experience of job loss and unemployment requires exploring both the lived experiences of job seekers themselves and how the support of their working spouse fits into the story they tell themselves— and others—about their unemployed status.

***

On a sunny fall day in 2004, I met Ed Donnelly for breakfast at a warehouselike used bookstore just east of Dallas. Ed, fifty-eight at the time of that interview, is a slight, intense man with piercing blue eyes, a sharp wit, and a quick laugh. I had first spoken with Ed two years before, after encountering him at a TechNet meeting. At that point, he told me about being laid off from his job as a computer programmer at Exalt, a major telecommunications company.

> My layoff was the Thursday before September 11th, and at first it didn't bother me too much. I knew that telecom was having troubles but I didn't figure that the rest of the market as well was going to be doing too badly. I hadn't really noticed how much effect the Internet crash was going to have on people. I don't know. It just didn't sink in I guess.

Although Ed did not see his layoff coming, he came to believe that he should have.

> They did what they had to do. If I had been at all aware of what was going on, I would have seen it coming. But, I just sat there at my desk coding—fat, dumb, and happy—and the world came crashing down around my ears.

Ed believed his former employer was "a little bit too greedy," but ultimately he saw them as just one of many victims of the dot-com crash, which pushed many of their customers out of business.

[A]ll of a sudden Exalt had no checks coming in and a bunch of used equipment sitting on their loading docks that they'd repossessed. They looked
around and realized, well, we're still one of the best switch makers in the
world, but nobody's buying switches. And everybody else was in the same
boat. So they were having bad financial problems. They still are. I didn't feel
like they treated me badly. Actually, I survived several waves of layoffs, and
I was glad I made it as long as I did.

Another reason Ed had little rancor for Exalt was that the company was
clear from the start that they neither wanted nor expected loyalty from
their employees.

One of the things they preached over and over and over again to us, through
management, through memos, whatever, was be loyal to yourself, not to
Exalt. They're right. No one but you is going to look out for you as well
as you can. You have to decide for yourself what you want and where you
can get it. Yeah, Exalt will do what they have to to keep employees, so
long as they need employees, but you have to decide for yourself what you
want.... It's the only perspective that makes sense these days. The old days
of cradle-to-grave employment are *long* gone. I'd say they first started dying
in the eighties, maybe the early nineties, and it's taken this long for a lot of
people to realize, but realize it they have.

CL: Do you put yourself in that category?

No, because IT was never a cradle-to-grave industry. But I thought that as
a *career* IT was cradle to grave, and I want to get back in the cradle! [*Laughs*]

As Ed's comments attest, if he blamed anyone for his layoff it was himself,
for not heeding Exalt's advice, for not embracing "the only perspective that
makes sense these days." In retrospect, he suspected that had he been a better career manager—less content to stay in one place, more aware of the
state of the industry, better poised to make a quick job change, and up-to-
date in the latest technologies—he could have avoided unemployment altogether. "I didn't jump sooner. Or rather I should say I didn't jump at all,
and the platform fell out from under me."

This was not Ed's first bout with unemployment—he had been let go
three other times in his long career—but it was by far the worst. After his
previous layoff, Ed was out of work about a month. "This time," he said

with frustration, "I haven't even gotten interviews. In seven months, I have had one interview with a recruiter. I've attended several job fairs, turned in lots of resumes, and I have yet to speak to an employer in any meaningful way. It has been hideously difficult." He attributed his difficulty finding work, or even landing interviews, to lack of demand for the kind of programming in which he specializes.

> I've looked at retraining. I'm taking a Java course, things like that. There are things I can do to try to update my skills. These people keep talking about keeping your saw sharp. I'm looking at new saws. But, in this climate, if you don't have several years' experience with the exact tools that they're using, they're not willing to look at someone who's changing specialties. And the fact that I have more than twenty years' experience, and a, I think, terrific track record, even an impartial observer would agree a very good one, in spite of that, since I don't have the specific skills they're looking for, they're willing to keep looking to find someone who does have them.

When we met again two and a half years later, Ed was still in the midst of what he called his "personal remake," accumulating certifications in new programming fields. A few months after his layoff, Ed, a long-time gardener, had stumbled into a part-time job at a small gardening supply store he had shopped at for years. He enjoyed the job and worked there for two years before moving to a big box electronics store that offered more hours and better pay and benefits. The new job, Ed said, kept him in shape, as he walked the sales floor all day and was often required to move heavy equipment. The constant influx of customers with unique and sometimes challenging problems, he said, kept "my brain working." Still, Ed would much rather have been programming computers than selling them, and he made significantly less money than he would as even an entry-level programmer. For the moment, however, he had stopped actively looking for programming jobs.

> I did that as long as I could and basically got tired of getting doors slammed in my face. So when I start seeing signs that things really are turning around, then I'll try to get serious about it again. Until then, all I can do is keep my ear to the ground because I don't have the psychic energy to keep beating my head against the wall.

Ed struggled with depression, for which he took medication and saw a therapist. "If I can get a decent job," he said, "I'll probably be able to drop the treatment... but until then keeping my attitude up is a real challenge." His major concern was not that the job market would not improve; he was confident that it would. "The economy will turn around. It's already started in a lot of sectors, but IT is lagging behind and Dallas is lagging behind, so Dallas IT is still in the dumper." What concerned Ed was not that the recovery would never happen, but that it might come too late for him. "I am," he said, "rapidly becoming obsolete, and if I don't do something to retool myself and be ready to look current to whomever is hiring, the upturn is going to pass me by. I'm fifty-eight. My age is against me."

Ed's fears for the future were serious ones, but they were tempered by the relatively secure financial position he and his wife Sarah, also a programmer, had been able to maintain. They paid off their mortgage in 2002, which eased their financial responsibilities considerably, and were getting by on Sarah's full-time income and Ed's earnings from the electronics store.

> Financially, we're quite well off. We've always lived fairly conservatively.... My wife got laid off a couple of months after I did. She has gotten a pretty decent job [full time but on a contract basis], so she is basically the breadwinner in the family and I am struggling to pay my share of the expenses.... And unlike a lot of guys I don't have a problem with me having the lower income.

Ed's presumption that "a lot of guys" would object to being supported by their wife did not bear out among male married job seekers in Dallas. Instead, many were in situations similar to Ed's, and they were quick to praise their spouses for their support, both financial and emotional, and, like Enrique Vivar, to reference the partnership ideal at the core of their marriages.[9]

TechNet leader Will Ericsson, for instance, mentioned repeatedly how lucky and grateful he was to have a supportive, employed spouse. He was well aware that her substantial salary as an executive at his former employer made his job search much less stressful.

> I've been fortunate that my physical needs have been taken care of [by my wife's income and our savings]. I see that others tend to panic when they

start to see that money running out. So people need to know that this is how long I've got and this is how long I need to take [to find a job]. Mine can take as long as it needs to take. Not everybody has that luxury. And I recognize that as a luxury.

Will's friend and fellow TechNet member, Peter Dumond, described a similar situation.

Financially, intellectually, I'd prepared for [my layoff] so I had a big nest egg built up. I just stopped spending money on expensive things for the months ahead. And unemployment [benefits provided by the government are] enough. Between that and the fact that my wife is working, I haven't been hurting. It's not like some people I know that are living in $2,000-a-month apartments and you add food bills to that and car payments, unemployment is just a drop in the bucket. They had to be working within a month. There's no way [they could get reemployed that quickly].

Although he had expected to be out of work for only four or five months, at seven months Peter was unconcerned. He was, he explained, still ahead of the "statistical average"; at that time, the average duration of unemployment for laid-off Dallas tech workers was fourteen months.[10] Peter was doing a bit of short-term contract work in the meantime to earn some money to get by, and, he said, "I relied a lot on my wife. There was not any way around it."

Whereas Peter's statement that "there was not any way around" relying financially on his wife suggests that for him the situation was less than ideal, forty-one-year-old Internet marketing expert Craig Murray reveled in his (admittedly temporary) transformation into a stay-at-home spouse.

I make a badass crème brûlée. I made cookies this morning. I've been doing a lot of June Cleaver–type things at home. The Mrs. likes it because, like, I made beef ribs last week. I seriously made cookies the other day. Chocolate chip with four kinds of chips that she took in to the office.... [Being unemployed is] not the end of the world. I think Americans probably identify too much of their self-worth with what they do for a living. And that's too bad.

With close-cropped dyed blonde hair, stylish but casual clothing, and funky black-rimmed glasses, Craig was something of a poster boy for the irreverent high-tech style of the time. His job loss in the first weeks of 2002 came as no surprise to him, as his employer had already held multiple rounds of layoffs. It did surprise him, however, when his usually high blood pressure immediately dropped fifteen points. Craig was not sure what sort of job he wanted to find, but he knew he wanted something less stressful and more fulfilling than his previous position. In the meantime—and perhaps for the long term—he was living up to the ideal of the career manager, pursuing various short-term freelance positions while his wife's steadier income as a management consultant paid the majority of their bills. He was also keeping himself busy around the house.

One study has found that married men who are not working, "despite their free time, do only 37 percent of the housework, on average."[11] Craig, however, was perfectly comfortable, even gleeful, doing what he described as "June Cleaver–type things at home," invoking traditional stereotypes of the gendered nature of domestic labor even as he subverted them in his daily life. Clearly, Craig was not fixated on achieving the role of male breadwinner, or even equal coearner, and neither were Will and Peter; although they were less exuberant about it. Although Ed Donnelly had a college-aged son, none of the other men quoted above have children, and it is worth investigating whether parenthood complicates job seekers' ease in relinquishing the role of steady earner. A 1997 study of gender and breadwinning in dual-earner couples found that young, highly educated couples without children were far more likely than other couples to embrace the ideal of "co-breadwinning," in which neither spouse's job is seen as the primary source of income or the more important career.[12] This finding explains in part why the educated, middle-class tech workers in this study appeared to be more comfortable relying on spousal income than other workers.[13] It also begs the question of whether and how fatherhood shapes male job seekers' attitudes toward unemployment and relying on a wife's income.

Alex Brodsky, whose "do what you have to do" mantra is described in the introduction, described his relationships with his wife, Hannah, and daughter, Ella, as his greatest source of strength in managing the challenges and discouragement of prolonged unemployment.

> The key to it, this is in the interest of getting maudlin, is my marriage. I've got a very, very strong marriage and a little kid who no matter what you do that day, no matter what's happened that day, you can't look at a little one

like that and be pissed off. She doesn't care that you feel like a schmuck. She doesn't care that you've had a bad day. When she sees you at the end of the day, she runs up to you and screams "Daddy" and you forget all the rest of it. I've been married ten years now as of March. This isn't my first time being unemployed.... And again that's put a big burden on [my wife]. She supported me through that. That's the key to it. She has taken on incredible burdens to help me to do the things that I need to do. Not to her complete detriment to the point that she completely loses [her] identity, but knowing that we're both working toward something. I'm doing my part, she's doing her part.

His part, he clarified, consisted of managing the household, caring for Ella during the hours she was not in day care, and working evenings at the steakhouse.

Theoretically, I'm free to interview and look for work...or meet with other people trying to find work. What it really kind of came down to or meant was that during the day I was doing laundry, running whatever errands needed to be done, paying the bills, taking care of all the domestic things that go into keeping a household running. Because I was the only one available and that was a job that I was able to do. Usually cleaning up after the pink tornado has run all over the house the night before. So that was sort of the routine that we got into. So it became less about looking for work and more about cleaning the garage or doing whatever else. Keep the laundry from piling up.

Despite the reduced time available for job searching and the frustrations of waiting tables, Alex and Hannah decided together that he would not accept the first full-time tech job that came along but would, instead, wait for a position that matched his skills and interests. Until then, they agreed, Hannah's teaching salary would continue to be the family's primary support, and Alex would retain his role as manager of the "second shift" of domestic work and child care.[14]

Like Enrique, Alex rejected the idea that a man's primary contribution to his family must be in the form of a monthly paycheck. He believed he was doing his part in supporting the family by caring for his daughter, keeping up with the housework, and waiting tables part time. He was therefore comfortable with his wife serving as the family's primary earner while he managed the house and Ella's care, an arrangement he saw as an effective division of labor for the time being. Within marriages conceived as egalitarian partnerships, then, the ideal of self-sufficiency can be reconceptualized as "couple self-sufficiency,"[15] in which getting by as part of a couple, rather than as an individual breadwinner, is the yardstick by which one's success is measured. This framing of the division of financial and other responsibilities within a marriage rejects the model of provider and dependent. Although Hannah earned the bulk of the family's income, Alex did not see himself as a dependent—with all of the emasculating implications such a positioning might incur.

The experiences and attitudes of the men I describe above represent a significant shift from the attitudes of unemployed men as documented in previous studies of white-collar unemployment. Mirra Komarovsky's 1940 study *The Unemployed Man and His Family,* for instance, alleged that the unemployed man "experiences a sense of deep frustration because in his own eyes he fails to fulfill what is the central duty of his life, the very touchstone of his manhood—the role of family provider."[16] Nearly a half-century later in 1988, Katherine Newman offered a similar assessment:

> Downward mobility strikes at the heart of the "masculine ideal" for the American middle class. When the man of the house has failed at the task that most clearly defines his role, he suffers a loss of identity as a man. When this is coupled with the admirable efforts of a wife to salvage the situation by going out to work, the man's response may be intensified feelings of impotence and rage culminating in abuse.[17]

Even more recently, in 2002, sociologist Nicholas Townsend argued, "Men's prestige, their value to others, and their self-worth are measured by their identity as workers and their earnings from their work. Men who do not have jobs are frequently branded as unworthy, morally inferior, and failures as men."[18] As these quotations demonstrate, studies of unemployment throughout the previous century have consistently equated job loss and unemployment with a crisis of masculinity that prompts depression, frustration, self-blame, and self-doubt among jobless men. Research like Townsend's confirms that the expectation that men should succeed at work and support their families has by no means disappeared in the contemporary United States. Yet the quotations above, from job seekers like Ed, Craig, and Alex, complicate the framing of unemployment as inherently devastating and emasculating.

The very notion of what it means to be a man is, of course, always in flux. As historian Gail Bederman argues, alleged crises of masculinity are often simply part of the "constant contradiction, change, and renegotiation" inherent in the ongoing ideological process through which gender is experienced and understood.[19] Indeed, Newman declares that the masculine ideal was already in flux at the time of her study, a casualty of increasingly insecure employment, rising numbers of working women, and a feminist movement that privileged female independence, male sensitivity, and egalitarian households.[20] To be clear, one model of masculinity—or femininity for that matter—is never neatly switched out for another, and "the ease with which gender bends in modern marriages should not be overestimated."[21] The masculine ideal that associates manly success with steady paid employment and providing for one's family still has a strong influence on how the American man sees himself and how he is seen by others. Yet as steady employment has become increasingly elusive and masculinity has been redefined to include other, less employment-based standards for success, the primacy of that breadwinner ideal has lessened. Instead, my research indicates, middle-class men who have lost their jobs now have alternative standards of masculinity, and alternative models of professional success, toward which they can turn.[22]

As Alex Brodsky explained in an expanded version of the quotation that introduced this volume, being laid off and taking a low-status interim position was part of what facilitated his embrace of a more flexible professional self-image, which in turn strengthened his identification with his other, non–work-related roles.

> I've worked from a very young age. Like a lot of people, I didn't really realize it so much until later on, but like a lot of people my self-image was so tightly aligned to what I did for a living. But when I was in a situation where I knew with absolute certainty that if somebody were to take a snapshot of this I could look at this and say, this is not my life. Because I knew that while for a living I was waiting tables, I was not a waiter. I began to think of myself more in terms of a collection of skills and traits that could be applied to any number of things, and if I felt like I needed

a label I was more satisfied with the idea of being Ella's dad than I was in being Alex the information architect, or Alex the project manager, or Alex the operations manager. The situation kind of forced me to shake loose that self-image.

As Alex's comments demonstrate, changing gender norms and family structures have interlinked with career management's ideology of the self as a flexible bundle of skills independent of a single job to create cultural and psychological space for some men to see themselves and their contributions as separate from their paycheck or professional title.

Just as career management reframes job loss within a different narrative of professional success, job seekers' conceptualization of marriage and self-sufficiency reframes the experience of relying on a spouse's income. Believing that marriage is a partnership and that men should respect and support their wives' professional achievements—along with the twin assumption that employed middle-class women should be comfortable assuming the role of primary breadwinner—allowed unemployed men to reconceptualize relying on a partner's income, at least temporarily, as evidence of their masculinity rather than a challenge to it. This also enabled them to continue to see themselves as independent companies of one despite the reality that the bulk of their daily expenses were covered not by the fruits of their own labor but by someone else's, someone on whom they depended, whether they used that term or not. Consequently, rather than seeing his dependence on his wife as evidence of his unmanliness, Ed Donnelly prided himself on being "unlike a lot of guys"—presumably unenlightened, less secure guys—secure enough in his manhood to comfortably rely on his wife's income. Ed's beliefs about gender equality, marriage, and the inevitability of job loss combined to allow him to be simultaneously unemployed and, in his view, an independent man.

The belief that job loss and unemployment provoke crises of masculinity in middle-class men is often paired with the assumption that they do not provoke similar crises for working women (of any class), who are generally believed to ground their identity and sense of self-worth primarily in emotional connections that transpire outside the world of paid employment. One might expect, then, that as men ground their identity less fundamentally in paid employment, their reactions to job loss will start to more closely resemble women's experiences. Yet my own research found that although the stigma and stress faced by unemployed middle-class men seem to be lessening, the opposite seems true for middle-class women.

I first met Natalie Lawson, a warm, engaging website manager in her early thirties, at a seminar on job searching at the public library. Although she later attended other networking and informational events, this was Natalie's first foray into organized job-seeking culture, and she admitted to being nervous. We met a few weeks later at a Starbucks, where Natalie told me how she first got involved in web design. After college Natalie bounced around for a few years, doing short stints at a variety of jobs, including traveling as a dancer with the performance group Cirque du Soleil. She eventually moved home to Dallas, where her parents lived, and stumbled into web designing just as the dot-com boom was taking off. She enjoyed the combination of creativity and technical skills that web design required, but found herself discontent with various employers. After a series of "good but not great" jobs, through a recruiter she eventually landed a job at a high-profile Internet consulting firm. The hours were long and the work was challenging, but theirs was a tight-knit office with a fun, lively culture.

> When you first started with that company, you went through…an orientation, and during that, especially for the people who were coming on who were just out of college, they were told by the chief marketing officer point blank, we are probably ruining you for every job you will have. And the thing was, it was really true. I know there were dot-com consultancies that had, like, climbing gyms, and we didn't have stuff like that. I mean, we had, like, an old pool table in our office and our kitchen was stocked. So I mean, nice work. Really nice work.… But it wasn't because of the games, it was just something about everyone who worked there, you felt like you could gain some kind of knowledge from. It was the kind of place where you find five mentors. And you were just so excited about the people around you and the things that were being done. Your own ability to have an opinion and make a difference.

In early 2001, amid a storm of rumors, Natalie's company, once the darling of the dot-com media, announced its first layoffs. The company reassured employees that this was a necessary "tightening of the belt," rather than the beginning of the end and vowed to eventually hire everyone back. But for Natalie, once the home office shut down, "you knew that it would never be anything close to what it had been."

It was customary at the company for anyone who left—voluntarily or not—to send a goodbye e-mail to the entire company through the global distribution list. After the first layoff, Natalie started her own ritual of acknowledging each departing employee by visiting their personal page on the company website. She looked at their picture and read about the projects they had worked on and what their hobbies were. As the layoffs proliferated, looking up every person who left "became quite a chore," and Natalie eventually stopped trying. She lasted another six months and a half dozen rounds of layoffs, by which point survivor's guilt and an evaporating workload had her actually looking forward to leaving the company she once adored.

The sense of togetherness Natalie experienced at that company was an enduring one; even years later she maintains touch with a number of former coworkers (company "alumni," as they call themselves, have a networking website of their own). One of these is her now-husband, Daniel Klein (he was her boyfriend at the time of her layoff), whose views on career management I quote in chapter 2. The two met at a company party at the firm's Silicon Valley headquarters and soon began a long-distance relationship. When Daniel lost his job in the company's first round of layoffs in 2001, he relocated to Dallas to be near Natalie. He quickly found a position at a firm providing software for health care providers. Being included in the first round of layoffs stung at the time, but Daniel came to believe that it worked in his favor because he faced a much better job market than the one Natalie entered just over a year later.

Just before her former employer announced their first round of layoffs, Natalie had purchased a new home in need of significant renovation. Between her severance pay and a contract job at Daniel's company, she was able to make her mortgage payments. When we met in April of 2002, however, the two-month contract position had ended, and she was about to start dipping into her savings.

> I've got a nice amount of savings, I just don't like going into it. So, movies stopped, going out to dinner stopped. Just little extras. I'm very good at spending nothing. It's not fun, necessarily, and I wasn't a huge spender anyway. I'm far more of a spender on tangible things, especially house stuff, and the theater, entertainment stuff. The thing that is bumming me out the most is [not being able to plant] stuff in my yard, since it's kind of that season. I'm cutting back with that. I'm paying more attention when I grocery shop to prices, I'm just getting the small basic stuff. I won't get lamb.

[*Laughs*] I think the biggest hit has been entertainment. My boyfriend loves to do all that stuff. It's kind of hard sometimes because he'll go, "Oh, let's go to the climbing gym." And it's just kind of an extra that I shouldn't be doing now. [So I say] "Let's go jogging." He also likes to go drinking here and there. We've actually been going to Barnes and Noble and just hanging out and reading, so we're kind of changing lifestyles a little bit. He takes me to the movies here and there, which is great, but I'm not really one to actually love someone paying for me all the time.

She described Daniel as incredibly supportive and encouraging of her job search efforts, but Natalie was concerned about the effect her unemployment was having on their relationship. Now that she had so much free time, she found herself relying on her boyfriend in ways that were new to them both.

I've probably become a little bit clingy with my boyfriend because I have so much time on my hands. [I'll say] "Oh, just take tomorrow off," "Come home for lunch, I'll cook for you." Which I would do normally, but it's coming from a different place now.... I'm reading more [since losing my job]. I've gotten some good books. I'm doing all sorts of great things for my cat. I'm starting to feed her a raw food diet, so I've been researching all kinds of remedies for my cat. I'm doing a lot of things for my boyfriend, which is nice. Actually I kind of enjoy doing things for him. We've had talks about me feeling at times that I don't offer as much because I'm kind of, and it's not money-wise, it's just that I don't feel like I'm extremely successful as a person right now. [*Begins to cry*] I'm sure that affects my feelings of insecurity around him.

Relying more on a spouse or partner was, for some male job seekers, a badge of their forward-thinking attitudes to marriage and gender roles. For Natalie, despite her financial independence, relying more on Daniel made her feel uncomfortably needy. Even though she was doing more for Daniel in terms of caretaking than she had when she was employed, Natalie felt that she did not "offer as much" to him because, as someone who was not employed as a professional, she was, in her own eyes, not successful as a person.

Like Natalie's, Erica Roth's fears about how her job loss had affected her relationship provide an interesting contrast to accounts of male job seekers. Erica, an athletic, soft-spoken woman in her early forties, lost her job at an international tech company in the beginning of 2002, just two months before we met for an interview. She had been laid off once before, and although that layoff was more financially challenging—at the time her husband was in graduate school and she provided the couple's entire income—this one was proving more stressful for Erica. Like the male job seekers described above, Erica was quick to express her good fortune at having a working spouse, but her comments reveal a more complicated mix of gratitude and guilt.

> At first, [my husband] was very, very good because unfortunately it was really challenging for us that it was totally unexpected for me to lose my job. My husband was in a position where he works for a hospital, and the hospital that he was working for, their company bought out another hospital. So the two are going to merge and...he inherited [responsibility for] the other hospital, which was three times the size of his operation. Basically he didn't get much of an increase, just a cost-of-living increase for managing something three times the size. And he's working twelve- to fourteen-hour days. If I hadn't lost my job, he would have had the flexibility of taking a severance package, and it would have been very easy for him to find another job being in the field that he is. But since I lost my job, he didn't feel he had the leverage. So he's in a very stressful situation.... And I think he thought that based on my contacts and everything else I'd be able to land a job really quick, and it hasn't been that way. And so I think it's starting to dawn on him that it's going to be a much rougher road than he originally thought. And then the stress of his own job. So it's starting to be very challenging.

When asked how she and her husband had been handling that stress, Erica began to cry. Still crying, she said, "I try not to overreact to what he says because he has every right to react that way. And I did put him in a bad situation." Wiping away her tears, Erica repeated, "It could be a lot worse. I'm lucky. I'm in a better position than a lot of people." Yet Erica felt guilty that her job loss had created a situation in which her husband no longer felt he had the option to leave a stressful and unsatisfying job. Rather than framing the couple's current situation as a simple reversal of the time when her husband was in school and she was the sole earner, Erica instead saw her current failure to contribute financially as placing an unfair burden on her husband. She blamed herself for "put[ting] him in a bad situation," even though she had no control over her layoff, the tight job market, or the recent changes in her husband's job satisfaction. The emotional cushion that self-sufficiency offered to job-seeking men like Alex was absent for Erica. Instead, she saw her obligation to contribute financially as independent of her husband's employment status.

Natalie's and Erica's feelings of dwindling self-worth and insecurity mirror in many respects those of the male managers in Newman's 1988 study, far more so than did the comments of their male peers. Whereas the grounding of masculinity in secure employment has weakened for middle-class men in recent decades, for women like Natalie and Erica, professional identity and self-worth appear to have become more closely intertwined, at least with regard to their role in personal relationships. In the past, researchers have presumed that women are less disturbed by job loss because they place such value on their personal relationships. Yet for Erica and Natalie, it was in part because their relationships mattered so much to them that they were so distraught about being unemployed.[23]

For a man to accept a wife's support suggests an open-minded, non-sexist attitude toward changing gender roles and women's professional achievements. Craig Murray could pride himself on the homemade cookies he sent to work with his wife, and Ed Donnelly could pronounce himself more enlightened than those other guys who might balk at living off a wife's income. For Natalie, however, the opposite was true. Gardening, cat caretaking, and cooking for her partner during her newly ample spare time actually undermined her sense of self-worth, making her feel less accomplished, less progressive, and, potentially, less attractive.

It is not surprising that job loss is discomfiting for women who came of age in a world in which paid labor is expected of educated, middle-class women (at least until childbirth). Indeed, for many middle-class women, it is the decision not to work for pay that has become the culturally fraught one and that is deployed as evidence in broader cultural debates over feminism and the family.[24] Women like Natalie and Erica have adopted the ideology of the independent provider—and its concomitant pressures—just as the white-collar men around them are discarding it for an alternative model that relieves them of the responsibility to provide for a dependent partner yet still manages to position them as autonomous, masculine agents. Natalie and Erica do not sound like their unemployed male peers in the 2000s; in their guilt and self-recrimination they sound instead like the displaced managers Newman interviewed in the 1980s, judging themselves according to an ideology of meritocratic individualism that equates unemployment with individual failure and unworthiness.

The ideology of career management is not explicitly gender specific—its adherents would vociferously object to the suggestion—but it clearly has a greater appeal, or applicability, for male workers. This is in part because, as discussed in chapter 2, career managers define themselves in opposition to the "dependent" organization man looking to a company for security and protection. Another component of that organization man mindset was always that the individual worker, while dependent on a corporation, was, in the familial context, a masculine provider for his dependent wife and children. That breadwinner role offered a masculine identity that compensated for the daily indignities of working for someone else and depending on a paycheck to survive. Career management is built around a different model of adult male autonomy. In adopting the illusion of complete self-reliance that career management provides, male workers have rejected the idea that they depend on anyone, a stance they maintain even when they rely on an employer for a paycheck or a spouse for the roof over their head and the food on their table. This historic ideological shift has dovetailed with equally significant changes in ideals of middle-class masculinity and marriage to create a situation in which unemployed men are able to conceptualize themselves as both independent (in the sense that they are companies of one and not employees) and, to an extent, without dependents. The decline of the provider-dependent model of marriage among middle-class couples has lessened men's obligation to provide financially—or at least to be a sole financial provider—for their families (though it has increased expectations that they will provide emotionally). White-collar women, on the other hand, because they have retained, or recently adopted, a model of professional identity built around steady employment and financial provision, are unable to share in career management's emotionally buoying effects, which seem better designed to shore up masculine identities than feminine ones.

Husbands and wives are not, of course, the only kinds of dependents out there. That Natalie and Erica had no children at the time of this study likely played a significant role in their response to job loss. (Natalie and Daniel have since married and have two children. In the epilogue I outline how this has affected their professional identities and division

of responsibilities.) As I note above, many of the most ardent male career managers I describe herein did not have dependent children, and
young couples without children are the most likely to see themselves as
co-breadwinners; couples with children tend to frame the issue of whether
to work as a choice for the woman but not for the man. In this study, only
three female interviewees were part of dual-earner couples with children.
Of these, one woman in her midthirties with two school-aged children
expressed feelings of guilt and discomfort similar to those of Natalie and
Erica. Another, a physicist in her late forties, was significantly less an-
guished than the two younger women over her job loss. She explained that
for her, unemployment felt uncannily akin to the time she stayed home to
raise her children while they were young. A third woman, a thirty-seven-
year-old African American web designer with four young children, shared
financial responsibility for the family with her husband even after her layoff. While she worked to get her own freelance web design business off the
ground, she did the bookkeeping and administrative work for her husband's small business, but insisted that she be paid for doing so. "He's not
supposed to get everything free," she said. "Business is business." It would
be presumptuous to draw conclusions from these few examples, but they
suggest that motherhood is indeed a factor in how women in dual-earner
couples experience unemployment and financial dependence on a spouse.

Shifting narratives of career, gender, and marriage have apparently had
a more positive effect on married men's experience of unemployment than
on married women's, but the situation is not so simple that one can proclaim men the winners and women the losers in these newly negotiated
models of work and family. Neither spousal support nor a more flexible
model of masculinity have entirely paved over the pitfalls and pressures
of job loss for American men. Being able to rely on a spouse's income does
make it easier to maintain the optimism and flexibility career management
requires, and staying afloat despite prolonged joblessness feeds job seekers' sense of themselves as resilient entrepreneurs successfully navigating a
challenging situation. And yet, the very dependence that enables job seekers to continue being good career managers also undermines the autonomous ideal at career management's core.

Job seekers might frame themselves as "companies of one," but those
companies are often capitalized through the labor of another worker, usually, although not always, one who is employed in a less volatile (and often

less lucrative) field than high tech.[25] As companies and, more ambivalently, individual workers celebrate the flexibility a dismantled social contract allows, they often fail to recognize the extent to which the changed institution of marriage has lessened the impact of the resultant insecurity. In their interviews with me, individual husbands and wives were openly appreciative of their spouse's support, but they rarely drew broader connections to the ways in which their very notions of themselves as proactive, flexible career managers depend on those secondary incomes. Just as the career model of the organization man was predicated on the services of a stay-at-home wife, the model of the career manager rests heavily, if often invisibly, on the presence of an employed, or at least employable, spouse. Without working spouses, immediate financial concerns might preclude the flexibility and perseverance career management demands. For job seekers who lack extensive savings or lucrative interim positions, and that accounts for most of them, it is the spouse's income that allows them to be good career managers—to retrain in a new field, obtain additional certifications, pursue advanced degrees, take on strategic volunteer work, and attend regular networking and job search events.

The same income that keeps the family afloat despite prolonged unemployment also softens any backlash that might be directed against the labor system and market economy that created these hardships in the first place. The fact that more laid-off workers have not lost their homes, declared bankruptcy, or had to go without necessities like food, shelter, and clothing obscures the extent to which public and private programs intended to protect unemployed workers are failing to do so. Absent a working spouse, the inadequacy of the current systems of unemployment benefits, workers' rights legislation, government-funded job training and employment programs, affordable child care, severance and pension payments, and an employment-based health care system would be far more visible and perhaps more likely to garner national attention. Instead, the burdens of a volatile and increasingly global labor market, an ailing economy, and the erosion of corporate welfare have been quietly transferred onto the shoulders of the dual-earner family.

Job seekers' acceptance of this burden can be traced to overlapping causes, both discussed in chapter 2. First, in times of unprecedented uncertainty, it is impossible to underestimate the appeal of individual agency. When all aspects of life seem shot through with insecurity and risk, the belief that I am the master of my destiny, that I can do this, and I can do it by my wits alone, offers inestimable comfort. Second, this acceptance is in line with a more general American tendency, particularly within the middle class, to prefer individual solutions over collective or institutional ones. Rather than objecting to the structural problems described above, tech workers tend to believe either that these problems are inevitable and intractable or, conversely, that they can and will be resolved through the workings of the market alone.

The individualist, pro-market philosophy of career management reinforces both of these instincts by celebrating the absence of protest as evidence of forward-thinking pragmatism and manly self-reliance. Yet job seekers' lack of anger at "the system"—the corporations, government policies, and labor market that shape their experiences of work and the lack thereof—is not a simple side effect of their allegiance to career management. It is neither accidental nor incidental. It is instead both a symptom of and an intended remedy for that system's enduring failure to protect and provide for individual workers and their families.

Epilogue

By the spring of 2010, unemployment was everywhere. More than fifteen million Americans were actively looking for work, and the national unemployment rate hovered just below 10 percent; *Up in the Air,* a movie featuring cameo performances by actual jobless Americans, had been nominated for Best Picture; a bevy of new books about happiness were citing the finding that job loss has a more significant and prolonged negative effect on happiness than even divorce or the death of a loved one.[1] Occasional suggestions that recovery lay just around the corner were tempered by comments such as those of one economist, who said, "I think the unemployment rate will be permanently higher, or at least higher for the foreseeable future.... The collective psyche has changed as a result of what we've been through. And we're going to be different as a result."[2]

That question, whether we, collectively, as Americans, will be substantively different as a result of this most recent recession and the soaring unemployment rates that accompanied it is one for which my own research can provide at least a partial and preliminary answer. Parallels between the

2007–2009 downturn and the one during which I conducted the research for this book are undeniable, although differences in their causes and consequences should not be overlooked.[3] The job seekers in this study are, of course, not representative of the entire U.S. workforce. Their social class, education, and professional experience—and, for some, their race and gender—garner privileges and opportunities not available to other workers. Access to savings, credit, personal loans, and interim jobs that pay well above minimum wage mean that these jobless workers rarely face losing a home or going without the essentials of life. Most important, the presence of two incomes in a majority of households—facilitated by changing norms around women's employment, the nature of marital partnership, and appropriate male gender roles and prompted by the increasing difficulty of attaining a middle-class standard of living on one salary—allows many families to get by for extended periods of time without the income of the laid-off spouse. Despite these particularities, as I note in the introduction, the tech workers I met in the earliest years of the twenty-first century can serve as canaries in the mines of insecure employment, indicating what lies ahead for this new generation of jobless U.S. workers.

The advantage of studying tech workers over studying canaries is that nearly a decade later one can reconnect with tech workers to find out how they have fared since that first trip down the mineshaft. And, so, in the spring of 2009, in the midst of yet another economic crisis—although one in which, in a reversal of the previous recession, Dallas's workforce was faring slightly better than the national average—I reinterviewed nine individuals whose words and stories figure most prominently in the preceding chapters.[4] I selected these nine in part because I assumed readers would be most interested in the fates of the book's main "characters," whom they had come to know through my descriptions and extended interview excerpts. Some of these were individuals to whom I had become close during my time in Dallas; others were those whose stories I presented at length because I found them either particularly representative or unique. In all cases, I, too, was curious as to what had happened to them and how their opinions and perspectives might have changed over the intervening years.

I had remained in occasional contact with three job seekers since leaving the field and knew how to contact them. For the rest, I sent a message to their last known e-mail address, asking whether they were willing to speak by phone about their experiences over the previous five years.

Some e-mails received immediate replies; others were "bounced back" due to defunct addresses. In the latter cases, I launched an online search, which usually consisted of googling their names, sometimes with "Dallas" added on, in order to locate new contact information. (The rise of online social networking served me well in this effort, which is not surprising, considering job seekers' emphatic commitment to networking in any form; I found most of my "lost" informants on LinkedIn, a professional networking site I have heard referred to as "Facebook for grown-ups.") My initial intent was to reinterview ten informants, but I never heard back from the tenth, and do not know whether that was because my e-mails never reached her or because she elected not to reply. Of the other nine, all readily agreed to speak with me. Although I emphatically believe that face-to-face conversations are far superior to interviews by phone or e-mail, a research trip to Dallas was not possible at that time, and so I settled for conducting my follow-up interviews by phone. Each interview lasted between one and three hours, and some were preceded or followed by e-mail exchanges in which informants offered additional updates and opinions.

The dramatic variation between these nine individuals' experiences over the five years since I last spoke with most of them is itself a testament to the complicated ways career management, and the structural and cultural changes that have accompanied its rise, shape the lives of its adherents. Some interviewees have fared well, others significantly less so. Perhaps most remarkably, career management, as an ideology and a way of life, has proved far more resilient than might have been expected, even among those for whom financial and professional security have been most elusive. I cannot claim with certainty that the fates of these nine are representative of the other sixty-six job seekers in the initial study, but the diversity of their experiences suggests that this group is neither overly homogeneous nor patently idiosyncratic; when possible, I offer comparative data at the regional and national levels to contextualize their experiences.

I open the introduction to this volume with the story of Alex Brodsky, and it seems fitting to begin the epilogue with him as well. Having done what he needed to do to make it through thirteen months of job searching, Alex is happy to be back doing what he wants to do. He landed an information architecture job at an online retail company in 2004 and has been there ever since. He now manages a team of eight people at a salary significantly higher than what he made at his prelayoff position. When I ask how he likes his job, Alex replies:

> What I always tell people is that I have this built-in barometer, because I live [forty miles from the office]. If I ever reach the point where I get up in the morning and I just can't bear the thought of getting in my car and driving out there every day, I know I've got a problem. I don't even have to know what it is. So I'm still making the drive and still happy doing it.... I like it there, and plan to stay there for quite some time as long as they don't get sick of me.

Hannah is still teaching, Ella is now in school, and a few years ago the family bought a new home in a Dallas suburb conveniently located between their two workplaces. Alex's bout with prolonged unemployment, coupled with the experience of bankruptcy, has made them financially cautious despite his high salary. They are not "wildly frugal," he says, but they have adjusted their cost of living so that, if Alex lost his job again, they could continue to meet their basic expenses, mortgage included, on Hannah's salary alone.

Alex's strategies for managing unemployment and looking for work appear to have served him well. His family is healthy and financially secure. His job is lucrative, challenging, and fulfilling. As he sees it, he did what he had to do, and it all worked out in the end. Yet when Alex hears about the millions of people currently out of work in the United States, he still thinks to himself, "There but for the grace of God go I." If his professional situation were to change, if he started dreading that long morning drive, or if the company laid him off, he could simply go back to waiting tables. "That's the comfort," Alex says, "that that to me is about as bad as it can get." He and his family would keep their home, keep relying on each other, keep doing what they have to do.

Alex's situation is not the norm—most people do not make more money following a layoff than they did before it, especially with a stint serving tables in between. Compared to the continuously employed, displaced workers suffer average earning losses of 10 to 15 percent; earning losses tend to be even higher among those laid off during economic recessions.[5] A 2004 study of laid-off Dallas tech workers found that of the quarter who had found full-time reemployment, nearly 60 percent experienced a pay cut.[6] Mine is not a statistically representative sample, but of the nine job seekers I reinterviewed in 2009, two make significantly more money than they did prior to their layoff in the early 2000s. One makes slightly more, another slightly less. Three have taken significant pay cuts (one-third to one-half of their previous salaries), one is currently unemployed, and another has voluntarily left the workforce. Together, their experiences, and how they explain them, tell the story of an ideology and its consequences.

Craig Murray is still baking cookies, but this time they are for his own colleagues not his wife's. In May 2009, Craig started a new job as a marketing researcher for a major food products company. "On Monday and Tuesday of last week when I took in chocolate chip *and* peanut butter cookies they were a real hit. I will tell you that, it's a great way to befriend everybody in the office." In the previous seven years, Craig has had to befriend many cadres of new coworkers. Since his layoff in 2002, Craig has held three different full-time positions (he left two voluntarily and one via layoff) and several contract jobs. He came to his current job through a recruiter, who found his profile on the professional networking website LinkedIn.[7] Craig liked his previous job, where he stayed for three years, but this company offered him a 30 percent pay increase and a chance to do work that he found far more interesting.

Craig credits his ability to move relatively quickly from one job to another, even following a layoff, in part to his active participation in professional associations. (Although getting up to speed in his new position has prevented him from attending the networking lunches he usually frequents, in the week before I spoke with him he had attended two evening events for marketing and branding consultants.) He advises those who are out of work to do the same: "I think you should manage your career like a brand and look for every opportunity to get your exposure out there, get your name out there." For Craig, as for Alex, the principles of career management, particularly the sense of oneself as an autonomous company of one and a faith in the efficacy of individual effort, remain firmly intact.

Also like Alex, Craig is aware that his wife's income has facilitated his professional success. His wife, "the same hilarious person that I married almost eighteen years ago," still works in management consulting, and her steady income continues to shape how he goes about looking for and choosing the work he does.

There's something to be said for having a spouse who makes a good salary. And she and I, over the years we have leapfrogged each other in terms of salary. And it's obviously something that puts you more at ease. At least I've gotten to a point where I feel more at ease when I'm discussing compensation issues with a prospective employer. If it's work that I'm really interested in doing and I don't really kind of care about the money all that much because the work is so interesting sounding, then that's something that I'll tell a prospective employer. I'll say, "Look, my wife is a consultant, she makes good money, I'm really interested in doing this work and salary is not really the primary driver or motivator for me in wanting to do this work." It's not because we're rich, but the reality is we're double income no kids, [that's] something that has certain advantages to it.

If Craig is something of a poster boy for career management—unflappable in the face of change, privileging project over paycheck, always looking for the next, more interesting position—his wife's salary and support are a good part of what makes such flexibility possible. As Craig notes, he and his wife are DINKs (double income, no kids). As noted in chapter 5, the absence of dependent children also factors into these job seekers' more flexible attitudes to employment. Craig does not have to be a provider (although he does not exactly position himself as a dependent either), not for his wife or for children, and this frees him to embrace an attitude to employment he could not otherwise afford.

The measure of a job seeker's success cannot, of course, be determined by reemployment or financial security alone. As many job seekers made clear, unemployment can be a messy, depressing, discouraging experience. The anxiety that experience produces does not always recede when a new job appears.

During his thirteen-month job search, former TechNet leader Will Ericsson relied on his wife's executive salary; by 2009, his wife had retired and their roles had reversed. The contract position Will e-mailed the group about in 2002 never turned into the full-time position he expected, nor did the next few contracts, but in 2003 a contract with a large aeronautical corporation in Fort Worth did lead to a permanent position, and Will has been there nearly six years. Now fifty-seven, Will hopes to retire from his current company. Although his target retirement date is only two years away, and he has no specific reason to believe his job is in peril, a part of him is still nervous that he might be laid off before then.

Thinking about it, I believe I do have an underlying anxiety about that, the fact that it [a layoff] could happen, and ten years ago I never would have had that anxiety. I think it's just having been laid off and going through what ended up being over a year of job search, I believe I would find it hard to find another job. Whether that's true or not, I have that belief. So [there is] this underlying anxiety about income stability, job stability, life in general.

For Will, as for most U.S. workers, insecurity has become a permanent component of life, shadowing even the relative security of his professional and financial situation.[8] The way he combats that insecurity, he says, is to surround himself with a supportive community of peers, something he believes all job seekers today need to do.

I think the message [I would have for people unemployed now] would be that the anxiety is normal, for one thing, but the other thing would be that they need to have a support network, or some kind of support group, close friends, somebody that they can talk to about their anxiety, about whatever they're going through. Because I know if I didn't have a support group when I was going through my job search and now, I think I would be in really bad shape emotionally.

I was surprised to learn that the group Will refers to as his source of support is not TechNet, to which he committed so much time and energy while unemployed, but a small Christian men's group that meets weekly. In his capacity as TechNet leader, Will regularly warned job seekers, "don't stop networking just because you land," but he has not followed his own advice. "When I landed my first job," he says, "I just kind of quit going and completely lost touch." In part, Will's decision to disengage from TechNet, which still meets on a weekly basis, stems from his expectation that there will not be a next job for him, at least not a paid one. His energy is now focused elsewhere, on his impending retirement and a nonprofit ministry group he recently founded. The anxiety he describes above, then, may eventually dissipate. A few more years of steady work, and Will and his wife (who were DINKs before his layoff and her retirement) will escape into the relative security of two fixed incomes and what they hope will be adequate retirement savings.

Mike Barnard, the former producer who described looking for a job as "a sucker's game" in chapter 2, is also imagining what his eventual retirement might look like.

> Retirement, for me, as for most people nowadays, is something that's becoming more and more of a remote sort of possibility....I've pretty much decided that whatever it is that I'm going to have as security is going to have to be generated by the gray matter between my ears.

To that end, five years ago, about the time we last spoke about his support for global offshoring, Mike started a company specializing in online video delivery. According to Mike, his business has been doing well; between it and a few contract jobs in related fields, he now makes approximately $85,000 a year. He used to make closer to $150,000, a salary he now sees as part of a "false economy" that reflected "the whole dot-com bubble." He lives comfortably, he says, particularly since he has only himself to support. He and his wife divorced soon after his layoff, and he attributes their breakup in great part to his job loss and subsequent decision to not seek full-time corporate employment.

> I had been thinking about going out on my own on and off for years, but the circumstances weren't right. It was just easy to fall back into the routine of, well, go get another job, or I didn't have an identity if I didn't have a job in some corporation....But when I left [my last employer] I was unemployed for a while, and basically found a situation where I was working full time [as a contractor] but it was very tenuous...and it seemed like our whole reason for being there was to be the fall guys whenever there was a downturn....So I would get laid off and then a few weeks later they'd hire you back, and I got very tired of that. And at the time I was married, and I told my wife I was pretty sick of that and didn't see much of a future in it, and she was really insistent that I remain employed, as she saw it. It was probably one of the big issues, one of the tiebreakers on our marriage [in] that I really was not wanting to go and continue to be a corporate whore, so to speak. So I got divorced, and I decided, well, it's as good a time as any to do this.

The significant reduction in income he has taken since his layoff places Mike among the ranks of the downwardly mobile. As Katherine Newman has noted, "It is a truism of downward mobility that the meaning of a loss...can only be understood relative to a particular starting point."[9] His current income places Mike in the top quarter of U.S. households, but it is still just over half what he made at his prelayoff job; through divorce, which he attributes in part to his job loss, he has also lost the additional income his wife provided.

Mike's use of the term "corporate whore" invokes once again a contrast between the allegedly feminized dependence of full-time, if erratic, employment and the manly independence of unemployment and (attempted) entrepreneurship. His conflict with his wife and their eventual divorce stem at least in part from her unwillingness to accept his framing of the situation. While Mike sees corporate employment as a form of dependence, his former wife (like the female job seekers in chapter 5) saw working for someone else as a safer, more responsible route. In the end, Mike chose to end his marriage rather than, as he saw it, surrender his masculine independence to corporate whoredom. Their marriage was one casualty of career management, the costs of which have taken other forms as well.

Keith Hartmann, the Japanese American job seeker and avid volunteer from chapter 3, has also sought a more secure alternative to traditional corporate employment, and he too has taken a dramatic pay cut. Now fifty-three, Keith was out of work for nearly two years before he found a management position in Japan at the subsidiary of a U.S. company. The company reorganized soon after he arrived, and he was promoted to president of the Japan operation at a salary of $230,000. The company refused to move his family to Japan, so Keith rented "a little bitty apartment that's about the size of my bathroom here." The plus side of his austere living arrangement was that he was able to send money home and pay off the debt they had accumulated during his time out of work. But Keith missed his wife and three children, and when his health started to suffer he resigned and moved back home. He immediately landed a contract position with a former client. After two years, a budget cut wiped out his position, and Keith found himself once again unemployed and looking for work in Dallas. He attended a few TechNet meetings but found the prospect of spending time with other job seekers less alluring this time around.

I remember there were times when I felt really, really desperate and hopeless, especially at the end of that two-year period when I was out of work, and it [going to networking events] just put me too close to being back in that bad place, and so I decided to distance myself psychologically from that, so I've pulled away. I get e-mails and things from some of these groups but I don't actively participate in any of them. And I understand now that they are just busting at the seams, because so many people are out of work again. I would say it's as bad if not worse than it was in the early 2000 era.

The same events that once gave Keith direction and encouragement now serve as painful reminders of his previous extended joblessness and the depression that accompanied it. Nearly all of the Dallas-area networking events I observed during my fieldwork continued to meet as of 2010, yet most of the tech workers who suffered repeat layoffs since I last spoke with them no longer attended organized networking events.[10] Their reasons ranged from Will's hope that he would not need another job, to Keith's emotional revulsion, to a more general belief that such events were not as professionally beneficial as those populated by employed people. Yet, as Keith notes, networking events for the unemployed continue to draw large crowds of new job seekers, and their structure and content continue to endorse career management and the importance of marketing oneself as an independent, never-complaining company of one.

After eight months of unemployment (with a few short but enjoyable interpreting gigs along the way), in 2007 a friend recommended Keith for a contract position in the Human Resources department of a government organization. Keith appreciates the relative security of a government job, even a contract one, but the position is far from the exciting international work he believes he was "born to do." His current job is "secure, but it's not challenging." "There are days," Keith says, "when I pass the entire day not doing anything." Still, he says, "I'm thankful that I have a job, even though there are days when I'm really bored and don't feel like I'm being used."

Keith longs for a chance to demonstrate and utilize the skill set he has cultivated over his long career. To be employed, for Keith, is not the same thing as being "used." In his lament lies one of the most painful consequences of the current system of insecure employment. There are millions of unemployed and underemployed people across the United States whose talents are being wasted. Their accumulated years of training, education, and experience, the immeasurable quantities of energy, creativity, and devotion they have put into their work, have ultimately come to nothing, or at least nothing even remotely resembling what they once expected.

For the time being, Keith is skeptical that he will ever find the sort of paid employment that makes him feel valuable and well used. He still checks the job boards during his ample downtime at work, and while Texas (along with California) has led the nation in the creation of new high-tech jobs since 2007, Keith sees few opportunities in his chosen field of international business.[11]

> I'm fifty-three now, which means I probably have about fifteen more [work] years left. So that's why I'm considering we've got to minimize our expenses and save as much as we can while we can both still work. Because I don't think the employment situation is going to get better. I don't think there are expat jobs overseas just hanging on low branches waiting to be picked any-more....In any case, I don't have that much time, I'd rather do something that's fulfilling to my heart.

A few years ago, Keith stumbled across a nonprofit organization that promotes self-discovery through weekend training seminars. "It sounds like it's kind of corny," he admits, but "it was an incredible experience for me to go through." He now volunteers for the organization, helping other people manage the crises in their lives.

> There's a lot of pain, there's a lot of desperation in this world. I get to see it firsthand. And when you see it firsthand, and you're helping somebody overcome what's happened in their past, it just puts money way down on the list. It would be great to be financially successful and be able to retire and have a leisurely life, but for me it's more about having meaning in my life than it is to be financially secure.

As detailed in chapter 3, Keith once used volunteer work to combat depression and occupy his mind and his schedule while he looked for work. Now he has a job, but it is not in his chosen field, and it is clear to him that the work he does is not valued by the people around him. To try to recapture that sense of himself as a valued contributor, not to mention a role of relative authority, he has turned once again to unpaid volunteer work. By privileging the values of generosity and emotional fulfillment over financial and professional gain, Keith conceptualizes his downward mobility as a welcome, if initially involuntary, opportunity to engage in more meaningful and important work.

Although it has its rewards, his volunteer work does not pay the bills, and Keith's family is living on a significantly reduced income. Keith believes his current $75,000 salary is generous for the type and amount of work he now does, but it is just a third of his former income, and he has two daughters in college. To get by, the family has slashed their spending, and, after more than two decades, his wife has reentered the workforce.

> She's got a bachelor's degree from UT Austin in marketing, but she has never worked since we've been married, so she started out working for the public school system here as a lunch room lady, passing out spoons to kids. And I think that must have been hard for her. [*She has since moved to an administrative position in the same school.*]...She's making, I think, $30,000, so that helps. So combined income we're making a little bit over $100,000. And we've cut our expenses down to the bare minimum. We don't go out, almost every meal we cook in. We go to the bookstore for a date, stuff like that, or we go to the dollar movies. [Now] I'm just thankful that the ice maker works, that hot water comes out of the shower. We've become much more thankful for a lot of basic things we used to take for granted. And there are so many other people around us that are in worse shape.

Keith, too, understands that downward mobility is relative. He mentions again and again in our interview that others are worse off than he, and that he is grateful for what he has, financially, professionally, and emotionally. He is especially thankful for the support he received from his wife and children during his time out of work. When I ask how he now feels about his two-year bout with unemployment, his mind goes to the same scaled-back Christmas he discussed in our first interview in 2001.

> What I remember the most is how my family bonded together, and how we relied on each other and not material things. I remember having Christmases when we borrowed a Christmas tree from my in-laws so we wouldn't have to buy a Christmas tree, and I remember giving my kids little gifts like tablets of paper. I mean they were cute, but stuff like that, and I also remember that my children never complained about anything that we gave them for Christmas. And I will never forget that. That will stay with me until my last day, that somehow my kids could see that we were doing the best we could and they never had a critical comment.... And so those are the kinds

of things that I will remember during that period, the good things that taught us character and persistence and not so much the financial stress.

Like many other job seekers, Alex Brodsky and his family included, Keith weaves the story of his unemployment and downward mobility into a narrative demonstrating the virtue of simplicity and the triumph of character over adversity. He credits unemployment with helping his family members take a hard look at their spending patterns and embrace a downscaled lifestyle they plan to continue even after their financial situation improves. By conceptualizing their frugality as a moral achievement, job seekers effectively transform an externally imposed hardship into an opportunity for the entire family's spiritual and moral growth.

Natalie Lawson and Daniel Klein, who married in 2004, also frame their scaled-back incomes as a fair exchange for other kinds of rewards. The couple now has two children—three-year-old Rose and six-month-old Max. By the time they married, Natalie, thirty-eight, was reemployed as a senior web designer, but she left that job after Rose's birth to become a full-time mother and homemaker. The family struggles a bit to get by on Daniel's salary, particularly since Max's birth and the purchase of a new home in need of renovation, but ultimately, Daniel says, the decision to give up a second income was an easy one.

> Before we had Rose, Natalie and I talked about it, because I was a high earner and she was a high earner, and together we had a very, very nice salary. We had a ton of disposable income. If we had done that for five years and just socked away all that extra income, we'd be doing incredibly well. But because we were both getting older, we knew that we couldn't really do that. So it was a very conscious [decision]; okay, we know we could live very comfortably without kids, financially, but that's not what we're looking for. I mean, we'd love to live well financially. [*Laughs*] But we definitely wanted to have kids.

Natalie's concerns, expressed in chapter 5, that not earning a salary made her a less attractive and overly dependent partner have mostly been alleviated by full-time motherhood, which she describes as both more challenging and more fulfilling than paid employment.

> I don't think there was ever a thought that [raising a child] was going to be easier [than paid employment], but it is so much harder! [*Laughs*] Holy cow! Physically and mentally, it's so much harder. And I think that took away so much of my concern or guilt or whatever about not earning physical cash because there's no question about contributing to the family. It's just contributing in a very different way.

Daniel shares Natalie's perspective on their new division of responsibilities.

> She has her job, I have mine, meaning her job is to take care of the kids, while I go to my job, which is over there. There are definitely guys out there who are just like, she's spending your money, and blah blah blah. I just think that that's not a very healthy partnership.

Despite the satisfactions of motherhood and her and Daniel's embrace of couple self-sufficiency, the urge to measure her value according to employment-based standards of success still creeps in now and then. When she and Daniel join dual-income couples for dinner, Natalie occasionally thinks, "I have nothing to add to this conversation. My life is just kids and diapers and toys." She hopes this feeling will diminish now that she has started contract work from home in the evenings ten to fifteen hours a week. Rather than choosing between two very different models of successful womanhood—the doting full-time mother and the professionally successful coprovider—Natalie measures herself according to both and, inevitably, finds herself wanting.

Daniel, thirty-six, has also made a professional transition. After yet another layoff, this one in 2006, he left the managerial track to pursue more technical positions that he believes will ultimately prove more secure, although less well remunerated. "The problem with a middle-management position," Daniel says, "is that you can be responsible for a lot, and you're a little more expendable...but if you're a good [software] developer, it's never going to be that hard to find a job." Daniel's most recent job search took two months. The family was in good shape financially, as he had received three months' severance pay from his previous position, but the job search was not without its stresses for Daniel.

> Especially now that we have two kids, I am the one who has to bring in the money and make sure that the kids are taken care of and my wife's okay.... As

the provider, it was definitely stressful to not have a job and to kind of have this nervousness about, "Okay, am I going to be bringing in money soon?" The fact that we had severance and plenty of savings definitely made that easier, but I actually wound up developing these weird itch attacks. All of a sudden my whole body would just instantly start totally itching. It was really weird. So we knew that was stress, just from the job search.

Daniel has been in his new position for two years. Rather than conceptualizing his lower pay and status as a move imposed on him by repeated layoffs and the disappearance of the sort of managerial positions he once coveted, he draws on larger cultural narratives of family and work–life balance to frame his new work situation as an improvement upon his old.

I was just thinking about this recently because I work with a bunch of young people—they seem young to me [*Laughs*]—but, just kind of how [much] more driven I was before the kids came. I was just a lot more interested in career growth, and in the fulfillment that that brought. And I think with kids now, I'm not looking for work to be the fulfillment as much as I was before. I get a lot of joy out of my kids and my wife and just being a family. And so it changes what I'm looking for.... I have no desire to go work at a place where I'm really going to have to put in a ton of extra hours. I don't mind doing a little.... But five years ago I was definitely envisioning management as my career goal, and maybe leading to upper management, and higher positions. Today, I don't have any career goals. [*Laughs*] In other words, management is *not* what I'm shooting for right now.

Like Keith Hartmann and Alex Brodsky, Daniel emphasizes that paid employment is no longer central to his identity or sense of self-worth. Yet when he explains his reduction in pay and status as voluntary, ultimately beneficial, and prompted by his children's births, Daniel rejects—or fails to see—alternative narratives that might explain his recent career moves. Like Keith's framing of frugality as a moral achievement, Daniel's interpretation of his situation emphasizes individual choice over necessity. Collectively, the men I reinterviewed in 2009 had been laid off more than a dozen times. When they take pride in having disconnected their identity and self-worth from the work they do for pay, they obscure the extent to which those old identities were pried away from them by the gradual dismantling of the social contract of employment.

It is certainly true, however, that the transition from DINK-hood to parenthood has dramatically altered Daniel and Natalie's views toward work and its place in their lives and identities. Although he still holds tightly to many of career management's tenets, upward mobility is no longer Daniel's ultimate career goal. Now a father of two, he is less willing than childless men like Craig and Mike to take on the risks of unsteady or entrepreneurial employment. This contrast suggests that even for white-collar males, there are limits on who can adopt career management and when. The ideal career manager not only depends on no one, he has no dependents. That is not the case for most job seekers, some of whom feel acutely responsible for providing for their families. The presence of an unemployed spouse and dependent children makes it difficult, if not impossible, to live up to the ideals of career management, adding sole providers to the growing list of individuals—working women, members of the poor and working classes—for whom career management and its promised rewards remain elusive if not unattainable.

This embracing of a more family-based and less employment-centered identity should not be taken as evidence that white-collar males have entirely rejected gendered ideas about work and family roles. Although he believes that Natalie's work as a full-time parent and homemaker is as much a job as his paid position, Daniel admits that he would be less comfortable if their roles were reversed.

> We've discussed the fact that if I for some reason hate my job or if I get laid off, Natalie can always go back to work. I think it would be very difficult just to take care of two kids full time, that's just a lot of work. I imagine that I'd have some amount of, I don't know what the word is, just like shame or embarrassment or something, about me being the stay-at-home dad....I'd have to have a good way of justifying it to other people to feel better about it. Because I think that people would probably just look down on you, like, why don't you work?...I think that stigma is still a little bit out there, even in the younger generation.

Daniel, like many members of his generation, is adamant that full-time parenting is a job, but he retains a sense that it is a woman's job. Men like Daniel and Alex clearly embrace a more engaged form of fatherhood and a more active role in the physical and emotional labor of maintaining a household than did most men of previous generations. Yet for Daniel, at least, social norms about gender and labor still shadow his egalitarian tendencies. In discussing his concern that others might judge him, he slips into a more traditional definition of work as paid labor outside the home. The role narrative plays in making sense of our lives is undeniable, but rarely is it so consciously acknowledged as when Daniel admits that it is not the choice to become a stay-at-home father that troubles him but the inability to explain it to others in a way that would maintain their positive image of him. He is, however, cautiously optimistic that if the opportunity presented itself, he would rise to the occasion. "If it happened," he says, "it would be okay. Even just for six months or something, or whatever, I think I'd be okay."

The opportunity to test Daniel's theory has presented itself not once, but twice, for Enrique Vivar. In 2002, while he looked for work, Enrique's wife took on two part-time jobs and he assumed responsibility for the house and their two children's care. After a year of searching, Enrique found a full-time position as a project manager; despite his new MBA, he took a salary cut of approximately $20,000 from his prelayoff job. A year later, he recouped that loss when he voluntarily moved to a similar position in another company at a starting salary of $80,000. Two years after that he moved again, eager for an opportunity to return to managing engineering projects in Latin America. This time he negotiated hard; the company, which had aggressively recruited him, eventually agreed to $110,000 a year and he jumped at it.

He enjoyed the puzzle-solving aspect of project management, and got positive reviews for handling a challenging project in his native Mexico. Traveling five days a week for months on end, however, started to wear on him. He butted heads with his boss on a number of topics, including his constant travel and the broken promise that his work would be concentrated in Latin America (he spent more than half of 2008 on a project in Minnesota). When in February 2009 his boss announced that they would be laying off one of the two managers on his current project, Enrique knew he would be the one to go.

> I could see the handwriting on the wall…and I was scared, scared to the bones that I was going to get laid off. I didn't want it to happen because I knew that I had been laid off before and I was fourteen months without a

job and all that stuff, and I knew that the economy wasn't at its best right now, so I didn't want it to happen. I managed to hold onto my job for about eight months, but ultimately, if the shoe ain't your size, it ain't gonna fit.

Enrique offers two competing narratives of his layoff. He first describes it as something he feared would be inflicted on him by his managers, a dreaded event he spent eight months trying, ultimately unsuccessfully, to avoid. His tone shifts significantly, however, when he compares his job to a shoe that did not fit. With this metaphor, Enrique frames insecure employment and job loss as personal, rather than societal, matters. He moves from describing himself as a worker competing in a tight labor market to hold onto and, later, to find, a job, to framing himself as an individual consumer, shopping for the right fit.

Enrique goes on to dismiss his initial fear as misplaced and his layoff as a positive event, saying, "I hated my job. I needed to be pushed out because I was scared." This idea that he is better off without a job than employed in a job he did not like functions to reposition Enrique's layoff not as a rejection of his value by his former employer (and the labor market more generally) but instead as an opportunity for him to pursue a better quality of life by finding a job that "fits." His metaphor of fit frames Enrique and his former employer as equals, both of whom walked away from a bad situation, but it obscures the reality that Enrique did not walk away—he was pushed. This way of interpreting (or disguising) his helplessness in the face of yet another layoff is not simply a psychological response to an unwanted event; it is part of the larger cultural logic of career management that relieves both employer and employee of culpability while retaining a sense of agency on both sides.

Discussing employment as a matter of personal compatibility also naturalizes the termination of the employment relationship—it was inevitable, because Enrique and his employer did not fit. Enrique extends this conceptualization of job loss as natural when, in response to a question about how he felt about his layoff, he spontaneously tells me about a neighbor of his who had recently passed away after a long, painful illness. Initially I do not understand the connection and ask him to explain.

It's one of those dualities that you have in life. I'm sorry that [she] died, but I'm glad [she] died. So it's kind of the same thing.... When you're not doing what you want to do in life, when the company is not taking you where you want to go, when your boss is being an asshole, when the company has to do what they have to do to survive, yeah, it's horrible that you die, or you got laid off, or stuff like that, but you know what, it's part of it. It's just part of the natural professional cycle I guess.

This belief that layoffs are part of the "natural professional cycle" is one of career management's core principles. Yet layoffs, unlike death, are not inevitable. Like death, they can be sudden and tragic, or expected and welcome, but they are cultural, not natural, phenomena. Layoffs are not ahistorical, nor are they apolitical. The proliferation of white-collar layoffs over the last half century is the product of specific decisions being made in the corporate world, decisions about, among other things, how to make money, how to treat workers, and how to manage an increasingly global workforce. The framing of layoffs as natural is itself a historically situated phenomenon, grounded in a particular form of neoliberal ideology and popularized through concrete systems of cultural dissemination. When they employ it, job seekers do so at the expense of other ways of seeing and understanding the events of their own lives and of the broader world around them.

Despite Enrique's avowed relief at having left a job he did not enjoy, this most recent layoff has placed incredible strain on his marriage. When Enrique returned to full-time work in 2003, Anna quit her part-time jobs and started freelancing as an event planner. Her business has grown gradually and turned its first profit of $15–20,000 in 2008. Since Enrique's layoff four months ago, she has become the family's primary source of support; he contributes, he says, "what my measly workforce unemployment insurance will provide" and has once again resumed responsibility for the household and their two children, now eleven and eight.

I am really a proud Dad. I've got to tell you. I cook for everyone, I make sure that the house is clean for everyone. I take care of the cars, I take care of the finances. . . . I am a lot less stressed, Carrie, because Anna's got an income and now it's her turn to maintain us. And if she didn't have that income I'd be walking on the streets now, I'd be trying to do whatever needed to be done to pay the mortgage. Whereas right now because she's working I am taking care of the kids and I'm taking care of the house and I'm taking care of a lot of things, and I'm not dying. The only thing is where I tell my true friends, I don't mind doing it, but I do mind not being acknowledged for it. [*Laughs*] Now I sound like the wife. See how it sounds like the wife?

Although he declared in chapter 5, "It's not a marriage for convenience...where I'm going to provide and she's going to care for the kids," Enrique is clearly ambivalent about fully embracing the partnership ideal of marriage. He takes pride in the work he does around the house and the time he spends with his children, and, as he emphasizes, it is Anna's "turn" to financially support the family. Yet his joke that he is the "wife," both because he does the housework and because he feels unappreciated for it, reveals his discomfort about the reversal of traditional gender roles in his marriage. Positioning himself as the wife in their relationship suggests the extent to which Enrique feels emasculated by his domestic responsibilities and his inability to fill the breadwinner role. At the same time, his joke shores up his damaged masculinity by invoking gender stereotypes and naturalizing the systematic devaluation of women's labor. What is supposed to be funny here is that it is a man who is performing work that is not valued by others, who feels unappreciated. A woman's complaint that her work is unacknowledged would hardly be funny; it would, the joke suggests, be the norm.

Enrique's ambivalence about depending on Anna is also revealed in their struggles over household expenses. As Enrique sees it, he has done a much better job of adapting to their new division of responsibilities than has Anna.

> It's sometimes hard to have her give it [money] to us, because she's like, "Well that's *my* money." And I go, "Well, you know, I have maintained you for the last fifteen years with *my* money."

This quotation bristles with contradictions that reveal Enrique's deep ambivalence about being "maintained" by his wife. He challenges Anna's presumption that the money she earns belongs to her, rather than the family, but then immediately refers to his own previous earnings as "my money." His framing of the situation suggests that it is Anna who has the problem, who balks at using the money she is earning to cover family expenses. But what Enrique actually says is that it is "hard to have her give it to us," suggesting that it is equally difficult for him to be on the receiving end of this exchange.

This tension over their respective responsibilities and performance thereof, and over money—the family is living on less than one-fifth of Enrique's former salary—have brought their marriage to a breaking point. They have been seeing a marriage counselor for years, and although he still loves his wife, Enrique is concerned about their future together. If anything, he says, what has kept them together this long is financial necessity—neither of them can get by on their current incomes alone. When he describes why his marriage might end, he uses the same tone, and almost exactly the same phrase, as he did to describe his layoff: "I've tried, I've tried, I've tried. It's just gotten to the point, I've stopped trying. It's time, because if the shoe ain't the right size, it ain't gonna fit." Here again, Enrique depicts as natural an event—his potential divorce—that is the product of specific cultural and economic circumstances. His marriage is not failing simply for lack of "fit"; it is failing, at least in part, because of the emotional and financial strains that insecure employment and a volatile labor market have placed on the family. Together they have experienced the stresses of multiple layoffs, two prolonged job searches, Anna's juggling of several part-time jobs, Enrique's grueling travel schedule and discontent with his work, Anna's struggle to get a new business off the ground, and the challenges of raising two children and supporting a family on a fraction of what they once earned. In addition, they are trying to navigate their new division of labor within a culture that—despite dramatic improvements over previous decades—undervalues and feminizes the labor required to maintain a home and raise children, discriminates against working women, and renders suspect men who eschew paid employment. It is not that the shoe did not fit. It is that this family was beaten repeatedly over the head with it.

Enrique's efforts to frame his job loss and ailing marriage as the natural products of incompatibility are poignant, but they are hardly unique. They are the products of a belief system that privileges individual agency while obscuring the role of broader social, political, and cultural forces in shaping individual lives. Career management's sway has not waned among the job seekers I discuss above, and this is nowhere as evident as in the advice they offer to those who are looking for work in the beleaguered labor market of 2009. They suggest spending less (Alex), saving more (Enrique), marketing yourself through networking (Craig), finding security through entrepreneurship (Mike), never growing complacent in a job (Daniel and Mike), staying positive (Will, Enrique), and seeking out supportive communities (Will). When they do offer broader social critiques, they tend to direct them at abstract forces, such as greed, rather than particular institutions or individuals.

Just before I conducted my follow-up interviews in 2009, Barbara Ehrenreich published an editorial in the *Los Angeles Times* lambasting nearly every aspect of the ideology of career management (although she does not call it by that name). Reconfiguring job seeking as a new form of work, structuring unemployment to resemble a corporate job, and "polish[ing] the 'brand called you,'" Ehrenreich argues, simply distract unemployed U.S. workers from what she sees as the more important work of "lobbying for universal health insurance or reading Marxist tracts on the 'reserve army of the unemployed.'"[12] Ehrenreich is not alone in asking, and trying to explain, why U.S. workers are not taking to the streets en masse, or at least joining political and social organizations, to protest rising layoffs, declining salaries, disappearing benefits, and inadequate or nonexistent government support.[13]

Curious to hear a jobless person's response, I ask Enrique his opinion on why U.S. workers are not taking to the streets.

> Well, it's a free society. We live in a free country. You can ask your government to do something about it.... The government is a representation of the people. That, to me, that's government. If everybody wants the government to step in and do something then you need to ask that. But I, on the other hand, I know what I want, so I'm not going to be told what I *should* be doing.

Rejecting the antipolitical stance that Henry Giroux has argued characterizes U.S. culture, Enrique asserts the power of the people to effect change through their political representatives.[14] Even as he does so, however, he distinguishes between what "everybody" wants and what he, as an individual, wants, bristling at the suggestion that he is mistaken or misguided in not adopting the agenda or methods social critics have endorsed.

I ask Enrique what it is, exactly, that he does want. His voice rising in anger, he explains that he wants pay equity between the salaries of CEOs and middle managers.

> There's gotta be a balance in between how much a CFO [chief financial officer] or a CEO [chief executive officer] or a C-level person earns versus a

general midlevel manager, or a low-level manager. Go back to the time of your dad or mom, when an employee of a company is making $2 an hour, the CEO of the company is making $10, $15, $20 an hour. Today, that employee is making $5 or $7 an hour, and the [CEO] is making $100,000 an hour, well, maybe not an hour.... We need to tell the government that fair is fair. That's where the government needs to step in.

Enrique does believe the government has a role in ensuring that people are treated fairly, and he has his own vision of what that fairness would look like. In 2009, for instance, he supported the Obama administration's implementation of a 65 percent health care subsidy for the unemployed, without which he says he would have been paying $1,500 a month for his family's health insurance. Yet as the quotation above demonstrates, even in his critique of corporate greed and inequality, Enrique speaks from the position of a middle manager, a job he no longer occupies, and has little faith he will return to anytime soon.

When I ask other interviewees why they think unemployed U.S. workers are not "taking to the streets," their responses embody the logic of career management in emphasizing the need for individual, rather than collective, solutions to unemployment and in posing government intervention into the economy as ineffective, unnecessary, or detrimental. Will Ericsson, for one, believes the extent of the current crisis has been exaggerated by "government leadership," which "needed a crisis to demonstrate their importance and to get their particular programs instantiated, programs like nationalizing banks, nationalizing auto companies, nationalizing other industries." Will opposes the government "taking over businesses" under any circumstances. He argues that the best way to speed the recovery is for "the person on the street [to] not lose hope in the future." Losing hope, he says, leads to depression, which in turn leads people to become chronically unemployed. Instead, he plans to "not get all wrapped up in what the news reports are, but try to just look at my own situation and do what I can to stay afloat." Casting chronic unemployment as a product of depression, Will positions the problem as an emotional rather than structural one, and goes so far as to consciously don mental blinders to avoid news that might suggest otherwise.

Will's belief that the state of the recession is being exaggerated for political ends is not shared by other job seekers, but his sense that the solution to the crisis lies with individual Americans is. Craig Murray attributes the lack of public protest to the United States' low unemployment rate relative to many other countries and the character of its citizenry.

> I guess I'd like to think that Americans at their core would be fairly optimistic. Certainly people who feel like in the long run they have greater control over what happens to them than feeling somebody else is responsible for their preservation or their success. I'd like to think those things. Maybe that kind of answer reveals more about me than is actually reflective of the American public in general.

Craig's comments juxtapose optimism and self-determination against political activism. People do not protest, he suggests, when they are optimistic and willing to take responsibility for themselves. Political activism, like corporate employment, is thereby framed as evidence of a dependent mindset, a public admission that you cannot, or will not, fend for yourself.

Keith Hartmann, whose current professional and financial situation is relatively secure, if far from ideal, shares Will's opposition to government intervention in economic affairs—he sees most government programs as ineffective and too expensive. He believes most Americans share his view, but currently lack the knowledge or motivation to do anything about it.

> Most Americans don't know how to effect change. They're up against this thing, and they really don't know how to identify what this thing is.... How does the individual force change? I think that Americans don't know how to do that. I certainly don't. I think that probably things are going to have to get worse before people just kind of say, no more, I'm not paying taxes, I'm not going to support this. If you push Americans against the wall, I think they'll start fighting back, but it's almost like when you put something in the water and start heating the water to the point where the animal doesn't realize it's being cooked. I think that must be what's happening. I think people are asleep here. I don't think people realize how bad it could get and I think that many people will have to be really in pain. I mean, in pain, out of work, in bad health, and fed up with having to support the government and all these lavish programs that at the end of the day are not going to help the economy, that's just my opinion. I think people are going to have to just get fed up before they start fighting back. I don't think we're there yet.

I ask Keith whether he, for one, is "there yet." "I'm fed up," he says, "but I don't know what to do to change it." Keith's metaphor of the animal slowly boiling in a pot is a powerful articulation of a particular model of how change occurs. The cultural logic he invokes, which is only one of many ways of thinking about change, is that when people are in pain, enough pain and for a long enough time, they will eventually fight back. According to this teleological model, departure from the pot is inevitable; the only variant shaping the animal's behavior is the extent of its suffering.

An alternative model, one that is better suited to explaining jobless Americans' relative political inaction, is that social change occurs only through a change in values, in ways of looking at the world and how it works. No matter how hot it gets in that pot, without a significant ideological shift, the animal, in this case, displaced workers, will continue to sit tight. Keith and other "companies of one" have trouble envisioning any solution other than individual responses to layoffs, job insecurity, and a labor market that devalues their skills and experience because they adhere to a cultural logic that renders such alternatives invisible, or at least unviable.

To explore this argument more fully, I offer a final update.

In chapter 5, Ed Donnelly, who is now sixty-two, joked that he once thought information technology would be a "cradle to grave" career, and he wanted back in the cradle. When I contacted him for a follow-up interview, I was curious to find out whether he had achieved that goal. When we spoke in 2004, Ed was making $10 an hour at an electronics store and relying on his wife's higher income while he looked for a new job in high tech. He stayed at the electronics store for four years, far longer than he expected. Although glad to have a job, he eventually grew frustrated with the irregular hours, rigid scheduling, and impatient customers. When his request to transfer to a store closer to home was denied, Ed quit and returned to his previous postlayoff job as a salesperson at a small gardening supply store. His hourly wage dropped from $10 to $8 (he has since received a raise to $9). It was, he says, "the most cheerful pay cut I ever took in my life. In return for that $2 pay cut, I got reasonable hours, I got a boss I could work with and be happy." What was initially a part-time job to make ends meet is now the job from which Ed hopes to ultimately retire in seven or eight years.

Despite the relative attractiveness of his new job, Ed is "hanging on teeth and toenails, paying expenses and trying not to dig into my savings to do that." While Ed's decline in income may be extreme, it follows a general pattern in which older workers experience a steep wage drop following a layoff. After the recession of the early 1990s, workers between the ages of fifty-five and sixty-four experienced an average wage loss of 27 percent, compared to just 7 percent for workers between the ages of twenty-five and thirty-four. Following the 2001 recession, rehired workers age forty-five to fifty-four lost 23 percent of their former wages, while younger workers lost just 6 percent.[15] As Ed commented in a previous interview, he believes age discrimination is especially common in the field of high tech, where maturity tends to be associated with obsolescence.[16]

Compounding this radical reduction in pay, Ed no longer has the option of relying on a spouse's income; he and his wife, Sarah, separated last year and plan to divorce. Although other factors contributed to their breakup, Ed's employment status played a central role. "Because I'm not employed as well as I was, and she is once again well employed," he says, "I don't feel like I'm contributing as much as I could be to the marriage. She said that she didn't worry about that, but her attitude seemed to say otherwise." More significant than how Sarah saw him, Ed admits, was the toll his failed IT job search took on how he sees himself. He is less self-confident than he once was, and, like the displaced managers of the 1980s, plagued by the question, "What's wrong with me that I can't hold down a good job like I used to? I still feel the same inside, but nobody else agrees that I'm worth it." If he had been more confident and less depressed, Ed believes, perhaps he could have contributed to the marriage as an emotional, if not financial, partner. As it is, he feels he has little left to give.

Although it has taken him a long time to get to this point, Ed has come to believe that, while it is still his "dream job," he will never work in software programming again. He is, he says, "stuck": "There are any number of things I could have done, but hindsight is 20/20. And once I was in this situation there was no way to get out of it, so I've just had to accept it." When I ask how he feels about that, Ed says that he is "resigned" and "a little angry." I ask at whom he is angry.

Myself, the IT world, the world in general, you know. Something goes wrong, you get angry. You don't have to have a rational reason for it. It bothers me that I didn't see it coming and take steps to avoid it. I'm irrationally angry that other people, having used me in the past, now refuse to find a use for me and have discarded me without what I, emotionally, at least, feel like is full return for the work I did.

What Ed describes as a conflict between rationality and emotion reflects the struggle between two different ways of explaining downward mobility: as the result of individual failure, or as a consequence of corporations' abandonment and exploitation of U.S. workers. The first, the one Ed privileges as "rational," resembles a modified version of the meritocratic individualism espoused by a previous generation of white-collar managers.

Although the two overlap, there are noteworthy differences between the philosophy of career management and that of managerial culture's meritocratic individualism. To see oneself as a company of one normalizes job loss, job change, and periodic unemployment, whereas previous models of professional success and upward mobility pathologized them. Career management also vilifies steady employment as evidence of a feminized, dependent mindset, reframing a volatile employment record as evidence of flexibility and masculinity rather than personal failure. Twenty-first-century job seekers are also less likely to see themselves as—and, in fact, to be—sole providers than were managers in the 1980s, a shift made possible by the preponderance of dual-income couples in the U.S. white-collar workforce today. This simultaneous eschewing of both dependence and dependents marks an important and significant shift from the mindset that prevailed among white-collar professional men just a few decades ago.

Despite these differences, meritocratic individualism and career management share an important central tenet: individual responsibility. What the individual is responsible for, however, may vary between generations; white-collar workers from different eras define the *merit* part of meritocratic individualism quite differently (modern-day career managers, for instance, pride themselves on strategically changing jobs, whereas earlier managers focused on keeping them). But at the bottom end of the scale of downward mobility, the end results—depression, discouragement, and self-blame—look about the same, as Ed's experiences attest.

Within this individualist framework that holds each worker entirely responsible for his or her own professional fate, Ed has only himself to blame for not having anticipated what skills would be in demand at a given time and retrained accordingly (on his own dime). In characteristic career manager fashion, he dismisses those who think otherwise as underskilled and overentitled: "Too many people feel like they have a right to a job regardless of what they know how to do. That, to me, is ludicrous. If you can't do something that pays your wages, then you don't deserve the wages." In contrast, Ed avows not once, but three times, that his situation is entirely his own fault.

> Intellectually, I know that I got paid well for what I was doing and it's my own fault that I didn't leave myself an out. The fact that my job skills are out of date is unfortunate from my perspective, but I consider it my own fault that I didn't see it coming and stay current so that I could jump to another job where I would have the current knowledge to keep working. That's my fault, not anybody else's.

Although his job loss, downward mobility, and the sorry state of his marriage and finances may be unfortunate, Ed takes some comfort, and not a little masculine pride, in the belief that they are the result of his choices and no one else's.[17]

Yet there is another way to frame Ed's experiences over the last decade, one Ed dismisses as irrational, but that clearly exerts a powerful pull on him. In this alternative narrative, Ed's expulsion from the high-tech workforce is not just unfortunate, it is infuriating and unjust. He has been "discarded," his skills, experience, and hard work—and, by association, Ed himself—dismissed as worthless by a labor market that, having used him in the past, refuses to find a use for him now. Again and again as we talk, particularly during moments of anger or frustration, this alternative explanation surfaces in Ed's comments, and repeatedly he pushes it away, dismissing it as emotional, irrational, something he feels but cannot justify according to his individualist, free-market worldview. He might not like to admit it, but there is a part of Ed that does believe he has a right to employment, a part that resents not having received "full return" for the work he did and, given the opportunity, would do again.

Ed's internal struggle over how to explain his predicament and where to place the blame for it reveals what is at stake in seeing oneself as a company of one. This ideology has its rewards. In some respects, career management is a life raft to which displaced tech workers can cling amid the roiling sea of insecure employment and prolonged joblessness. Seeing oneself as an independent company of one (rather than a discarded employee) can bolster the optimism and self-esteem of job seekers while providing them with tangible strategies for finding reemployment. Casting secure employment as a situation of foolish, emasculated dependency provides some protection against the emotional upheaval of an unexpected layoff or prolonged job search. Conceptualizing job seeking as just another kind of job allows tech workers to retain a resilient sense of self-worth and professional value in the prolonged absence of paid employment.

On a pragmatic level, the specific strategies career management recommends—to network and keep abreast of industry trends—make a good deal of sense in today's labor market. The skills and sorts of knowledge that are most in demand on the labor market change rapidly—particularly in high-tech fields—and although retraining is no panacea, it is preferable to obsolescence. Innumerable research studies confirm that most white-collar jobs are obtained through networking of one sort or another. In addition to functioning as a job search method, participation in organized networking events provides job seekers with camaraderie, community, and daily structure. These meetings also allow the unemployed to reaffirm their professional identities through ritualized self-presentation, the public demonstration of professional and job search expertise, and other activities that mimic corporate life. Finally, the experiences of some tech workers over the previous decade—Alex Brodsky, Craig Murray, Mike Barnard, and Will Ericsson, for instance—confirm that even in an ailing economy, individual agency and flexibility, particularly when paired with a spouse's income, can purchase for some workers, at least temporarily, the sort of security and prosperity that corporate loyalty and longevity no longer can.

But although career management can be conceptualized as a buoying life raft to which job seekers cling in a stormy sea, it can just as reasonably be imagined as a stick with which they are beaten, and with which they beat themselves, as they try to stay afloat. To see it one way without also seeing the other is to sacrifice a fuller view of these job seekers and the cultural logic they inhabit. Over the previous five years, the small group of tech workers I reinterviewed have experienced four layoffs and more than a dozen job changes, not including short contract positions, between them. They have lost tens of thousands of dollars in annual income (although some have reversed those losses) and depleted savings accounts intended for college tuitions and retirement expenses. Some who wished to remain full-time parents have gone back to work out of financial necessity. Others have suffered from anxiety, depression, and panic attacks. Three marriages have ended in, or are headed for, divorce. Not only has adherence to the principles of career management not prevented these misfortunes, it has in some cases prompted them.

Despite these tangible and often painful losses, the ultimate cost of career management lies in its naturalization of these losses. When Enrique sees job loss as "just part of the natural professional cycle I guess" and Ed laments, "once I was in this situation, there was no way to get out of it, so I've just had to accept it," they frame as natural and inevitable situations that are neither. The dismantling of the social contract of employment, mass layoffs, global offshoring, the expansion of part-time and contract work, and the disappearance of employer-provided benefits are all the result of specific corporate decisions and government policies. It is their acquiescence to this naturalizing of decidedly politically and historically situated events that undergirds tech workers' "fundamental inability to resist—and tacit collusion with— the forces that threaten to destroy [them]."[18] This acquiescence, which takes multiple forms, is itself built into the logic of career management.

These job seekers accept layoffs because they believe job change is healthy and manly, and because, as companies of one, they take pride in identifying with corporations' relentless privileging of the bottom line. They relieve employers of the responsibility to provide retraining or to avoid sending jobs overseas because to do so would suggest that they, like those dependent foils against whom they define themselves, are unable to fend for themselves in a competitive labor market. By denying the agency of any entity larger than the individual, career management obscures the fact that individual workers and corporations are not entering into employment contracts on a level playing field; they do not have access to equal resources, and the law vastly favors corporations over individual workers. These job seekers oppose most forms of political activism, particularly labors unions, because they believe, in the words of Ed Donnelly, "I can do better for myself negotiating with an employer than I can with group negotiations."[19] (How well Ed's solo negotiations have served him is debatable.) By conceptualizing themselves as companies, rather than employees, and doggedly favoring individual agency over collective action, these workers liberate their employers from the employment contract generations of labor activists worked diligently to erect and maintain.

Most of the burdens corporations are no longer expected to bear have been transferred onto individual workers and their families, who accept them because they can imagine no alternative. They then draw on broader cultural narratives of partnership, family togetherness, and frugality to re-frame those sacrifices as moral achievements. The twin themes of divorce and depression that run through job seekers' accounts demonstrate the extent to which families bear the emotional, as well as financial, burdens of managing insecure employment and extended joblessness. The narrative of the optimistic job seeker, however, constantly and confidently engaged in the hard work of looking for work, allows no space to acknowledge, in any but the most fleeting of ways, the feelings of self-doubt, helplessness, and resentment that plague even the most committed career managers. And yet those feelings peek through again and again in the spaces between job seekers' attestations of their optimism and agency. Enrique "felt like a piece of furniture" upon his layoff and was "scared to the bones" at the thought of facing another. Natalie and Erica cried in coffee shops because they worried their loved ones would think less of them for not finding new jobs. Daniel was plagued by phantom itch attacks. Will was anxious despite having been employed full-time for more than six years. Alex struggled to remain patient with customers who "desperately need the shit choked out of them." Keith still cannot shake the memory of that sparse, sad Christmas when he could not afford to buy his children presents. And while Ed "still feel[s] the same inside," he finds it increasingly difficult to convince himself "that there's nothing wrong with me, it's the outside world that's changed."

These wrenching moments, repeated endlessly across a workforce of tens of millions, represent the true costs of a system of increasingly insecure white-collar employment. Even as they and their families stagger under the heavy burden of those costs, job seekers continue to conceptualize the situation as inevitable, looking for ways to manage it, rather than change it. Even in those rare moments when anger wins out over resignation, few high-tech workers can identify exactly what event or institution to hold accountable. The at-times comforting notion of having made one's own choices—to accept a pay cut, change careers, downsize one's lifestyle, engage in constant networking, accept the risks of entrepreneurship—masks the extent to which these workers, indeed all workers, are ultimately subject to forces outside their control. Their adherence to the principles of career management renders other ways of explaining and reacting to the situation invisible. Indoctrination into the culture of job seeking exacerbates this absence by rewarding a can-do attitude while silencing doubt and discouraging political activism or debate. The unemployed thus find themselves, as Keith says, "up against this thing, and they really don't know how to identify what this thing is."

It is an unhappy accident that I am completing this project during yet another period of economic crisis characterized by rampant layoffs and high unemployment. As I write this epilogue, we are allegedly witnessing the downfall of neoliberal ideology and modes of governing and a resurgence of interventionist economic and social programs. It is possible that career management, with its decidedly neoliberal leanings, might also be in its final throes. Yet the experiences of these tech workers suggest otherwise, as does other evidence that attests to career management's continuing sway in U.S. popular culture. Ehrenreich's editorial, for instance, identifies source after source—self-help gurus, career coaches, individual job seekers—who urge the unemployed to approach job seeking as a job. Simultaneously, networking groups continue to issue support and admonition in equal measure to unemployed attendees in re-created corporate environments across the country.[20] The 2008 book *No Job? No Prob!* assures readers, if "you regard your joblessness as a mere life pothole—albeit one that may shake, rattle and roll you for a moment or two—you'll find yourself in the enviable position of total control of your situation."[21] And while job fair organizers might admit to a journalist that there are few jobs to be had, an optimistic job seeker waiting in the long line outside reports, "Nothing gets me down.... Everything is an emotion; you discipline yourself to be happy."[22] If there is a sea change underway, it is a very gradual one.

Yet history offers ample evidence that neither this way of organizing work and workers nor this way of looking at redundancies is engraved in stone. They are the product of specific historical, political, and cultural trajectories and, as such, are open to change. Career management itself is not a static ideology—what ideology is?—nor does it entirely preclude political awareness. It is instead part of a much longer intellectual history of American ideas about hard work, individualism, and upward mobility. To zero in on just one segment of that history, career management is a reworked version of the tenets of the managerial culture Katherine Newman documented so thoroughly in the 1980s, which was itself an ideological descendent of the organization man mindset of the postwar era. These ideologies share an overarching faith in the power of individual agency to determine one's professional fate, but they differ significantly in their conceptualization of what security should look like, who is obligated to provide it, and how to go about obtaining it. The differences between them—forged in response to specific structural and cultural changes around work, family, and the meanings of dependence and self-reliance—serve as evidence that, although resilient, these ideologies are not immutable.

The current downturn, and the decades to follow, will undoubtedly result in structural changes that will shape the lives of new generations of white-collar workers in novel and significant ways. Just as certainly, those decades will witness cultural shifts that will exert their own influence on those workers' jobs, families, and identities. These changes are bound to alter the cultural landscape within which individual Americans and their families go about making sense of the world and their place in it.

For now, however, the experiences of these high-tech workers, although not representative of all U.S. workers, testify to broader truths about U.S. culture: that ideology of any sort is relentlessly resilient, even in the face of material hardship; that people will agree to shoulder extensive financial and psychological burdens to maintain a sense of themselves as self-reliant, valuable members of a professional community; and that paid employment, however insecure and elusive it might be, remains central to Americans' sense of who we are and what, at core, we are worth.

NOTES

Preface

1. Bureau of Labor Statistics (2009); Dean Baker, quoted in Mishel and Shierholz (2009).

2. Goodman and Healy (2009).

3. See, e.g., Barley and Kunda (2004); Benner (2002); Darrah (1994 and 2000); English-Lueck (2002); English-Lueck and Saveri (2000); and Saxenian (1996).

4. Dallas has been curiously overlooked by humanities and social science scholars in general, unless one counts cultural studies texts on the *Dallas* of J. R. Ewing fame. Anthropologist Robert V. Kemper has called Dallas "perhaps the most under-studied major city in the country" (Ragland 2002), in part because research on Texas has tended to focus on the border communities over 300 miles to the city's south (e.g., Foley 1990; Hagan 1994; Limón 1991; Madsen 1964). Historical studies of the city are equally rare. When I asked a prominent historian of Texas about research on Dallas, he could think of only two significant books to suggest, one published in 1940, the other in 1982, although Michael Phillips's 2006 *White Metropolis: Race, Ethnicity, and Religion in Dallas, 1841–2001* marks an important recent addition to the list.

5. Cf. Clifford and Marcus (1989), Sanjek (1990), and Van Maanen (1988).

6. See Lane (2010) for further exploration of this subject and its implications for ethnographic research.

Introduction

1. "Alex Brodsky" is a pseudonym, as are the names of all job seekers mentioned herein. I do not use composites; each person I describe is an actual interviewee. I have, however, changed descriptive information and story details to protect the anonymity of individual study participants.

For the same reason, I also employ pseudonyms for the networking groups and companies described herein.

2. Greenspan (2008: 2, 3).

3. Harvey (2005). E.g., Giroux (2008); Hackworth (2006); Klein (2007); Mensah (2008); Ong (2006); Rose (1990, 1999).

4. Harvey (2005: 3).

5. Collins, di Leonardo, and Williams, eds. (2008).

6. Boyd (2008); Pérez (2008).

7. Xiang (2007). See also Kipnis (2008) for an ethnographic examination of how cultures and processes analyzed by anthropologists as examples of neoliberalism can be interpreted in decidedly different ways within specific cultural milieus, in this case among Chinese teachers and Chinese immigrants workers in the United States.

8. I use the terms "interviewee" and "study participant" where others might say "informant." Substituting one term for another does not dissipate the fraught power relations of ethnographic research or erase the ethical concerns of researching and representing human subjects. My choice of terms is simply intended for purposes of clarity and accessibility to readers outside the field of anthropology.

9. Of the seventy-five interviewees approximately 30 percent were women; over 80 percent were white; nearly 11 percent were Japanese American, Chinese American, Indian American, or Pakistani American; 4 percent were Hispanic; and 3 percent were African American. The racial diversity reflected in those numbers allowed me to conclude that my findings were not limited to white tech workers, but the small numbers of nonwhite study participants made a more extensive race-based analysis difficult at best. Future research in this area would prove fruitful, particularly a study that took as its subject the handful of Dallas professional groups geared specifically to Indian American tech workers.

10. See Durkheim (1965).

11. Dudley (1994, 2000); Newman (1988, 1993).

12. See Spindler and Spindler (1983) for a detailed overview of anthropological research on the United States; Overbey and Dudley (2000) for an updated synopsis of qualitative anthropology and sociology of the U.S. middle classes; and Baba (1986, 1998), Burawoy (1979b), Forsythe (1999), and Nash (1998) for histories of the anthropology of work.

13. Ehrenreich (2005).

14. Sennett (1998).

15. Geertz (1973: 14).

16. William H. Whyte (1956) characterized the postwar organization man as a conformist who willingly subordinated his own goals and personality in return for secure employment and "belongingness." *Who Moved My Cheese?* (Johnson 1998), published forty-two years later, encourages its own version of conformity. The brief book, which spent over five years on the *New York Times* business bestseller list, is a parable of four mice forced to rethink their attitude to change and entitlement when their cheese supply disappears. It advocates that workers embrace the opportunities that insecurity brings and has achieved the status of cultural shorthand among many U.S. white-collar workers. Several job seekers mentioned it in their interviews (usually mocking the book's hokeyness but accepting its message); Thomas Frank lampoons its "breathtaking[ly] obscen[e] call for childlike innocence before the gods of the market and…scheme for gulling, silencing, and firing workers who are critical of management" (2000: 248–249).

1. Silicon Prairie

1. Primeau (1985).

2. "The Crystal Palace Story," brochure by Infomart (2001).

3. Dillon (1985); Goldstein (1995); "The Crystal Palace Story" (2001).

4. Petre (1985).

5. Mitchell (1985a).

6. In Sumner (1985: 2C) and Bailey (1985: 33A), respectively.

7. Maxwell (2010a); McElhaney and Hazel (2010); Read and Youtie (1994).

8. Dallas is distinct from other high-tech regions in that its tech growth centered not around a major research university—such as Stanford University in the Silicon Valley, MIT along Route 128, Duke University in the Research Triangle, and the University of Texas in Austin—but around corporations themselves (Saxenian 1996).

9. Wysocki (1989); Kelly (1992).

10. Riche, Hecker, and Burgan (1983); Slater (1985).

11. On the causes and implications of this downturn, see Saxenian (1996: 83–104).

12. E.g., Hurlock (1986); Mitchell (1985a, 1985b, 1987); Petre (1985).

13. Shelp and Hart (1986: 1).

14. Petersen and Thomas (1995).

15. Bajaj (2000).

16. See, e.g., Abbate (1999); Cassidy (2002); Hauben and Hauben (1997); Lewis (2001); Mahar (2003); Randall (1997); Segaller (1998).

17. Atkinson and Gottlieb (2001: 1).

18. Cassidy (2002: 166–181). See Shiller (2000) on the cultural and psychological roots of the investing epidemic around Internet stocks.

19. Hoffman (1998).

20. Habal (2000).

21. Habal (2000: 74).

22. Carson (2001); Maxwell (2010b). See also Govenar and Brakefield (1998).

23. Gladwell (2000). On the idiosyncratic management styles and corporate cultures of Internet companies and their high-tech predecessors, see Marshall (2001), Ross (2003), and Saxenian (1996: 50–57).

24. With the growth of the Internet, the presence of the DFW airport once again bolstered Dallas's technology growth. 70 percent of e-commerce sales depend on express delivery, making Dallas's central location a major attraction to Internet-based companies (Kotkin 2000).

25. Lowenstein (2004: 159).

26. Oppel (2001).

27. See Lowenstein (2004: 127–226) for a more detailed account of the telecom bubble.

28. Lowenstein (2004: 149–150).

29. Telecom executives saw the issue differently, bragging that "we are using, at most, one-fiftieth of our domestic backbone capacity" and optimistically proclaiming that "no matter how much bandwidth is available, it will get used" (Lowenstein 2004: 150, 152).

30. Cassidy (2002: 314).

31. Conlin (2001); Stevens (2001); Warner (2001).

32. Cassidy (2002: 301).

33. Gale and Palfini (2001: 72); Howe (2002); "University Study Shows Area Has Lost 30 Percent of Tech Jobs" (2004); Bureau of Labor Statistics (2010a).

34. Texas led the nation in tech job losses in 2001 and ranked second behind California for the next three years. Texas's high-tech employment began to expand again in 2005, a trend that continued until 2008, when the state began to shed high-tech jobs once again (TechAmerica 2009).

35. Statistics in this paragraph are drawn from Bajaj and Harrison (2001); Godinez (2002); Oppel (2001); "Santa Clara, Dallas Counties Lead Nation in Employment Decline" (2003); and "University Study" (2004). Comparison of statistics from these sources is difficult because some tally numbers of job lost, while others tally net job losses, taking into consideration new jobs

created over the same time period. As well, sources vary in their definition of what constitutes the Dallas area, although the region is usually considered to include Collin, Dallas, Delta, Denton, Ellis, Hunt, Kaufman, and Rockwall counties.

36. Schwartz (2003).

37. Economic Policy Institute (2004).

38. McGill (2002).

39. Bajaj and Harrison (2001); Housewright and Farwell (2003).

40. Even with the timely shift from housing offices to housing data, Infomart occupancy faltered in the mid-2000s; the group of investors who acquired the building through foreclosure in 2007 returned to the tenancy (rather than data storage) model of occupancy (Brown 2007).

2. A Company of One

1. High-tech workers interviewed during the more prosperous late-1990s by English-Lueck (2002), Marschall (2001), and Ross (2003) also dismissed the idea of corporate loyalty and expressed willingness to change jobs whenever something more interesting or higher paid came along.

2. Sennett (1998).

3. Enrique's framing of the employment relationship as akin to a marriage is revisited in the epilogue where he draws similar parallels between his last layoff and his recent marital struggles.

4. Dudley (1994); Doukas (2003); Nash (1989); Moore (1990). See also Uchitelle (2006) on the rise and implications of increasingly insecure employment in the United States.

5. Schwartz (2003).

6. Although the recession that began in 2007 officially ended in June 2009, more than a year later the economy's growth remained slow and unemployment remained high.

7. Mishel, Bernstein, and Boushey (2003); Stettner and Wenger (2003); Shierholz and Mishel (2009).

8. See Benner (2002) and Barley and Kunda (2004) for comprehensive studies of flexible work and employment relationships in Silicon Valley's high-tech industry. On the rise and implications of flexible work arrangements, see also Atkinson and Meager (1986a, 1986b); Bradley et al. (2000: 51–70); Gordon (1996); Harvey (1990); Pink (2001); Piore and Sabel (1984); Standing (2002).

9. Dudley (1994: 177).

10. Newman (1988: 42–94). This is by no means a new development in U.S. history; Bakke's famous Depression-era studies (1934, 1940) argued that blaming one's self for one's circumstances was the last refuge of self-respect among the unemployed.

11. Joint Venture: Silicon Valley Network (1999: 10); Bureau of Labor Statistics (2002); "The Future of Work" (2000: 90).

12. See Sennett for a fuller discussion of how "risk has become a daily necessity shouldered by the masses" (1998: 80).

13. A 1996 poll found that 66 percent of people who had never been laid off believe that companies are less loyal to their employees than they were ten years ago, and 55 percent say workers are less loyal to their employers than ten years ago (*New York Times* 1996: 294).

14. For historical and statistical analysis of the demise of corporate loyalty and the decline of the lifetime employment model, see Benner (2002: 20); Boyett and Conn (1992); Cappelli (1999); Heckscher (1995); Moore (1996); *New York Times* (1996); Osterman (1996, 1999).

15. The book Mike describes is *The Media Lab: Inventing the Future at M.I.T.,* by Stewart Brand (1988).

16. The figures for job seekers in this study are slightly higher than those found in another study of laid-off high-tech workers in North Dallas, which found that 46.6 percent of respondents had been laid off more than once (Virick 2003). This discrepancy might be attributed to my informant recruitment methods. Individuals who have been laid off in the past tend to champion the

importance of networking, which leads them to the kind of events where I recruited many of my participants. Job seekers with previous layoff experience are also perhaps more likely to feel comfortable speaking about job loss and unemployment than those experiencing it for the first time.

17. Dixon and Van Horn (2003).

18. Virick (2004).

19. Ross (2003: 218).

20. Generations X and Y's penchants for frequent job change and distrust of long-term employment are well documented (see, e.g., Connelly 2003; Feldman 2000; Tulgan 2003: 6–7). Yet while nearly half (48%) of workers aged eighteen to twenty-nine believe they or a family member will be laid off in the next three to five years, this figure is not much higher than that for workers aged thirty to forty-nine (41%), and even slightly less than the rate for workers of all ages who were laid off in the previous three years (50%) (Dixon and Van Horn 2003: 10).

21. Mike is quoting from Shoshana Zuboff's *In the Age of the Smart Machine* (1988), a book he recommended to me, in which Zuboff argues that the increased use of computers requires a rethinking of traditional management roles.

22. Throughout this book I use the term *career manager* in reference not only to job seekers in this study, all of whom advanced aspects of this ideology at some point in our discussions, but also to other workers and management experts who espouse this perspective on employment.

23. In this sense, the tenets of career management resemble the perspectives and strategies of the independent contractors Barley and Kunda (2004) interviewed in Silicon Valley in the late 1990s. There are three main differences between Barley and Kunda's informants and my own: First, most contractors in Barley and Kunda's study made a conscious decision to pursue contract rather than permanent positions, whereas many of my informants accepted contract jobs but did not necessarily prefer them to longer-term positions. Second, as Barley and Kunda note in their epilogue, the booming economy and low unemployment of the late 1990s, especially in high tech, made for a seller's market in high-tech expertise, whereas job seekers in the early 2000s faced a decidedly bleaker labor market. Finally, and perhaps most important, the workers in my study advocated looking at all work as contract and temporary, at least in theory, whereas Barley and Kunda's informants still drew a distinction, albeit a sometimes blurry one, between contract and permanent positions.

24. Barley and Kunda (2004: 264–284) document how independent contractors go about building, maintaining, and utilizing their professional networks and demonstrate how crucial this form of social capital is to securing employment, particularly on short notice, in the high-tech industry.

25. Cappelli (1999: 32).

26. Wallulis (1998: 8).

27. Goffman (1961: 127–169).

28. Dudley (2000: 8).

29. Barley (1989: 56). Kathryn Dudley brought this parallel to my attention and suggested the connection between tech workers' industry and their worldview.

30. Marschall (2001: 121–122).

31. Recent ethnographic research among downsized blue-collar U.S. workers suggests the view of independent contract work as a source of autonomy and security is not limited to white-collar workers. In Broughton and Walton (2006), a laid-off Maytag assembly worker looks forward to completing computer classes because, "That is gonna give me somewhat of an independence because I don't have to rely on nobody for a job. I'm kind of going to be my own consultant. I'm gonna be working in the computer field and I'm gonna be my own supervisor" (9).

32. Spherion Emerging Workforce Study (2003).

33. Kunda and Van Maanen (1999: 74).

34. Davis (2000).

35. Hall (1976).

36. Kunda and Van Maanen (1999: 73).

37. Anthropologists Bishop and Foley were prescient in arguing, in 1992, that as declarations like these reshape the "initial understanding between employer and employees, job security should gradually retreat as a workplace issue" (1992: 14).

38. Hall and Mirvis (1995: 326).

39. Ross (2003: 17).

40. See Ehrenreich (2009) and Kipnis (2008).

41. See Barley and Kunda (2004: 22) and Pink (2001).

42. Giroux (2001: 2). Thomas Frank makes a similar argument but blames this erasure of the economic as a legitimate subject of social criticism on the rise of political conservatism in the United States (2004: 128–129, 242).

43. Some anthropologists and other social scientists have studied the people and cultures on the other side of the offshoring relationship, e.g., Balakrishnan (2001); Freeman (2000); Krishnamurthy (2004); Sonntag (2004); Xiang (2007).

44. Sirohi (2004). See Chet (2005) for an extended discussion of job seekers' attitudes to offshoring and globalization.

45. Thanks to Jean-Christophe Agnew for bringing this point to my attention.

46. Reich (1991: 177).

47. Hannerz (1996: 84).

48. See Dudley (1994: 73–83; 2000: 85–102).

49. Talent (2007).

50. Osterman (1999) outlines various forms government and community support for a mobile workforce might take.

51. Harrington (2001: 2).

52. Kunda and Van Maanen (1999: 75).

3. The Hardest Job You'll Ever Have

1. Barley and Kunda (2004) outlines the advantages and disadvantages of independent contracting in the high-tech industry.

2. See Ezzy (2001) for an excellent overview and critique of psychological studies of the unemployed.

3. Newman (1988: 93); Turner (1969).

4. On the cultural need to define and maintain such boundaries, see Mary Douglas's classic *Purity and Danger* (1966).

5. Keith is referring here to organized networking events for job seekers, which are the subject of chapter 4.

6. Kübler-Ross (1969).

7. Bureau of Labor Statistics (2004).

8. Field (2002); Stettner and Wenger (2003).

9. Challenger, Gray & Christmas (2009). Like most calculations of unemployment, these figures exclude "discouraged workers," those who remain unemployed but have stopped actively looking for work. In June 2010, for example, the official U.S. tally of 14.6 million unemployed did not include more than 1.2 million out-of-work individuals classified as "discouraged" (Bureau of Labor Statistics 2010b).

10. Blanton (2003).

11. Virick (2004).

12. See Briar (1978) on the effects of long-term employment.

13. Newman (1988: 18).

14. Cappelli (2001: 139–146); Marschall (2001: 121–124).

15. Pew Internet Project (2002).

16. Noguchi (2009).

17. Bolles (2003); Ligos (2003: 1). In their high popularity and low efficacy, online job boards mirror the low-tech help-wanted ads that preceded them (Mangum 1982: 36).

18. See, e.g., Burawoy (1979a); Dudley (1994: 118–126); Harris (1987); Lamphere (1979).

19. Goffman (1959: 164–165).

20. Although such resume-writing services do exist—and are sharply critiqued in Barbara Ehrenreich's (2005) investigation of white-collar job seeking—neither Enrique nor any other job seeker I met used such services. Instead, they turned to friends, fellow job seekers, and the free resume-review services (also usually run by job seekers) offered at many networking events and job fairs.

21. See Urciuoli (2008) on the history of this discursive model of the "worker-self-as-skills-bundle" in the United States and its dissemination through websites marketing skills-related products and services.

22. Dunn (2004) employs the related term "entrepreneurs of themselves" (22) to describe the self-image U.S. managers attempted to foist on factory workers in post-socialist Poland.

23. Marschall (2001: 1–5)

24. Similar arguments are made in Ehrenreich (2005: 234) and Sennett (1998).

4. Rituals of Unemployment

1. Newman (1988: 52, 56–60); Torres (1996).

2. Milgram (1974).

3. Milgram (1967). See Watts (2003: 37–39, 130–134) for an excellent overview of Milgram's work on networks and the flaws belatedly discovered therein.

4. Granovetter (1973; 1995 [1974]).

5. Azrin and Besalel (1980: 107–111); Bolles (2003); Carbasho (2002); Feldman and Klaas (2002: 182); Fernandez, Castilla, and Moore (2000); Granovetter (1995); Harrington (2002: 160); Mangum (1982: 51, 70).

6. Fitzgerald (2003).

7. Breen (1997: 8); Licht (1988: 23).

8. Kaufman (1982: 169).

9. Forty Plus of New York (2010). Newman (1988: 42–94) and Ehrenreich (2005: 41–51) offer rich descriptions of Forty Plus events. Although Forty Plus was the first event of its kind, those interested in a history of job clubs should not overlook the work of Nathan Azrin. In 1970, Azrin, a behavioral psychologist, apparently unaware of Forty Plus and its methods, pioneered and popularized the "Job Club Method" for finding work. While teaching vocational skills to emotionally disturbed patients in Illinois's Mental Health Department, Azrin noticed that after completing training the patients were still unable to find jobs. After conducting extensive research on how people find jobs (his conclusions presaged Granovetter's, though the latter is the more famous of the two), Azrin applied behavioral psychology to the job search process and eventually designed a program, similar to Forty Plus, that included motivational procedures, written materials, well-equipped office facilities, and intensive daily instruction. His program was widely utilized in state and federal job search programs, including those of the Department of Labor. Azrin later designed treatment procedures for other behavioral arenas, including "potty training in 48-hours or less." See Azrin et al. (1980: 137); Azrin and Besalel (1980, 1982); Jones and Azrin (1973); Wax (1976: 25).

10. Hansen (2003).

11. Bakke (1934); Briar (1978: 47); Granovetter (1995: 136); Newman (1988: 54, 58–9).

12. Ehrenreich (2005).

13. Byrne (1999); Stein (2000).

14. Mangum (1982: 68–69).

15. Cnaan (1999).

16. Robinson (2002). A 2009 survey found that nearly one-third of Protestant churches had or were considering offering programs for the unemployed (Michelsen 2009).

17. 1996–1997 Texas Almanac (1995: 325); Kosmin and Lachman (1993: 83).

18. Gilbreath (2002). Most Dallas churches are Baptist, Methodist, Catholic, or Church of Christ.

19. Postrel (2002).

20. Drentea (1998); Granovetter (1995: 133); Huffman and Torres (2002); Mangum (1982: 40–43); McPherson and Smith-Lovin (1982); Torres and Huffman (2002).

21. BrainBench (2009).

22. "Apparently," wrote Barley and Kunda (2004: 221), "even in the land of individualism, independence required interdependence."

23. Dudley (1996). In its careful balancing of collective reliance and individual accountability, TechNet resembles the shop floor culture described in Dudley's study of auto factory workers (1994: 110–115).

24. This tendency is not unique to unemployed tech workers but is a characteristic mode of self-presentation for professionals across occupational fields. "Sociologists of work have repeatedly shown that lawyers, scientists, police, carpenters, machinists, accountants, and members of other occupations construct their identities and organize their practice not only around their employer or the market for their services, but also around their occupational affiliations. Ask a doctor what she does for a living and she'll first tell you her specialty, not that she works for Kaiser Permanente" (Barley and Kunda 2004: 26).

25. Geertz (1973: 448).

26. Layne (2000: 503).

27. Malinowski (1948).

28. Layne (2000: 502).

29. Malinowski (1948).

30. Smith (2001: 145–150) found a similar censuring of workers who fell into "the pity pit" in the job search club she studied in the late 1990s.

31. Kunda and Van Maanen (1999: 75).

32. Smith (2001: 154).

5. Man Enough to Let My Wife Support Me

1. Over three-quarters of laid-off technology workers in and around Dallas significantly reduced their savings accounts during their time out of work, and a majority reduced their spending as well (Virick 2004).

2. Echoing popular financial experts, many of the job seekers I spoke with stated that every household today needs to maintain a savings "cushion" in case of job loss or financial emergency (this was also a common refrain among presenters at organized networking and job search events). Job seekers and experts alike disagree on exactly how big this emergency fund should be, but most suggest at least six to twelve months' worth of income or living expenses.

3. Newman (1988: 124–128).

4. Konrad (2002); Mahler (2003); Muldoon (2002).

5. Newman (1988: 72).

6. See Mahoney (1995).

7. Warren and Tyagi (2003). For an opposing viewpoint on the efficacy and prosperity of dual-income families, see Barnett and River (1996).

8. Virick (2003); Bureau of Labor Statistics (2008: 2). These statistics are not directly comparable; the Dallas study reports only the percentage of *total* job seekers (including the unmarried)

who lived with another earner. Nationally, in 83 percent of married-couple families in which one spouse lost his or her job the other spouse remained employed (Bureau of Labor Statistics 2008: 1). Dual-earner couples account for 62 percent of married-couple families with children under 18, and 52 percent of married-couple families without children under 18. Only 30 percent of married couples with children (themselves a minority among U.S. households today) now match the increasingly mis-titled "traditional" model in which the father is employed and the mother is not (Bureau of Labor Statistics 2008: 2). For couples without children, or whose children are all over 18, the figure drops to 52 percent. For statistics on the percentage of dual-worker families since 1940, see Hayghe (1990: 16–17). The statistics cited above refer specifically to legally married couples. In this chapter I also consider the experiences of unmarried couples in long-term partnerships. These partnerships are all heterosexual, as none of my seventy-five interviewees were in a long-term gay or lesbian relationship at the time of their job loss. Whether the experiences of the unemployed men and women described herein differ from those of partnered gay men or lesbians remains to be studied. Focused as it is on two-earner households, this chapter also does not cover the experiences of single men and women, for whom relying on spousal income was not an option.

9. Unlike husbands in Potuchek (1997: 119), job seekers in this study did not minimize or criticize their wives' labor force participation.

10. Virick (2003).

11. Peck (2010: 52).

12. Potuchek (1997).

13. Townsend (2002), for instance, conducted his research entirely among working-class and lower-middle-class men, which might explain why his study, undertaken between 1989 and 1992, found a more traditional model of male breadwinning than I found among middle- and upper-class men.

14. See Hochschild (1989).

15. Townsend (2002: 10).

16. Komarovsky (1940: 74).

17. Newman (1988: 140).

18. Townsend (2002: 117).

19. Bederman (1995: 11).

20. Newman notes that many children of downsized fathers adopted more "progressive" stances toward appropriate male and female roles (1988: 117–119). In their own families, these grown children often saw supporting the family in a crisis as the responsibility of both parents. Grown daughters of unemployed men were especially likely to reject the idea of female dependence and to seek professional and financial security of their own. Historians disagree over the causes and timeline for the demise of the ideal of the male breadwinner, but most concur that this is no longer the dominant ideal for men in the United States. According to Barbara Ehrenreich (1983) the "breadwinner ethic" came loose from its moorings in the 1970s as a result of men's self-interested abdication of the breadwinner role. Michael Kimmel, in contrast, dates the shift later, arguing that the success of the feminist movement provided a political model for "male liberationists" who sought to free men from the fetters of traditional masculinity (1996: 261–290).

21. Peck (2010).

22. Other anthropologists have identified similar, although not identical, shifts among laid-off and insecurely employed blue-collar U.S. men, for whom "strict interpretations of a gendered division of labor have proved incompatible with the survival of the family unit" (Broughton and Walton 2006: 5).

23. The few single women in my study did not have the option of relying on a partner's income. Some of them complained that married women were "taking" jobs from single women who needed them more. Interestingly, unmarried women did not direct the same critique at male job seekers with working wives.

24. Consider, for example, the furor that erupted over Lisa Belkin's 2003 article about Ivy League–educated women leaving the workforce to care for their homes and children full time.

25. There are striking parallels here to the findings of Biao Xiang's 2007 ethnography of Indian IT workers participating in the system of global body shopping, a global labor management system under which tech workers migrate to complete project-based contracts. Xiang demonstrates that the flexibility of the allegedly de-territorialized and unfettered New Economy depends to a great extent on mundane and decidedly un-abstract realities like a revitalized Indian dowry system. Xiang also found that wives' incomes provided an important source of security for entrepreneurial Indian IT workers attempting to start their own body-shopping businesses. As one such business owner explained, "The family needs some money coming in on a regular basis. Otherwise it would be too scary for us" (2007: 55–56). Thus, although Indian IT workers aggressively positioned themselves and their industry as flexible, global, and autonomous, they depended on the structure of the dual-career family and on the decidedly less flexible jobs of their usually government-employed spouses.

Epilogue

1. Kolbert (2010: 73); Peck (2010).

2. Mark Zandi, quoted in Associated Press (2009).

3. See, e.g., Mishel and Shierholz (2009).

4. Journalist Michael Winerip (2010) undertook a similar endeavor in March 2010 when he reinterviewed sixteen job seekers he met at a job fair one year before. His updates, most with workers over fifty, echo my findings that although some laid-off workers have prospered most continue to struggle with un- or underemployment.

5. Couch and Placzek (2010); Couch, Jolly, and Placzek (2009: 1).

6. Virick (2004).

7. By 2009, not having a profile on professional networking sites such as LinkedIn had become, "for some employers," particularly in the high-tech field, "not only a major liability but a sign that the candidate is horribly out of touch" (Noguchi 2009).

8. See Gusterson and Besteman (2009).

9. Newman (1988: 277).

10. I learned that the founder of one popular high-tech happy hour had transferred leadership of the group to a friend and moved two hours south, where he joined his parents in running the family farm; he now applies his tech skills to maintaining the farm's website, which offers hogs, sheep, and chickens for sale.

11. TechAmerica (2009).

12. Ehrenreich (2009).

13. See, e.g., Greenhouse (2009) and Venkatesh (2009).

14. Giroux (2001).

15. Winerip (2010).

16. See, e.g., Weinberg (1998).

17. Newman (1988: 233) outlines more fully the compensatory rewards of shouldering responsibility for one's own downward mobility.

18. Dudley (2000: 165).

19. The incompatibility of individualist ideologies such as career management with organized labor movements is also noted by Smith (2001: 172) and Wacquant (2002: 1517–1518).

20. Luo (2009).

21. Nigro (2008: 3–4).

22. Clines (2009).

BIBLIOGRAPHY

1996–1997 Texas Almanac. 1995. Dallas: Dallas Morning News. Abbate, Janet. 1999. *Inventing the Internet.* Cambridge, MA: MIT Press.

Adler, Rachel H. 2004. *Yucatecans in Dallas, Texas: Breaching the Border, Bridging the Distance.* Boston: Pearson Allyn and Bacon.

Alexander, Karen. 2003. "Unemployed Discover They Must 'Use It or Lose It.'" *Taipei Times,* September 14.

Applebaum, Herbert. 1981. *Royal Blue: The Culture of Construction Workers.* New York: Holt, Rinehart, and Winston.

Associated Press. 2009. "Uh, Oh, Higher Jobless Rates Could Be The New Normal." *Daily News,* October 19.

Atkinson, John, and Nigel Meager. 1986a. *New Forms of Work Organisation.* Brighton, England: Institute for Employment Studies.

———. 1986b. *Changing Work Patterns: How Companies Achieve Flexibility to Meet New Needs.* London: National Economic Development Office.

Atkinson, Robert, and Paul Gottlieb. 2001. *The Metropolitan New Economy Index.* Washington, DC: Progressive Policy Institute.

Azrin, Nathan H., and Victoria A. Besalel. 1982. *Finding a Job.* Berkeley: Ten Speed Press.

———. 1980. *Job Club Counselor's Manual: A Behavioral Approach to Vocational Counseling.* Baltimore: University Park Press.

Azrin, Nathan H., R. A. Philip, P. Thienese-Hontos, and Victoria A. Besalel. 1980. "Comparative Evaluation of the Job Club Program with Welfare Recipients." *Journal of Vocational Behavior* 16: 133–145.

Baba, Marietta L. 1998. "The Anthropology of Work in the Fortune 1000: A Critical Perspective." *Anthropology of Work Review* 18, no. 4: 17–28.

———. 1986. *Business and Industrial Anthropology: An Overview.* Washington, DC: American Anthropological Association.

Bailey, Brad. 1985. "Infomart: Where the Future Is Present." *Dallas Morning News,* May 12.

Bajaj, Vikas. 2000. "Federal Panel Targets Shortage of Tech Workers." *Dallas Morning News,* February 25.

Bajaj, Vikas, and Crayton Harrison. 2001. "With 7,000 Lost Tech Jobs, Area Economy Feels Pinch." *Dallas Morning News,* July 20.

Bakke, E. Wight. 1940. *The Unemployed Worker.* New Haven, CT: Yale University Press.

———. 1934. *The Unemployed Man.* New York: E.P. Dutton and Co.

Balakrishnan, Radhika, ed. 2001. *Hidden Assembly Line: Gender Dynamics of Subcontracted Work in a Global Economy.* Bloomfield, CT: Kumarian Press.

Barley, Stephen R. 1989. "Careers, Identities, and Institutions: The Legacy of the Chicago School of Sociology." In *Handbook of Career Theory,* edited by Michael B. Arthur, Douglas T. Hall, and Barbara S. Lawrence, 41–65. Cambridge: Cambridge University Press.

Barley, Stephen R., and Gideon Kunda. 2004. *Gurus, Hired Guns, and Warm Bodies: Itinerant Experts in a Knowledge Economy.* Princeton, NJ: Princeton University Press.

Barnett, Rosalind C., and Caryl River. 1996. *She Works, He Works: How Two-Income Families are Happy, Healthy, and Thriving.* Cambridge, MA: Harvard University Press.

Bederman, Gail. 1995. *Manliness and Civilization: A Cultural History of Gender and Race in the United States, 1880–1917.* Chicago: University of Chicago Press.

Belkin, Lisa. 2003. "The Opt-Out Revolution." *New York Times,* October 26.

Benner, Chris. 2002. *Work in the New Economy: Flexible Labor Markets in Silicon Valley.* Oxford, UK: Blackwell.

Bishop, Ralph J., and Peter Foley. 1992. "Job Security and Other Jokes: Employee Comments on a Broken Social Contract." *Anthropology of Work Review* 13, no. 2–3: 12–15.

Blanton, Kimberly. 2003. "Technical Knockout." *Boston Globe,* March 9.

Bolles, Richard. 2003. *What Color Is Your Parachute 2003: A Practical Manual for Job-Hunters and Career Changers.* New York: Ten Speed Press.

Boyd, Michelle R. 2008. "Integration and the Collapse of Black Social Capital: Nostalgia and Narrative in the Neoliberal City." In *New Landscapes of Inequality: Neoliberalism and the Erosion of Democracy in America,* edited by Jane L. Collins, Micaela di Leonardo, and Brett Williams, 91–111. Santa Fe, NM: School of American Research Press.

Boyett, Joseph H., and Henry P. Conn. 1992. *Workplace 2000: The Revolution Shaping American Business.* New York: Plume.

Bradley, Harriet, Mark Erickson, Carol Stephenson, and Steve Williams. 2000. *Myths at Work.* Cambridge, England: Polity.

Brand, Stewart. 1988. *The Media Lab: Inventing the Future at M.I.T.* New York: Penguin.

BrainBench. 2009. "Predicting Employee Success." BrainBench. http://www.brain
bench.com/xml/bb/business/hiring/hireemployees.xml (accessed February 14, 2009).

Braverman, Harry. 1975. *Labor and Monopoly Capital: The Degradation of Work in the Twentieth Century*. New York: Monthly Review Press.

Breen, William J. 1997. *Labor Market Politics and the Great War: The Department of Labor, the States, and the First U.S. Employment Service, 1907–1933*. Kent, Ohio: Kent State University Press.

Briar, Kathleen H. 1978. *The Effect of Long-Term Unemployment on Workers and Their Families*. San Francisco: R&E Research Associates.

Broughton, Chad, and Tom Walton. 2006. "Downsizing Masculinity: Gender, Family, and Fatherhood in Postindustrial America." *Anthropology of Work Review* 27, no. 1: 1–11.

Brown, Steve. 2007. "New Owner Filling Infomart." *Dallas Morning News*. http://www.dallasnews.com/sharedcontent/dws/bus/columnists/sbrown/stories/082407dn busrecol.361189c.html (accessed March 26, 2010).

Burawoy, Michael. 1979a. *Manufacturing Consent: Changes in the Labor Process under Monopoly Capitalism*. Chicago: University of Chicago Press.

——. 1979b. "The Anthropology of Industrial Work." *Annual Review of Anthropology* 8: 231–266.

Bureau of Labor Statistics. 2010a. Current Employment Statistics Survey. http://data.bls.gov/PDQ/servlet/SurveyOutputServlet?series_id=CES5051700001&data_tool=XGtable (data extracted March 26, 2010).

——. 2010b. "The Employment Situation: June 2010." http://www.bls.gov/news.release/empsit.nr0.htm (accessed July 26, 2010).

——. 2009. "The Employment Situation: May 2009." Bureau of Labor Statistics. http://www.bls.gov/news.release/empsit.nr0.htm (accessed June 22, 2009).

——. 2008. "Employment Characteristics of Families in 2007." Washington, DC: U.S. Department of Labor.

——. 2004. "Employment Characteristics of Families in 2003." Washington, DC: U.S. Department of Labor.

——. 2002. "Numbers of Jobs Held, Labor Market Activity, and Earnings Growth among Younger Baby Boomers: Results from More Than Two Decades of a Longitudinal Survey." BLS Press Release, August 27. http://www.bls.gov/news.release/nlsoy.nr0.htm (accessed March 27, 2010).

Byrne, David. 1999. "The Search for the Young and Gifted." *Business Week*, October 4: 108.

Cappelli, Peter. 1999. *The New Deal at Work: Managing the Market-Driven Workplace*. Boston: Harvard Business School Press.

Carbasho, Tracy. 2002. "Jobseekers Who Continue to Network, Hone Skills Will Make Lasting Impressions." *Pittsburgh Business Times,* June 24.

Carson, L. M. Kit. 2001. "Deep_Ellum.Com." *D Magazine: Special Edition: eDallas,* July: 75–79.

Cassidy, John. 2002. *Dot.Con: The Greatest Story Ever Sold*. New York: HarperCollins.

Challenger, Gray & Christmas. 2009. "More on White-Collar Job Loss." *@Work,* October 6. http://challengeratworkblog.blogspot.com/2009/10/more-on-white-collar-job-loss.html (accessed March 26, 2010).

Chet, Carrie Lane. 2005. "Like Exporting Baseball to Japan: U.S. Tech Workers Respond to Offshoring." *Anthropology of Work Review* 25: 18–26.

Clifford, James, and George Marcus. 1989. *Writing Culture: The Poetics and Politics of Ethnography.* Berkeley: University of California Press.

Clines, Francis X. 2009. "Are They Depressed? Nowhere Near." *New York Times,* March 15.

Cnaan, Ram A., with Robert J. Wineburg and Stephanie C. Boddie. 1999. *The Newer Deal: Social Work and Religion in Partnership.* New York: Columbia University Press.

Collins, Jane L., Micaela di Leonardo, and Brett Williams, eds. 2008. *New Landscapes of Inequality: Neoliberalism and the Erosion of Democracy in America.* Santa Fe, NM: School of American Research Press.

Conlin, Michelle. 2001. "Labor Laws Apply to Dot-Coms? Really?" *Business Week,* February 26: 96, 98.

Connelly, Julie. 2003. "Youthful Attitudes, Sobering Realities." *New York Times,* October 28.

Couch, Kenneth A., Nicholas A. Jolly, and Dana W. Placzek. 2009. "Mass Layoffs and Their Impact on Earnings during Recessions and Expansions." Occasional Paper Series 2009-1. Wethersfield, CT: Connecticut Department of Labor Office of Research.

Couch, Kenneth A., and Dana W. Placzek. 2010. "Earnings Losses of Displaced Workers Revisited." *American Economic Review* 100, no. 1: 572–589.

Darrah, Charles N. 2000. "Techno-Missionaries Doing Good at the Center." Paper presented at the annual meeting of the American Anthropological Association, San Francisco, November 17.

——. 1994. "Skill Requirements at Work: Rhetoric Versus Reality." *Work and Occupations* 21, no. 1: 64–84.

Davis, Clark. 2000. *Company Men: White-Collar Life and Corporate Cultures in Los Angeles, 1892–1941.* Baltimore: Johns Hopkins University Press.

Dillon, David. 1985. "Borrowing from the Past." *Dallas Morning News,* January 13.

Dixon, K. A., and Carl E. Van Horn. 2003. *The Disposable Worker: Living in A Job-Loss Economy.* Work Trends 6, no. 2. Brunswick, NJ: John J. Heldrich Center for Workforce Development, Rutgers University. Joint project with Center for Survey Research and Analysis, University of Connecticut (Storrs, CT).

Douglas, Mary. 1966. *Purity and Danger: An Analysis of the Concept of Pollution and Taboo.* London: Penguin.

Doukas, Dimitra. 2003. *Worked Over: The Corporate Sabotage of an American Community.* Ithaca, NY: Cornell University Press.

Drentea, Patricia. 1998. "Consequences of Women's Formal and Informal Job Search Methods for Employment in Female-Dominated Jobs." *Gender and Society* 12, no. 3: 321–338.

Dudley, Kathryn. 2000. *Debt and Dispossession: Farm Loss in America's Heartland.* Chicago: University of Chicago Press.

——. 1996. "The Problem of Community in Rural America." *Culture and Agriculture* 18, no. 2: 47–57.

———. 1994. *The End of the Line: Lost Jobs, New Lives in Postindustrial America*. Chicago: University of Chicago Press.

Dunn, Elizabeth. 2004. *Privatizing Poland: Baby Food, Big Business, and the Remaking of Labor*. Ithaca, NY: Cornell University Press.

Durington, Matthew. 2003. "Discourses of Racialized Moral Panic in a Suburban Community: Teenagers, Heroin and Media in Plano, Texas." PhD diss., Temple University.

Durkheim, Emile. 1965 [1963]. *The Division of Labor in Society*. Translation by George Simpson. New York: Free Press.

Economic Policy Institute. 2004. "JobWatch: June 2004." Economic Policy Institute. http://www.jobwatch.org/email/jobwatch_20040604.html (accessed August 1, 2010).

Ehrenreich, Barbara. 2009. "Trying to Find a Job Is Not a Job." *Los Angeles Times*, May 3. http://articles.latimes.com/2009/may/03/opinion/oe-ehrenreich3 (accessed June 18, 2009).

———. 2005. *Bait and Switch: The (Futile) Pursuit of the American Dream*. New York: Metropolitan Books.

———. 1983. *The Hearts of Men: American Dreams and the Flight from Commitment*. New York: Doubleday.

English-Lueck, Jan. 2002. *Cultures@Silicon Valley*. Stanford, CA: Stanford University Press.

English-Lueck, Jan, and Andrea Saveri. 2000. "Silicon Missionaries and Identity Evangelists." Paper presented at the annual meeting of the American Anthropological Association, San Francisco, November 17.

Ezzy, Douglas. 2001. *Narrating Unemployment*. Aldershot, England: Ashgate.

Feldman, Daniel C. 2000. "From the Me Decade to the Flee Decade." In *Relational Wealth: The Advantages of Stability in a Changing Economy*, edited by Carrie Leanu and Denise Rousseau, 169–182. Oxford: Oxford University Press.

Feldman, Daniel C., and Brian S. Klaas. 2002. "Internet Job Hunting: A Field Study of Applicant Experiences with On-line Recruiting." *Human Resource Management* 41, no. 2: 175–192.

Fernandez, Roberto M., Emilio J. Castilla, and Paul Moore. 2000. "Social Capital at Work: Networks and Employment at a Phone Center." *American Journal of Sociology* 105, no. 5: 1288–1356.

Field, Anne. 2002. "When a Job Hunt Is Measured in Seasons or Even a Year." *New York Times*, December 8.

Fitzgerald, Thomas J. 2003. "Help Wanted: Customizing a Job Search." *New York Times*, March 20.

Foley, Douglas E. 1990. *Learning Capitalist Culture: Deep in the Heart of Tejas*. Philadelphia: University of Pennsylvania Press.

Forsythe, Diana E. 1999. "Ethics and Politics of Studying Up in Technoscience." *Anthropology of Work Review* 20, no. 1: 6–11.

Forty Plus of New York. 2010. "About Us." Forty Plus of New York. http://www.fortyplus-nyc.org/Forty_Plus_of_New_York/Welcome.html (accessed August 10, 2010).

Francis, David R. 2003. "Finally, A Jobs Tally with a Positive Surprise." *Christian Science Monitor*, October 6.

Frank, Thomas. 2004. *What's the Matter with Kansas? How Conservatives Won the Heart of America*. New York: Metropolitan Books.

——. 2000. *One Market under God: Extreme Capitalism, Market Populism, and the End of Economic Democracy.* New York: Random House.

Freeman, Carla. 2000. *High Tech and High Heels in the Global Economy: Women, Work, and Pink-Collar Identities in the Caribbean.* Durham, NC: Duke University Press.

"The Future of Work." 2000. *Economist,* January 29: 89–92.

Gale, Ivan, and Jeff Palfini. 2001. "Who Got Fired?" *Industry Standard,* April 30: 72–73.

Geertz, Clifford. 1973. *The Interpretation of Cultures.* New York: Basic Books.

Gilbreath, Edward. 2002. "The New Capital of Evangelicalism." *Christianity Today* 46, no. 6: 38.

Giroux, Henry. 2008. *Against the Terror of Neoliberalism: Politics Beyond the Age of Greed.* Boulder: Paradigm.

——. 2001. *Public Spaces, Private Lives: Beyond the Culture of Cynicism.* New York: Rowman and Littlefield.

Gladwell, Malcolm. 2000. "Designs for Working." *New Yorker,* December 11: 60–70.

Godinez, Victor. 2002. "Rebound in Tech May Be Slow." *Dallas Morning News,* May 13.

Goffman, Erving. 1961. *Asylums.* New York: Anchor Books.

——. 1959. *The Presentation of Self in Everyday Life.* New York: Anchor Books.

Goldstein, Alan. 1995. "A Decade of Data." *Dallas Morning News,* January 17.

Goodman, Peter S., and Jack Healy. 2009. "No End in Sight to Job Losses; 663,000 More Cut in March." *New York Times,* April 3.

Gordon, David. 1996. *Fat and Mean: The Corporate Squeeze of Working Americans and the Myth of Managerial "Downsizing."* New York: Free Press.

Govenar, Alan B., and Jay F. Brakefield. 1998. *Deep Ellum and Central Track: Where the Black and White Worlds of Dallas Converged.* Denton: University of North Texas Press.

Granovetter, Mark. 1995 [1974]. *Getting a Job: A Study of Contacts and Careers.* 2nd ed. Chicago: University of Chicago Press.

——. 1973. "The Strength of Weak Ties." *American Journal of Sociology* 78: 1360–1380.

Greenhouse, Steven. 2009. "In America, Labor Has An Unusually Long Fuse." *New York Times,* April 5.

Greenspan, Alan. 2008. Testimony to the Committee of Government Oversight and Reform. October 23. http://oversight.house.gov/images/stories/documents/2008 1023100438.pdf (accessed August 1, 2010).

Gusterson, Hugh, and Catherine Besteman, eds. 2009. *The Insecure American: How We Got Here and What We Should Do About It.* Berkeley: University of California Press.

Habal, Hala. 2000. "Dallas.com." *D Magazine,* March: 74–83.

Hackworth, Jason. 2006. *The Neoliberal City: Governance, Ideology, and Development in American Urbanism.* Ithaca, NY: Cornell University Press.

Hagan, Jacqueline María. 1994. *Deciding to Be Legal: A Maya Community in Houston.* Philadelphia: Temple University Press.

Hall, Douglas T. 1976. *Careers in Organization.* Glenview, IL: Scott, Foresman.

Hall, Douglas T., and Philip H. Mirvis. 1995. "Careers as Lifelong Learning." In *The Changing Nature of Work,* edited by Ann Howard, 323–361. San Francisco: Jossey-Bass.

Hannerz, Ulf. 1996. *Transnational Connections: Culture, People, Places.* London: Routledge.

Hansen, Katherine. 2003. "For Networking and Support, Join or Start a Job Club." Quintessential Careers Website. http://www.quintcareers.com/job_club.html (accessed June 6, 2003).

Harmon, Amy. 2001. "Virtual Revenge and the Decline of the Dot-Coms." *New York Times,* July 15.

Harrington, Ann. 2002. "Make That Switch." *Fortune,* February 4: 159–162.

Harrington, Brad. 2001. "An Interview with Tim Hall." *The Network News* 3, no. 2. http://wfnetwork.bc.edu/The_Network_News/3-2/TNN3-2_Hall.pdf (accessed December 13, 2008).

Harris, Rosemary. 1987. *Power and Powerlessness in Industry: An Analysis of the Social Relations of Production.* London: Tavistock.

Harvey, David. 2005. *A Brief History of Neoliberalism.* Oxford: Oxford University Press.

———. 1990. *The Condition of Postmodernity: An Enquiry into the Origins of Cultural Change.* Cambridge, MA: Blackwell.

Hauben, Michael, and Ronda Hauben. 1997. *Netizens: On the History and Impact of UseNet and the Internet.* Los Alamitos, CA: IEEE Computer Society Press.

Hayghe, Howard. 1990. "Family Members in the Workforce." *Monthly Labor Review* 113, no. 3: 14–19.

Heckscher, Charles. 1995. *White-Collar Blues: Management Loyalties in an Age of Corporate Restructuring.* New York: Basic Books.

Hochschild, Arlie. 1989. *The Second Shift: Working Parents and the Revolution at Home.* New York: Viking.

Hoffman, Jeffrey. 1998. "Too Rich to Risk?" *D Magazine,* January 25: DB4–DB8, DB22.

Housewright, Ed, and Scott Farwell. 2001. "All Built Up, Nobody Home." *Dallas Morning News,* November 5.

Howe, Peter J. 2002. "Layoffs Shrink in Some Sectors." *Boston Globe,* July 15.

Huffman, Matt, and Lisa Torres. 2002. "It's Not Only 'Who You Know' That Matters: Gender, Personal Contacts, and Job Lead Quality." *Gender and Society* 16, no. 6: 793–813.

Hurlock, Jim. 1986. "Slow Starters—or White Elephants?" *Business Week,* February 17: 78.

Johnson, Spencer. 1998. *Who Moved My Cheese?: An Amazing Way to Deal with Change in Your Work and in Your Life.* New York: G.P. Putnam's Sons.

Joint Venture: Silicon Valley Network. 1999. *Workforce Study: An Analysis of the Workforce Gap in Silicon Valley.* San Jose: Silicon Valley Network.

Jones, R. J., and Nathan H. Azrin. 1973. "An Experimental Application of a Social Reinforcement Approach to the Problem of Job-Finding." *Journal of Applied Behavioral Analysis* 6: 345–353.

Kaufman, Harold G. 1982. *Professionals in Search of Work: Coping with the Stress of Job Loss and Unemployment.* New York: John Wiley and Sons.

Kelly, Kevin. 1992. "Hot Spots: America's New Growth Regions." *BusinessWeek,* October 19: 80–84.

Kemper, Robert V. 2002. "Dallas-Fort Worth." In *Encyclopedia of Urban Cultures,* edited by Melvin Ember and Carol Ember. Bethel, CT: Scholastic/Grolier.

Kemper, Robert V., and Anya Peterson Royce, eds. 2002. *Chronicling Cultures: Long-Term Field Research in Anthropology.* Lanham, MD: AltaMira Press.

Kenney, Martin, ed. 2000. *Understanding Silicon Valley: The Anatomy of an Entrepreneurial Region.* Stanford: Stanford University Press.

Kimmel, Michael. 1996. *Manhood in America: A Cultural History.* New York: The Free Press.

Kipnis, Andrew. 2008. "Audit Cultures: Neoliberal Governmentality, Socialist Legacy, or Technologies of Governing?" *American Ethnologist* 35, no. 2: 275–289.

Klein, Naomi. 2007. *The Shock Doctrine: The Rise of Disaster Capitalism.* New York: Metropolitan Books.

Kolbert, Elizabeth. 2010. "Everybody Have Fun." *New Yorker,* March 22: 72–74.

Komarovsky, Mirra. 1940. *The Unemployed Man and His Family: The Effect of Unemployment on the Status of the Man in 59 Families.* New York: Dryden Press.

Konrad, Rachel. 2002. "The World of the Laid-off Techie." *ZDNet News,* February 8. http://www.zdnet.com/news/the-world-of-the-laid-off-techie/120632?tag=content; search-results-rivers (accessed August 1, 2010).

Kosmin, Barry A., and Seymour P. Lachman. 1993. *One Nation Under God: Religion in Contemporary American Society.* New York: Crown Trade Paperbacks.

Kotkin, Joel. 2000. "The Capital of Capitalism." *D Magazine: Special Edition: eDallas,* December: 10–11.

Krishnamurthy, Mathangi. 2004. "Resources and Rebels: A Study of Identity Management in Indian Call Centers." *Anthropology of Work Review* 25, no. 3: 9–18.

Kübler-Ross, Elisabeth. 1969. *On Death and Dying: What the Dying Have to Teach Doctors, Nurses, Clergy, and Their Own Families.* New York: Macmillan.

Kunda, Gideon. 1992. *Engineering Culture: Control and Commitment in a High Tech Corporation.* Philadelphia: Temple University Press.

Kunda, Gideon, and John Van Maanen. 1999. "Changing Scripts at Work: Managers and Professionals." *Annals* 561: 64–80.

Lamphere, Louise. 1979. "Fighting the Piece Rate System: New Dimensions of an Old Struggle in the Apparel Industry." In *Case Studies on the Labor Process,* edited by A. Zimbalist, 421–446. The Hague: Mouton.

Lane, Carrie. 2010. "'If the Shoe Ain't Your Size, It Ain't Gonna Fit': Ideologies of Professional and Marital Instability among U.S. White-Collar Workers." *Iowa Journal of Cultural Studies* 12/13: 37–54.

———. 2009. "Man Enough to Let My Wife Support Me: How Changing Models of Career and Gender Are Reshaping the Experience of Unemployment." *American Ethnologist* 36, no. 4: 681–692.

Layne, Linda. 2000. "The Cultural Fix: An Anthropological Contribution to Science and Technology Studies." *Science, Technology & Human Values* 25, no. 4: 492–519.

Lewis, Michael. 2001. *The New New Thing: A Silicon Valley Story.* New York: Penguin.

Licht, Walter. 1988. "How the Workplace Has Changed in 75 Years." *Monthly Labor Review* 111, no. 2: 19–25.

Ligos, Melinda. 2003. "In Job Search, Warm and Fuzzy Beats Online and All-Business." *New York Times,* February 2.

Limón, José E. 1991. "Representation, Ethnicity, and the Precursory Ethnography: Notes of a Native Anthropologist." In *Recapturing Anthropology: Working in the Present,* edited by Richard G. Fox, 115–135. Santa Fe, NM: School of American Research Press.

Lowenstein, Roger. 2004. *Origins of the Crash: The Great Bubble and Its Undoing.* New York: Penguin.

Luker, William Jr., and Donald Lyons. 1997. "Employment Shifts in High-Technology Industries, 1988–96." *Monthly Labor Review* 120, no. 6: 12–25.

Luo, Michael. 2009. "For Growing Ranks of the White-Collar Jobless, Support With a Touch of the Spur." *New York Times,* January 25.

Madsen, William. 1964. *The Mexican Americans of South Texas.* New York: Holt, Rinehart and Winston.

Mahar, Maggie. 2003. *Bull!: A History of the Boom, 1982–1999: What Drove the Breakneck Market—and What Every Investor Needs to Know about Financial Cycles.* New York: HarperBusiness.

Mahler, Jonathan. 2003. "Commute to Nowhere." *New York Times,* April 13.

Mahoney, Rhona. 1995. *Kidding Ourselves: Breadwinning, Babies, and Bargaining Power.* New York: Basic Books.

Malinowski, Bronislaw. 1948. *Magic, Science and Religion.* New York: Doubleday.

Mangum, Stephen L. 1982. *Job Search: A Review of the Literature.* San Francisco: Olympic Research Centers.

Marschall, Daniel J. 2001. "Ideology and Career Consciousness in the Occupational Community of Internet Technologists." Master's thesis, Georgetown University.

Maxwell, Lisa C. 2010a. "DALLAS COUNTY." Handbook of Texas Online. http://www.tshaonline.org/handbook/online/articles/DD/hcd2.html (accessed August 1, 2010).

———. 2010b. "DEEP ELLUM." Handbook of Texas Online. http://www.tshaonline.org/handbook/online/articles/DD/hpd1.html (accessed August 1, 2010).

McElhaney, Jackie, and Michael V. Hazel. 2010. "DALLAS, TX." Handbook of Texas Online. http://www.tshaonline.org/handbook/online/articles/DD/hdd1.html (accessed August 1, 2010).

McGill, Adam. 2002. "Deep Ellum's Growing Pains." *D Magazine,* November: 22–23.

McPherson, J. Miller, and Lynn Smith-Lovin. 1982. "Women and Weak Ties: Differences by Sex in the Size of Voluntary Organizations." *American Journal of Sociology* 87, no. 4: 883–904.

Mensah, Joseph. 2008. *Neoliberalism and Globalization in Africa: Contestations on the Embattled Continent.* New York: Palgrave Macmillan.

Michelsen, Michael W., Jr. 2009. "Career Counseling in Church." *Christianity Today,* October 2. http://www.christianitytoday.com/ct/2009/august/37.38.html (accessed March 26, 2010).

Milgram, Stanley. 1974. *Obedience to Authority: An Experimental View.* New York: Harper & Row.

———. 1967. "The Small World Problem." *Psychology Today* 2: 60–67.

Mishel, Lawrence, Jared Bernstein, and Heather Boushey. 2003. *The State of Working America 2002–03.* Ithaca, NY: Cornell University Press.

Mishel, Lawrence, and Heidi Shierholz. 2009. "Seven Million Jobs Needed to Return to Pre-Recession Employment Levels." Economic Policy Institute, May. http://www.epi.org/publications/entry/jobspict_200905_preview/ (accessed June 16, 2009).

Mitchell, Jim. 1987. "Infomart Begins to Compute." *Dallas Morning News,* January 17.

———. 1985a. "Infomart Takes Central Stage Monday." *Dallas Morning News,* January 21.

———. 1985b. "Infomart's Future Still In Question." *Dallas Morning News,* August 17.

Moore, Michael. 1990. "Roger & Me." Burbank, CA: Warner Home Video.

Moore, Thomas S. 1996. *The Disposable Workforce: Worker Displacement and Employment Instability in America.* New York: Aldine deGruyter.

Muldoon, Bob. 2002. "White-Collar Man in a Blue-Collar World." *Newsweek,* February 4: 13.

Nash, June C. 1998. "Twenty Years of Work Anthropology: A Critical Evaluation." *Anthropology of Work Review* 18, no. 4: 1–6.

———. 1989. *From Tank Town to High Tech: The Clash of Community and Industrial Cycles.* New York: State University of New York Press.

Newman, Katherine. 1993. *Declining Fortunes: The Withering of the American Dream.* New York: Basic Books.

———. 1988. *Falling from Grace: Downward Mobility in the Age of Affluence.* Berkeley: University of California Press.

New York Times. 1996. *The Downsizing of America.* New York: Three Rivers Press.

Nigro, Nicholas. 2008. *No Job? No Prob!: How to Pay Your Bills, Feed Your Mind, and Have a Blast When You're Out of Work.* New York: Skyhorse Publishing.

Noguchi, Yuki. 2009. "Job Seekers Find New Rules of Recruitment." National Public Radio, June 28. http://www.npr.org/templates/story/story.php?storyId=105483848&sc=nl&cc=es-20090628 (accessed June 29, 2009).

Ong, Aihwa. 2006. *Neoliberalism as Exception: Mutations in Citizenship and Sovereignty.* Durham, NC: Duke University Press.

Oppel, Richard A. 2001. "Dallas Bleeds as Job Cuts Hit Its Tech Sector." *New York Times,* August 5.

Osterman, Paul. 1999. *Securing Prosperity: The American Labor Market: How It Has Changed and What to Do About It.* Princeton: Princeton University Press.

———, ed. 1996. *Broken Ladders: Managerial Careers in the New Economy.* New York: Oxford University Press.

Overbey, Mary Margaret, and Kathryn Dudley, eds. 2000. "Anthropology and Middle Class Working Families: A Research Agenda." Arlington: American Anthropological Association. http://www.aaanet.org/gvt/mcwf.pdf (accessed Aug. 1, 2010).

Peck, Don. 2010. "How A New Jobless Era Will Transform America." *Atlantic Monthly,* March: 42–56.

Pérez, Gina M. 2008. "Discipline and Citizenship: Latina/o Youth in Chicago JROTC Programs." In *New Landscapes of Inequality: Neoliberalism and the Erosion of Democracy in America,* edited by Jane L. Collins, Micaela di Leonardo, and Brett Williams, 113–130. Santa Fe: School of American Research Press.

Petersen, D'Ann M., and Michelle Thomas. 1995. "From Crude Oil to Computer Chips: How Technology Is Changing the Texas Economy." *Southwest Economy* (a publication of the Federal Reserve Bank of Dallas), November: 1–5.

Petre, Peter. 1985. "Computer Marts: A New Way to Hawk High Tech." *Fortune,* February 4: 64.

Pew Internet Project. 2002. "Online Job Hunting: A Pew Internet Project Data Memo." Pew Internet Project. July 17. http://www.pewinternet.org/Press-Releases/2002/Online-Job-Hunting-A-Pew-Internet-Project-Data-Memo.aspx (accessed August 1, 2010).

Phillips, Michael. 2006. *White Metropolis: Race, Ethnicity, and Religion in Dallas, 1841–2001.* Austin: University of Texas Press.

Pink, Daniel. 2001. *Free Agent Nation: How America's New Independent Workers Are Transforming the Way We Live.* New York: Warner Books.

Piore, Michael J., and Charles F. Sabel. 1984. *The Second Industrial Divide: Possibilities for Prosperity.* New York: Basic Books.

Postrel, Virginia. 2002. "Come All Ye Faithful." *D Magazine,* July: 47–50.

Potuchek, Jean L. 1997. *Who Supports the Family?: Gender and Breadwinning in Dual-Earner Marriages.* Stanford: Stanford University Press.

Primeau, Marty. 1985. "A French Feast to Herald a Palace of Information." *Dallas Morning News,* February 3.

Ragland, James. 2002. "Great to Know You, Dallas." *Dallas Morning News,* November 22.

Randall, Neil. 1997. *Soul of the Internet: Net Gods, Netizens and the Wiring of the World.* London: International Thomson Computer Press.

Read, William H., and Jan L. Youtie. 1994. "Texas Telecom Corridor." *Economic Development Review* 12, no. 3: 27–31.

Reich, Robert. 1991. *The Work of Nations: Preparing Ourselves for 21st-Century Capitalism.* New York: Vintage Books.

Riche, R. W., D. E. Hecker, and J. U. Burgan. 1983. "High Technology Today and Tomorrow: A Small Slice of the Employment Pie." *Monthly Labor Review,* November: 50–58.

Robinson, David. 2002. "Networking in the Pews." *Time,* July 15: 17.

Rose, Nikolas. 1990. *Governing the Soul: The Shaping of the Private Self.* London: Routledge.

——. 1999. *Powers of Freedom: Reframing Political Thought.* Cambridge: Cambridge University Press.

Ross, Andrew. 2003. *No-Collar: The Humane Workplace and Its Hidden Costs.* New York: Basic Books.

Sanjek, Roger. 1990. *Fieldnotes: The Making of Anthropology.* Ithaca, NY: Cornell University Press.

"Santa Clara, Dallas Counties Lead Nation in Employment Decline." 2003. *Dallas Business Journal,* November 4.

Saxenian, Annalee. 1996. *Regional Advantage: Culture and Competition in Silicon Valley and Route 128,* revised ed. Cambridge, MA: Harvard University Press.

Schwartz, Nelson D. 2003. "Down and Out in White-Collar America." *Fortune,* June 23: 79–82, 86.

Segaller, Stephen. 1998. *Nerds 2.0.1: A Brief History of the Internet.* New York: TV Books.

Sennett, Richard. 1998. *The Corrosion of Character: The Personal Consequences of Work in the New Capitalism.* New York: W.W. Norton.

Shelp, Ronald K., and Gary W. Hart. 1986. "Understanding a New Economy." *Wall Street Journal,* December 23.

Shierholz, Heidi, and Lawrence Mishel. 2009. "Highest Unemployment Rate Since 1983." Economic Policy Institute Jobs Picture Preview. June 16. http://www.epi.org/publications/entry/jobspict_2009_july_preview/ (accessed March 26, 2010).

Shiller, Robert J. 2000. *Irrational Exuberance.* Princeton, NJ: Princeton University Press.

Sirohi, Seema. 2004. "Impatient Jobs." YaleGlobal Online. January 20. http://yaleglobal.yale.edu/content/impatient-jobs (accessed August 1, 2010).

Slater, Wayne. 1985. "Silicon Prairie?" *Dallas Morning News,* September 22.

Smith, Vicki. 2001. *Crossing the Great Divide: Worker Risk and Opportunity in the New Economy.* Ithaca, NY: Cornell University Press.

Sonntag, Selma. 2004. "Appropriating Identity or Cultivating Capital? Global English in Offshoring Service Industries." Paper presented at the annual meeting of the American Anthropological Association, San Francisco, November 19.

"Spherion Emerging Workforce Study." 2003. Fort Lauderdale, FL: Spherion.

Spindler, George D., and Louise Spindler. 1983. "Anthropologists View American Culture." *Annual Review of Anthropology* 12: 49–78.

Standing, Guy. 2002. *Beyond the New Paternalism: Basic Security as Equality.* London: Verso.

Stein, Nicholas. 2000. "Meet-Markets for the New Economy." *Fortune,* July 10: 257–258.

Stettner, Andrew, and Jeffrey Wenger. 2003. "The Broad Reach of Long-Term Unemployment." *Economic Policy Institute Issue.* Brief #194. May 15.

Stevens, Laura Roe. 2001. "On the Firing Line." *Industry Standard,* January 15: 154, 156.

Sumner, Jane. 1985. "Out-takes." *Dallas Morning News,* January 27.

Talent, Jim. 2007. "Beyond the Bottom Line: Redefining Corporate Social Responsibility." *Huffington Post.* http://www.huffingtonpost.com/sen-jim-talent/beyond-the-bottom-line-re_b_51449.html (accessed July 17, 2009).

TechAmerica. 2009. "Cyberstates 2009: A Complete State-by-State Overview of the High-Technology Industry." Washington, DC: TechAmerica.

Torres, Lisa. 1996. "When Weak Ties Fail: Shame, Reciprocity, and Unemployed Professionals." Master's thesis, University of California, Santa Barbara.

Torres, Lisa, and Matt L. Huffman. 2002. "Social Networks and Job Search Outcomes among Male and Female Professional, Technical, and Managerial Workers." *Sociological Focus* 35, no. 1: 25–42.

Townsend, Nicholas W. 2002. *The Package Deal: Marriage, Work, and Fatherhood in Men's Lives.* Philadelphia: Temple University Press.

Tulgan, Bruce. 2003. *Generational Shift: What We Saw at the Workplace Revolution: Executive Summary: Key Findings of Our Ten Year Workplace Study, 1993–2003.* New Haven, CT: Rainmaker Thinking.

Turner, Victor. 1969. *The Ritual Process: Structure and Anti-Structure.* Chicago: Aldine.

Uchitelle, Louis. 2006. *The Disposable American: Layoffs and Their Consequences.* New York: Knopf.

"University Study Shows Area Has Lost 30 Percent of Tech Jobs." 2004. *Dallas Business Journal,* September 15.

Urciuoli, Bonnie. 2008. "Skills and Selves in the New Workplace." *American Ethnologist* 35, no. 2: 211–228.

Van Maanen, John. 1988. *Tales of the Field: On Writing Ethnography.* Chicago: University of Chicago Press.

Venkatesh, Sudhir. 2009. "Feeling Too Down to Rise Up." *New York Times,* March 29.

Virick, Meghna. 2004. "Research Report: Follow-Up Survey on the Effect of Layoffs in the North Texas Region." Dallas: North Texas Technology Council and University of Texas at Arlington.

———. 2003. "Research Report: The Effect of Layoffs in the North Texas Region." Dallas: North Texas Technology Council and University of Texas at Arlington.

Wacquant, Loïc. 2002. "Scrutinizing the Street: Poverty, Morality, and the Pitfalls of Urban Ethnography." *American Journal of Sociology* 107, no. 6: 1468–1532.

Wallulis, Jerald. 1998. *The New Insecurity: The End of the Standard Job and Family.* Albany: State University of New York Press.

Warner, Melanie. 2001. "Pity the Poor Dot-Commer (a Little Bit)." *Fortune,* January 22: 40.

Warren, Elizabeth, and Amelia Warren Tyagi. 2003. *The Two Income Trap: Why Middle-Class Mothers and Fathers Are Going Broke.* New York: Basic Books.

Watts, Duncan J. 2002. *Six Degrees: The Science of a Connected Age.* New York: W.W. Norton.

Wax, Judith. 1976. "Mission Employable." *New York Times Magazine,* June 20: 24–25, 56.

Weinberg, Neal. 1998. "Help Wanted: Older Workers Need Not Apply." *CNN.com,* September 14. http://www.cnn.com/TECH/computing/9809/14/tooold.idg/index.html (accessed July 31, 2010).

Whyte, William H. 1956. *The Organization Man.* New York: Simon and Schuster.

Winerip, Michael. 2010. "Time, It Turns Out, Isn't on Their Side." *New York Times,* March 14.

Wysocki, Bernard, Jr. 1989. "The New Boom Towns." *Wall Street Journal,* March 27.

Xiang, Biao. 2007. *Global "Body Shopping": An Indian Labor System in the Information Technology Industry.* Princeton, NJ: Princeton University Press.

Zuboff, Shoshana. 1988. *In the Age of the Smart Machine: The Future of Work and Power.* New York: Basic Books.

INDEX

Page numbers followed by f indicate figures.